The Growing Edge presents...

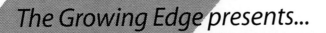

Hydroponic Solutions

Volume 1

Hydroponic Growing Tips

new moon publishing, inc.

341 S.W. Second Street
P.O. Box 1027
Corvallis, OR 97339
USA

(541) 757-8477
(541) 757-2511 editorial
(541) 757-0028 fax
www.growingedge.com
newmoon@growingedge.com

Copyright © 2004, New Moon Publishing, Inc.
First printing, March 2004
Printed in the United States of America
ISBN: 094457-04-X

Published by Tom Alexander
Compiled by Douglas J. Peckenpaugh
Edited by Douglas J. Peckenpaugh and Tom Weller
Layout and Design by Ashley Cobb
Advertising Coordination by Sherry Littlefield

Introduction

Questions Put, Answers Delivered

Since the 1989 launch of Growing Edge magazine, our flagship publication, readers have sent us questions about hydroponics. In the beginning, we would print in the magazine the questions and their answers provided by our experts. Later, when we expanded our website (www.growingedge.com), we added a question-and-answer section to it, and you responded by sending us about four times more questions.

Since that time we have collected enough Q&A to fill several books. You are now holding in your hands the first volume in our planned Q&A book series.

We're confident you'll find solutions to your hydroponic questions in these pages. We expect you'll have other questions as well. Simply log on to www.growingedge.com and send them to us. Before you know it, one of our experts will get back to you with free advice.

As the hydroponic industry expands in the coming years, we hope growers—new growers especially—will benefit from the Growing Edge Q&A forum. If we can help them avoid common pitfalls in hydroponic growing, or direct them to a key product or supplier, then we've done our job. We hope our grower-readers will continue to read Growing Edge and visit The Growing Edge website often. If, in your work as a grower, you've found a solution to a hydroponic problem and want to share it, please by all means send it to us so that we can share it with your fellow grower-readers.

The hydroponic industry is constantly changing, with new techniques and products to solve your problems. Growing Edge will always be there to help by reporting on these new developments! I hope you find the solution you're looking for!

Tom Alexander
New Moon Publishing

Right: Douglas J. Peckenpaugh.
Below: Lynette Morgan, Ph.D.

The Growing Edge magazine is fortunate to have a readership comprised of enthusiastic and curious hydroponic growers. They seem to have an unquenchable thirst for knowledge about hydroponics. Growing Edge staff are reminded every day of readers' enthusiasm and curiosity for hydroponics, because for years they've been sending us questions via the Growing Edge website (www.growingedge.com). These questions display an amazing range of interests, and this book would not have been possible without this contribution. Thanks, readers!

When the questions arrive at Growing Edge, they are evaluated for degree of difficulty. Most of the questions—and all of the tough ones—are forwarded to Lynette Morgan, an expert in hydroponics, for a response. The rest are handled by the Growing Edge editor.

Contributors

Lynette Morgan

Readers of the Growing Edge are already familiar with Lynette. She is a regular contributor to the magazine, answering readers' questions as well as writing features for beginning and advanced hydroponic growers.

Lynette earned a Ph.D. in horticulture in 1996, with a specialty in hydroponic vegetable production, from Massey University, New Zealand. Her thesis covered many aspects of hydroponic tomato production, including fruit quality, the single truss system of production, and seasonal variations in yield.

Lynette is scientific director for SUNTEC International Hydroponic Consultants, New Zealand. SUNTEC provides consultancy advice to hydroponic growers, educators and manufacturers around the world, as well as carrying out product development and research trials. A main focus of this research has been organic hydroponic methods and ways of making hydroponic production systems more efficient.

In addition to writing for Growing Edge and other horticultural journals, she has authored three technical publications on hydroponic production: "Hydroponic Lettuce Production" (1997), "Hydroponic Capsicum Production" (2000) and "Fresh Culinary Herb Production" (2002). Her current writing projects focus on hydroponic strawberry and tomato production.

She's also worked as a hydroponic lettuce grower and has held positions at various other horticultural operations. Lynette can be reached via The Growing Edge website (www.growingedge.com).

Lynette can also be reached at the following:
email: suntec@suntec.co.nz
website: www.suntec.co.nz/consultants.htm
Mail: P.O. Box 41, Tokomaru 5450, Manawatu, New Zealand

Douglas J. Peckenpaugh

A former editor of Growing Edge, Doug is a year-round gardening enthusiast with a special interest in hydroponics. He was editor when questions in this book were submitted, and in that capacity he answered many of the questions in this book. Doug lives with his family in the Chicago area, where he edits a food industry magazine.

Q: I currently use NFT as a preferred growing system. I am now going to experiment with an aeroponic system of my own making and would appreciate any comments you may have.

Four heavy gauge plastic 4-inch tubes that are 6 feet long are coupled together, resting on a frame that allows natural drainage. Each tube has 8 holes cut along the top and equidistant into which cups fit tightly. In each of these cups a seedling sits in a one inch cube. Roots, therefore, grow down through holes in each cup and into the tube. In between each cup is inserted a misting nozzle that delivers nutrients. Excess nutrients will either drain into a tank for recycling or discharge away. One aspect I am uncertain to is the misting cycle.

A: There are two options for the misting cycle in your aeroponic system: continuous and intermittent. Many aeroponic systems use continuous misting, particularly where the root system is large and dense to ensure the roots never dry out and this also has the benefit that the amount and frequency of misting does not have to be constantly adjusted as the plants grow and develop. Other aeroponic systems use intermittent misting. The frequency and length of time the misters are on and working is dependent on a number of factors, such as the stage of growth of the plants, rate of growth, ambient air temperatures, type of mister, pump capacity, etc. I would suggest you start with a cycle of misting 5 minutes in every 30 and keep a check on the root system to make sure the roots do not dry out between mistings. This can be increased in frequency as the root system gets larger and fills the tubes. You will also need to ensure you can check and unblock the misters daily (and they will tend to block up often) so access into the tubes will be important. You might also like to try net or lattice pots to put the seedlings in as they allow maximum root outgrowth and good initial wetting of the propagation cube and seedling root system. —*Lynette Morgan (L.M.)*

Q: I would like to start my own hydroponic system but I would like a possible system layout for a small-scale enterprise that will include all the necessary requirements and also alternative items that can be used instead of the expensive ones. Also, the possible mixtures of the system nutrients and various pictures of a hydroponic system.

A: I would recommend that you buy and read "Home Hydroponic Gardens" by Peggy Bradley. This book describes how to build and maintain simplified hydroponic systems with readily available materials. It is actually based on research that was performed through the United Nations in Africa and other countries around the world.

These UN projects were designed to help people better grow their own food in areas that feature poor soil or harsh climates, but the principles of the systems apply to any climate or location. Some simplified instructions for how to build one of the systems described in the book can be found on our Website. Also, if you are new to hydroponics, the book will help you learn more about the basic principles involved in soilless cultivation. The book includes information on how to create your own hydroponic nutrient solutions from naturally occurring substances (organic materials). —*Douglas J. Peckenpaugh (D.J.P.)*

Q: I am planning a new DWC hydroponic garden. I prefer to build a simple garden rather than buying a costly system. I have done extensive research and decided on this basic plan. I am looking for advice on how I can improve this DWC system. I am wondering if this is the most efficient way to run the buckets.

The system is a 5-gallon DWC bucket garden with 6-inch net pots for grorocks. This system should run about five 5-gallon buckets. The lids will have a hole for an air line to connect the air stone. A Hagen "The Pump 40" air pump will run to the air stones in the bottoms of the buckets. All five buckets will be hooked up with a flexible hose to a controlling 5-gallon bucket. The controller bucket will have five straight barbs in the bottom with rubber hose connected to the five garden buckets. I plan to have a 30-gallon reservoir to mix the nutrients and adjust the ppm and pH. Here I would like to have a 700-900 Mag Drive pump to pump the nutrient from the reservoir to the controller. The nutrients will then flow to the other five buckets after passing the controller. A float valve will also be added to the controller bucket to keep the correct level of nutrients toped off. To change the nutrients, I'll place the Mag Drive in the controller bucket and pump the nutrients out to my organic garden. I'll remix the fresh nutrients in the reservoir and refill the controller/garden.

Does this seem like the most efficient way to run this type of DWC growing system? Are there any improvements I could make to the system more user friendly? Please feel free to offer any comments and suggestions.

A: I'm not familiar with the "DWC" hydroponic garden. However, your design seems to be a good one and I can't foresee any major problem with the system itself. The only suggestion I would have is to keep a close check on the electrical conductivity (EC) of nutrient solution when the float valve is used to top up the water and readjust the EC as necessary to prevent the nutrient from becoming too dilute. Also, keep a close eye on the root systems. There should be more than sufficient oxygen in the nutrient with the air stones, but

sometimes, particularly if the system is being run under artificial lights, the temperature of the nutrient can increase and this means less oxygen is available for root uptake. —*L.M.*

Q: I tried using the floating system, but I have problems with less oxygen in the system. How can I avoid this problem? In other words, how can I add more oxygen to the system?

A: One of the best ways to introduce oxygen into the nutrient solution in a small floating hydroponic system is to use an aquarium pump. Just run a line from the pump into the nutrient and connect the end to an air stone (also commonly used in aquarium setups). It can be set to constantly bubble oxygen into the nutrient at a gentle rate or you can set it up to oxygenate the nutrient every so often. If you are going to hook the pump up to a timer and have it run periodically, make sure the pump is situated higher than the system so that gravity will not permit nutrient solution to run down the tube and into the pump apparatus when it turns off.

Another option is to manually stir the nutrient solution once or twice a day. However, this method is more time-consuming and less effective than using an aquarium pump. —*D.J.P.*

Q: I have a question regarding the angles of decline for NFT trays—specifically an issue regarding stagnant water gathering in the trays. Is there a limit to the angle of declination? I haven't used a consistent method in the past, but realize I have exceeded the usual measurements (1 inch for every 10 feet of tray, or something like that).

I didn't have any problems with nutrient solution gathering or pooling in the trays due to the sharper decline. The plant growth was great and I really didn't encounter any serious issues. I intend to build a couple of braces in the greenhouse for a half dozen trays I will be setting up there and was just wondering if there was a rule to follow.

A: There isn't one universal slope ratio for nutrient film technique (NFT) systems. Some growers determine the best slope for their particular type of system and crop by trial and error. Others have used published, recommended gradients only to find they end up suffering from nutrient ponding and stagnation. The problem with NFT channels is that it's very difficult to get an even slope along the channels since most PVC is fairly flexible and spots can occur where the nutrient doesn't flow as well as it should. Given that at the objective of NFT is to have only a very thin film of nutrient—1-2 millimeters deep—and plant roots usually grow into a fairly dense, thick mat on the base of the gully, sometimes the best solution is to have a system that allows the slope on each channel to be increased as the crop develops or as otherwise required.

A slope of 1:40 is a good figure. Some growers start with a slight slope of 1:100 and gradually increase it to 1:40 or even higher as the root system fills the gully. Crops with a large root system that are grown for a long term, such as 18-month tomato crops, will need a higher slope than a short-term lettuce crop, which has a smaller root system. There isn't really an upper limit for the slope. Growers tend to be limited regarding how much gradient they can put on their trays or channels since they need to access the plants at both ends of the system and wouldn't want one end of the channels above head height and the other end sitting on the floor!

I would suggest that you start with the slope you have been using successfully but design the system so that you could jack up the inlet end a little to increase the slope rate if any ponding is noted when the crop is mature. Keep a good check on the depth of the nutrient in the channels and the general health of the root system and let this determine the best gradient for your particular system and crop. —L.M.

Q: What is the proper slope ratio for an NFT hydroponic system with 10-foot gullies?

A: Rob Smith, author of Hydroponic Crop Production, recommends a minimum slope of 1:40 for NFT gullies. Howard Resh, author of Hydroponic Food Production, recommends a slope of 1:25. These two gentlemen are looked upon as authorities in the hydroponic world.

So if your gullies are 10 feet long, the side your nutrient solution is delivered to needs to be 3 inches (7.62 cm)—at the least—higher than the other end of the gully (according to Smith). Following Resh's guidelines, the delivery end should be 0.48 inch (1.22 cm) higher than the other end. If you shoot for between these numbers, you should be fine. Make sure that the ground you situate your gullies on is perfectly level. You shouldn't have any depressions in the middle of the gully. The nutrient solution should be able to flow at a constant rate along the entire path of the gully. The actual slope of the gullies can also sometimes depend on the type of plants that are being grown since larger root systems can occasionally impede the flow of nutrient down the gully. Some experimentation would be recommended to see what works best for you in your particular location and crop choices. —D.J.P.

Q: What are the advantages and disadvantages of modified NFT (adding inert media, such as perlite) compared to the normal NFT system?

A: Modified nutrient film technology (NFT) systems that incorporate an inert media, such as perlite, have the advantage that the media will hold a reserve of nutrient and moisture should the NFT irrigation stop for some reason. Therefore, these types of systems are most useful where blockages in the NFT delivery system may occur or where electricity cuts are common. With normal NFT, there usually isn't a reserve of nutrient held around the root system should the system shut down for any length of time. The disadvantage is that often, where a continually running or recirculating NFT system is in operation with a media that retains moisture (such as perlite, coconut fiber, rockwool, vermiculite, etc.), the media can become water-logged and overly wet

Q: I need to know what I need and how to construct a homemade drip system.

A: A homemade drip system for hydroponics is fairly easy to make. The simplest system has a tank where you make up your liquid fertilizer or nutrient solution and an outlet tap. The tank can be placed up above the level of the plants and the tap opened manually each day (or how every often you want to irrigate the plants) and the solution will flow out through the tubing via gravity. If the tank can't be placed above the level of the plants, a pump can be used to deliver the nutrient. The pump can then be set run automatically at selected intervals with a timer, which is a little more convenient than manual systems.

Thin-walled alkathene can be used for most home systems. These components simply push together and you an purchase the tubing and fittings at most garden centers or hardware stores. For a more permanent system, you could use rigid PVC pipe, but this requires a lot of messing around with gluing joiners and so on and is not really required for small systems. Drip irrigation tubes or emitters need to be joined to the main lateral pipe, which is attached to the pump. Alkathene tubing (4-mm) is usually fine for most systems but you can buy a rage of emitters that you can then use to adjust the flow rate into each plant, if required. You may want to install a nutrient collection system under each pot or container if you plant to recycle or reuse the leachate or waste nutrient.

Here are a couple of Websites with some information on drip systems which might be useful:

www.ces.ncsu.edu/hil/hil-33-a.htm
jessstryker.com/install.htm

—L.M.

since the nutrient is continually applied. This can rob oxygen from the root zone and cause root death and pathogen attack. Often, with media-based NFT system, fungus gnats and shore flies are common since they are attracted to the continually damp media. Whenever media is being used in an NFT system, the volume of media should be limited and it should be reasonably free draining and allow the nutrient to easily percolate through and out to the drainage channel. In many cases, it may be better to use an "intermittent NFT" system that applies some nutrient, turns off for a certain length of time to allow the media to drain, and then applies another irrigation on a frequent basis.. —*L.M.*

Q: What ways can I power my hydroponic system without using electricity? Can I use natural gas to power it?

A: If you have good levels of sunlight throughout the year, you could probably use solar power to run your hydroponic system for much of the time. This would involve having a few solar panels, which would be used to charge up large batteries that you can then plug your pumps and other hydroponic equipment into. The batteries (depending on how many you have) can store energy for cloudy days or nighttime and there are systems running in this way.

Solar power has the advantage of being free. However, you may need an emergency backup system, such as battery power, should you have a long period of insufficient radiation levels.

A: There are numerous small, well-designed hydroponic systems that could be used indoors to grow the plants you want to produce. Hydroponic retailers have a good range of attractive systems that might suit your needs. There might be a local hydroponic retailer in your area. Buying from a local merchant can be a great way to start a growing relationship. Your system choice will really depend on which one appeals to your particular taste—and budget. An alternative, less expensive option would be to design your own system using components from hydroponic and home improvement outlets. Many retailer and hobbyist Websites can provide quality plans and advice. I would suggest that you chose a nutrient film technique (NFT) system to avoid long-term media costs. NFT systems are a great way to learn about hydroponics.

Sometimes, when people refer to "organic," what they're really driving at is a final product that hasn't been exposed to pesticides. This is quite achievable in a home hobbyist system. There are also many brands of organic nutrient solutions on the market. However, these take a greater degree of skill to manage and can cause problems if not used correctly.

When starting to experiment with hydroponics, buying a good brand of commercially available nutrient solution—made from "inorganic" fertilizer salts—is the best option. If complete organic operation is one of your goals, you can try an organic solution after you've learned some of the basics of hydroponic gardening. —*L.M.*

> *When starting to experiment with hydroponics, buying a good brand of commercially available nutrient solution—made from "inorganic" fertilizer salts—is the best option.*

I assume natural gas could be used to power pumps and other equipment. However, you would probably have to invest in specialty equipment and systems to make this possible. —*L.M.*

Q: I'm interested in starting a small indoor hydroponic garden to experiment with growing organic produce, such as herbs, tomatoes, salad greens, and perhaps some other vegetables. I would love some advice on a system to start with—a beginner setup that's easy to use, doesn't take up a lot of space, and isn't very expensive. I'm looking for something that's user-friendly . . . something that I could use to get the hang of this method of gardening. Do you have any suggestions or know where I could pick up such a system?

Q: What are some benefits and drawbacks of using the wick system?

A: Wick hydroponic systems are usually best used with single plants and therefore is geared toward hobbyists. Wick systems are dependent on someone to fill the tray that holds the nutrient solution every so often. If the tray runs out of nutrient solution, and nobody fills it, the plant media will dry out, killing the plant's roots.

But for someone who just wants to grow one or a few soil-less plants, the wick system can work just fine. You just have to remember to check the level of nutrient solution in the system every so often. For more information on passive, media-based hydroponic systems, see www.growingedge.com/basics/easyplans/selfwater.html. —*D.J.P.*

Q: What are the principles of aeroponics? What are some uses and benefits of this growing technique? And is there a simple way in which I can build a system with minimal costs?

A: Aeroponics is a variation on hydroponics that involves misting a plant's roots, which hang into a closed chamber, with nutrient solution. The runoff is collected and usually reused. Some systems mist the roots in cycles while others constantly mist the roots.

Our magazine, The Growing Edge, has run a few articles on aeroponics, including "From Desert, to Laboratory, to Backyard Aero-Hydroponics," by Lawrence L. Brooke, (Volume 2, Number 1); "The Land . . . A Touch of Reality in a World of Fantasy," by Delthia Ricks, (Volume 8, Number 1); and "Hybrid Hydro: Aeroponics in Texas," by Don Jensen (Volume 11, Number 6).

You also might check out the Aeroponics International Website at www.biocontrols.com/. They have the best dedicated aeroponics Website that I know about. I know that some people really enjoy operating aeroponic systems. And I'm sure you could build one once you have learned the basics of the technique. —D.J.P.

Q: I am new to hydroponic gardening, my intention is to set up a hobby system in a greenhouse. I don't know what type of system it will be. Is it correct that only food grade plastics should be used for components of a hydroponic system which the nutrient solution contacts? Is it questionable or dangerous to use non-food grade plastics in a system which will be producing food crops? Black polyethylene or white PVC potable water pipe, white PVC drain pipe, and Rubbermaid type containers are some examples of the materials I'm wondering about.

A: These days, the majority of the plastics you buy which are designed to carry water for human use such as PVC water pipes and other plumbing supplies are suitable for contact with the nutrient solution—if you are concerned about this, buy your gullies and pipes from a reputable hydroponic retailer (there are a number listed in The Growing Edge magazine), that way you know you will be safe. If you want to adapt other plastic containers as growing beds or planters then it's best to select the food grade ones and stay away from ones that have used a larger percentage of recycled materials since the plasticizers used in these can sometimes be toxic to plants. There is an excellent and simple test you can carry out on your plastic material if you are concerned about it—this is detailed in Rob Smith and Lon Dalton's book Hydroponic Crop Production (page 60) where there is also a good description on phytotoxic plastics. The test involves placing a small piece of the plastic material into

a container and pouring boiling water over it, if you can then smell a plastic odor coming off the heated material, be wary, allow the water to cool and then take a tiny sip, if you can now also taste the plastic content, be extremely wary of using this material. While this test if not foolproof, its certainly a good indicator if something is likely to be toxic in the material. —L.M.

Q: I live in Hawaii and would like to set up a rooftop hydroponics system. I would like to have about 50 plants growing at one time. Can you steer me in the right direction for information?

A: Growing on a rooftop isn't really much different than growing in the backyard. However, you just need to make sure you don't put too much weight on your roof! One good article on rooftop hydroponics is "Higher Ground," which appeared in The Growing Edge, Volume 10, Number 2 (November/December 1998).

I would also recommend researching the type of system you are going to use, the requirements of the plants you are gong to grow, and the nutrient solutions you are going

Q: I want to do a project on aeroponics but cannot find information about what nutrients are required for it, what the procedure is, etc. Could you kindly help me?

A: Aeroponics is a form of hydroponics where the plant's roots are constantly or intermittently misted in an enclosed lightproof chamber. The aboveground portion of the plant is treated normally (striving to provide the optimal light, temperature, and humidity levels in a well ventilated area). The nutrient solution is usually collected at the bottom of the misting chamber and then returned to the nutrient solution reservoir.

The nutrient solution used should be of good quality and designed for hydroponic use. For vegetative plants, such as lettuce, only one type of nutrient solution is needed (usually called "grow"). If fruiting plants will be grown, two nutrient solutions will be needed ("grow" and "bloom"). Premixed, reliable nutrient solutions are available at hydroponic retailers or over the Internet. For more information on aeroponics, see: www.growingedge.com/community/archive/search.php3?query=aeroponic&c=all www.biocontrols.com —D.J.P.

to use. By growing in a tropical area like Hawaii outdoors, chances are, you won't need to use any supplemental lighting. You might, however, need some sort of shade cloth to avoid giving your plants too much light (depending on what you are going to grow). Just make sure you are providing your plants with the correct nutrient and light levels. —D.J.P.

Q: I've been working on making my own version of an air-lift top-feeding system analogous in concept to the General Hydro Waterfarm system. However, I have run into one problem. In the reservoir, where the air pump tube meets the t-valve underwater, all too often when the system is switched on the pressure from the air pump is so great that air is forced through the bottom of the t-valve and into the reservoir instead of just going up and pushing the water up to the plants. At first I thought I fixed it by adding a valve to the bottom of the t-valve, which widened the opening from the 0.17-inch to 3/4-inch, but that still didn't fully fix the problem. The system works great once it's flowing, but sometimes to get it started I either have to block the bottom for a second or siphon from the top end to get it flowing right.

A: This system works on the venturi principle, whereby a certain amount of air pumped through the hose is released

into the solution and water replaces the lost air, which is then carried up the pipe by the bulk air flow. For the system to work effectively, a balance needs to be reached between the amount of air displaced by solution and the flow of air in the pipe being sufficient to carry the solution up to the top of the container. If the air pump is too powerful, the solution won't be able to flow into the pipe at the same time air is being released, air will just blow out of any orifice and not be displaced by nutrient solution. Conversely, if the pump is not powerful enough, there won't be enough airflow to carry the air/water mixture up to the container surface. Usually, a fairly small opening works better than a large one, so increasing the diameter of the opening would be unlikely to have the right effect. The amount of solution entering the pipe can be increased by increasing the depth of solution in the reservoir and positioning the opening in the pipe at the lowest point in the loop as the pipe begins to turn upwards out of the solution. By maximizing the depth, this maximizes the pressure of water at the point where the air is being released, improving the chances of solution entering the pipe. This will also help with priming the system between operation. —L.M.

Q: I am doing an experiment on hydroponics with a group of students aged 9–12 since we are on the topic at the moment. In the experiment, they are to grow seeds in hydroponic solution and in normal tap water to study and compare the growth of plants in the solutions given.

The materials and methods used are basic: two plastic containers holding seeds in the two different solutions with a Styrofoam lid cut with holes to allow the growth of the plant to sprout through. We are not intending to use any media for the seed, save for being half submerged in water at the beginning.

I am concerned with the stagnation of the water during the initial stages. I do not know for certain whether it will work—especially since aeration for the roots is important.

Can you please advise me on the feasibility of this basic experiment as well as how to create air in the solutions? One child suggested if they could use a stick and stir the solution once a day to allow air into the solution. Is that probable?

A: It sounds like you have a good experiment worked out! Stirring the water and nutrient solution once or twice a day will work for aeration. If you use this method, be sure to stir somewhat vigorously.

However, another way to accomplish oxygen introduction would be to use a standard aquarium pump (that pump air and is commonly used in fish tanks; in the United States, a small one costs around $7 at pet stores). Just split the line with a small plastic two-way splitter (should also be available at the pet store; very inexpensive) and run one line to each container that is holding the water and nutrient solution. Then, if you really wanted to get sophisticated, you could hook the pump up to an appliance timer set to go on for 15 minutes or so every morning and afternoon. The pump should come with a "bleed valve" that can be turned to control the rate of aeration. Make sure it is set to bubble the water and nutrient solution at a very gentle rate. With such a setup, the entire aeration system would be automated. —D.J.P.

Q: My biology and chemistry class is putting together a hydroponic system. We need some basic information. We would like to make one with a pump with 12 different places for each person to do their own plant. We haven't been able to find info on how to do something like that ourselves—and we don't want to spend $1,000.

A: From what you have told me, I would recommend a Dutch pot type of hydroponic system. In such a setup, you would have one central nutrient solution tank (a large, covered bucket will do). A submersible pump distributes nutri-

ent solution via a plastic tube (like what is used with fish aquariums or for irrigation) that travels around the growing area and drains back into the nutrient tank. Split the line with tee connectors, running a line to each individual growing container (for 12 plants you split the line twelve times, running a line to each growing container). You can just poke the line into the growing medium in the top of each growing container.

When everything is in place, turn on the pump and see how long it takes to adequately water the plants. Each growing container should have a way to collect any runoff nutrient solution. This could be accomplished with something as simple as a saucer, like traditional houseplants. Then you can pour the extra runoff nutrient through a filter (to remove any growing media that could clog the distribution lines) and return it to the nutrient solution tank. However, if you want to get creative, you take this concept a step further. You could have all of the growing containers sitting on and draining into a gully (like a wide rain gutter or something similar) that would be slightly sloped to return the excess nutrient solution to the nutrient tank by itself. Just outfit the runoff gully with a strainer or filter at the end by the tank. If you can cover the runoff gully, you will reduce algae buildup.

Once you have figured out how long it takes to irrigate the plants, you can hook the pump up to a timer so that your system is completely automated. Depending on how much light the plants are receiving and the stage of growth, you might want to water the plants once or twice a day. Then, all you would have to do is regulate and monitor the system and plants.

The choice of growing media will depend on what you are going to grow. Some good choices are a mix of perlite and peat moss, coir (coconut fiber), or expanded clay pellets. Monitor the nutrient solution's electrical conductivity (EC) and pH to make sure it stays in the proper ranges for the plants you are growing. Make sure you have at least 30 percent more nutrient solution in the tank than will be used to water the plants every day. This extra solution acts as a buffer.

Dutch pot kits are sold through most hydroponic supply outlets and a 12-pot system runs around $500. However, they aren't very difficult to construct. You should be able to purchase all of the materials needed for this project at home improvement centers, pet stores, garden centers, or hydroponic shops. The total cost for a setup like this should run under $100 for 12 plants (not including high-intensity discharge lighting—however, warm and cool fluorescent lights might work in some situations where some natural sunlight is available). I would imagine that a class could construct this system in a week, working on it for one hour or so a day.

Here's a good link to get a better visual idea of what a Dutch pot hydroponic system might look like: www.homeharvest.com/hydrosysgh.htm

I hope this helps you along your way toward a fun hydroponic project! This is just a brief outline for how to proceed. Make sure you investigate all of the variables involved when constructing your own growing system. The Growing Edge Website has a lot of practical growing information in the Hydroponic Basics section (www.growingedge.com/basics/start.html). And there is a ton of great information in different areas around the Web. —D.J.P.

Q: Who builds the best greenhouse for the Pacific Northwest area? I am going to purchase a greenhouse that will also double as a pool and spa house. I will also put in a hydroponic system for personal vegetables and flowers. I will use alternate methods of sanitizing pool and spa water—I will not be using chlorine. I want a unit approximately 20x30 feet that has the best glazing system with automatic vents. I want an all aluminum frame unit, top-of-the-line manufacture. I'm not interested in inferior products, I need the best available.

A: It's good to hear you are not going to be using chlorine for your pool and spa. Many plants have died a very rapid death in spa and pool rooms! There is a huge number of greenhouse manufacturers in the United States so I can't really comment on which is the best or top of the line. I would suggest that since you really want to the best structure possible for your multipurpose greenhouse that you contact the National Greenhouse Manufacturers Association and see which of their members they recommend for this project. The National Greenhouse Manufacturers association is a professional trade organization for the manufacturers and suppliers of greenhouses and greenhouse components. You can check out the products and services of NGMA members on their Website at www.ngma.com/ngmahome1.htm. Another good site is the directory of garden buildings, which lists a large number of greenhouse suppliers (see www.gardenbuildings.com/directory/United_States/). —L.M.

Q: Where can I find information for converting my garage to a greenhouse? I have metal roof that could be replaced by translucent panels. What things do I need to think about when planning such a project?

A: Whether this type of growing structure is feasible or not will depend on what plants you want to grow. If the garage has a clear roof (it will still need considerable structural beams, etc.) with solid walls, there will not be sufficient light entering the inside of the garage for most crop plants unless you intend on supplementing radiation levels with artificial lighting (which is expensive to install and run). Plants that may possibly grow in such a structure with limited light would be houseplants, such as orchids, ferns and a few other low light species. You may be able to grow some lettuce and herbs, but quality is likely to be compromised unless incoming radiation levels are very high all year round. With supplementary lighting on the sides of the garage, you could grow many of the salad greens and herbs, but you would have to be careful with heat buildup in such a structure. The garage also needs to have some form of ventilation to allow fresh air into the cropping area to provide sufficient carbon dioxide (CO_2) for plant growth and extractor fans or vents to allow the moist air from the crop out of the growing structure. The growing area may need heating and/or cooling equipment for maximum plant growth (depending on your climate) and a supply of good quality water for your hydroponic system. I would suggest you start out small and trial a number of different plants to see how much production you can get from your new grow room. —L.M.

Q: Is it more beneficial to have a greenhouse for your hydroponic and aquaponic systems? Are there fewer or virtually no plant disease problems using these modalities?

A: Yes, a greenhouse is an ideal location for a hydroponic or aquaponic system. Greenhouses make the most of available natural sunlight and can be outfitted with safeguards (such as fine mesh screens over any openings to the outside) to help prevent the introduction of insect pests. Greenhouses also help prevent problems with birds and other outdoor animals that could trouble some edible crops. Greenhouses also provide gardeners with a focused area for their activities. It becomes their haven.

Hydroponic techniques can dramatically cut down on the incidence of the pests and diseases associated with soil (since soil isn't used in hydroponics). However, some pests and diseases can still be a problem in hydroponics. The best treatment for pest and disease problems is preventative: Make sure all gardening tools and equipment are sterile before beginning and maintain a clean growing environment throughout the life of the crops. You will also want to make sure any media used (if media is used) is completely sterile. Following these simple guidelines will help you prevent any problems before they can get a foothold. —D.J.P.

Q: If a greenhouse is 11 feet on the south by 16 feet on the east, how much area should be glass on the south- and east-facing sides? Is there a formula? How much can be vertical and how much can be on the roof, at an angle based on our latitude? Does the formula depend in part on the quality of the glazing?

A: The main factors determining the height of walls of your greenhouse will be the crop(s) you wish to grow in the greenhouse, the height required for comfortable access, the building materials used, and the expertise of the builder. Your plan sounds like a "lean-to" structure based on the height of the building to which it is attached. The pitch of the roof needs to be sufficient to shed rain (and snow) and can also influence the ventilation area (percent of floor area). Despite common misconceptions, it has little to do with the latitude.

Most modern greenhouses feature clear cladding all the way to the floor, so the answer to your question is "all of it." There is no hard and fast formula for calculating this fact, it is just a case of maximizing the light entering the greenhouse, producing a practical structure that is cost effective and meets the needs of the grower, and conforms to some general principles. —*L.M.*

Q: I am planning on converting my greenhouse to hydroponic. I was wondering if I can use a combination of coconut-fiber and vermiculite as a medium for plants, using it similar to regular dirt, with a layer of rocks on the bottom, for drainage, with a layer of landscape fabric

The drip irrigation hose might need regular maintenance since hydroponic nutrient solutions can cause salt buildup in the tiny holes, creating blockages. Also, the hose shouldn't be left exposed on the top of the growing beds. Doing so could cause the nutrient solution inside to heat to very high levels—especially if the hose is black—and burn the plants. —*L.M.*

Q: What would be the best greenhouse covering for a desert location? I had a very nice one that I built of dual-pane, tempered glass and redwood. I am going to buy or build a new one, approximately 1,000 square feet, strictly for hydroponic use. Would two layer poly coverings work for me or would the blowing sand cause it harm? My temperature range is 10–120° with very high winds. I live in the Mojave Desert, about 60 miles southwest of Las Vegas, Nevada. I was leaning toward buying my greenhouse from a major manufacturer. But since they were a little pricey, I was wondering if you had any ideas. Also, with my last greenhouse, I had a terrible problem with whitefly even though I used a screen for the openings and sprayed with diazinon. Any suggestions?

Greenhouses make the most of available natural sunlight and can be outfitted with safeguards (such as fine mesh screens over any openings to the outside) to help prevent the introduction of insect pests.

to separate the two. I was thinking of using a recovery system, with drip irrigation hose that I already have. I could set the timer for as often as necessary. I plan on changing the nutrient solution as needed, and diverting it to the garden outside. Is this a feasible plan, or do I need to rethink?

A: Your plan sounds like a good one—and it's always smart to plan what you're going to do with the spent nutrient solution. You don't need to mix up a combination of coconut fiber and vermiculite for the growing medium—just coconut fiber on its own would be better and is likely to be more cost-effective. Good quality coconut fiber has ideal physical properties for hydroponics and usually does not need to be amended with any other substrates.

I would recommend that you grow in raised beds with coconut fiber on top and coarse gravel at the base. Using raised beds—which can easily be constructed of timber—ensures that the nutrient solution will drain down and out of the root zone and makes planting and removing crops much easier.

A: One of the best greenhouse cladding materials is polycarbonate sheet. You should find that it's cheaper than glass, is easier to work with, and is easily fixed to a basic timber frame. The result is a very durable and practical structure, which should maintain its original condition despite the harshest of environments. There is usually no need for dual layers of cladding. If extra insulation is thought to be necessary, a single layer of polyethylene or other "thermal screen" can be attached below the rafters to create an air space in the eaves. At the same time, this will reduce the volume of air that needs to be heated. Excess solar radiation and heat buildup can be alleviated by covering the outside of the structure with 50 percent shade cloth. Also, consider evaporative cooling for the vents—especially the intake vents at the base of your greenhouse—to cool the interior. The ventilation area is the most important consideration for maintaining an optimum environment within the greenhouse and should be greater than 30 percent of the floor area. You will probably find that a home-built greenhouse will work out to be cheaper than ready-made kits or buying an existing structure from a greenhouse manufacturer. Your own design can also have a level of flexibility for your particular location, taste, and growing needs. On the other hand, experienced manufacturers can provide proven designs that can be quickly constructed quickly and easily serviced. Check around your area and see if you can find any growers who have purchased a ready-made greenhouse from any manufacturers you are considering and get their opinions before investing. Whitefly can quickly become resistant to diazinon. It is best to alternate the sprays you use on a regular basis. Also, try combining the knockdown pesticides with insect growth regulator sprays to control all stages of the insect lifecycle. Repeat this combination at three day intervals for approximately two weeks after a whitefly infestation commences. If you suspend yellow plastic strips covered with oil at intervals throughout your greenhouse, some adult whiteflies will get trapped and provide an early warning of when to commence spraying. An alternative to spraying with inorganic pesticides is to use predator insects or botanical remedies for control. Glasshouse whiteflies can be controlled with the predator wasp, Encarsia formosa. Botanical compounds derived from custard apple, sweetsop, the neem tree, and others have shown effectiveness against whitefly. Such remedies usually work best in small, closed greenhouses. —L.M.

Q: I am used to growing my plants in rockwool. Recently, I tried transplanting some plants into an ebb-and-flow system filled with leca. I am having problems finding a good watering schedule. When I first transplanted, I almost killed my plants by overwatering. Now, they have recovered but I can't seem to tell when they need to be watered. Any information or advice about leca and how it works would be very helpful!

A: It can be difficult to gauge how much watering is required in ebb-and-flow systems, particularly when you have been used to growing in rockwool which has a very high capacity to retain moisture compared to leca. Leca is light expanded clay aggregate, which is widely used in ebb and flow systems since it supports the plants well and drains completely during the irrigation cycle, thus preventing waterlogging of the root systems. Leca also allows good air penetration around the root system as the nutrient flows in and then out, creating a suction effect that drags fresh air into the plant's root zone.

However, these same properties also mean that irrigation cycles need to be frequent as leca does not hold a great deal of nutrient within its structure between waterings. You may also need to increase the frequency of the flood cycles as the plants increase in size as they will remove more moisture and dry out quicker. You can buy one of the those soil moisture indicators, which are used for potted plants, and push it into the leca around the base of one of the plants to use this a guide as to how often you need to have a flood cycle to keep the plants growing well.

Another method is to push your finger down into the leca around the plants between irrigations to try and determine when the moisture levels have fallen sufficiently to apply more nutrient—if your finger doesn't appear to be wet after reaching the root zone. Also, you can gauge the flood cycle by observing the plants. If you notice the plants beginning to wilt, the irrigation cycles need to be more frequent. You might also need to have frequent flood cycles but only let the nutrient sit for one or two minutes before draining out again to prevent waterlogging. Good luck with your new system. —L.M.

Q: I would like to know what the recommended depth or volume per plant is for hydroponic and aeroponic containers. I will most likely be using PVC piping. Just to give you an idea of my thoughts: I would like to build a small ebb-and-flow system using a 5-inch-diameter piping. I know that root systems can get rather massive so I'm wondering what a suggested minimum space for the roots would be.

Q: How long does rockwool hold its water? If it was watered well once every day, would it still have enough moisture?

A: Rockwool will hold a certain degree of moisture between irrigations. However, how often you need to irrigate depends largely on the stage of plant growth and the type of plants being grown. For example, most seedlings will not need a lot of water and can usually be irrigated once a day. However, a mature, fruiting tomato plant will need much more water and nutrient on a daily basis and might need to be irrigated a few times a day. The environmental conditions also play a part in the amount of water that needs to be available to plants. Plants growing in hot, sunny conditions will need more water than plants growing in cool, cloudy conditions. Your best bet would be to monitor your plants and the moisture of the rockwool during different stages of growth to make sure the rockwool is not drying out too much before the next irrigation cycle and adjust your feeding schedule accordingly. —D.J.P.

A: The depth required for the root system differs depending on what types of plants you are growing (small salad greens, strawberries, herbs, etc., or large, fruiting plants, such as tomatoes, peppers, cucumbers, etc.). It also differs depending on the type of system you are using—nutrient film technique (NFT), aeroponic, ebb and flow, media-based, float, or others.

PVC pipes are best for NFT systems, as they only have to contain a thin film of nutrient flowing along the base. The rest of the space inside the PVC pipe can rapidly become filled with root systems. Aeroponic systems, where the nutrient is misted onto the plant roots as they dangle in a moist chamber, needs a larger volume, particularly for larger plants such as mature tomatoes. In aeroponics, since the root system is hanging downward and the nutrient is usually misted upward, a good depth (usually more than 30 centimeters is required) to contain the growth of the root system and also allow the misting of the nutrient to wet a good portion of the roots in the chamber. For smaller plants, aeroponic systems made from large diameter PVC have been used.

Normally, for ebb-and-flow systems, the plants are grown in pots of a heavy media (that doesn't float) inside another larger tank or container that is flooded and then drained on a regular basis. In these systems, there has to be sufficient room for both the plant's roots (which can grow to take up a large volume in many species) and the media that holds them (and prevents the plants root system from floating during the flood cycle). For this reason, ebb-and-flow systems are usually based on a large container or tank with sides of at least 25 centimeters to prevent any overflow during the flood cycle.

However, for small plants, 5-inch PVC pipes could potentially be used, provided you carefully monitor the flood cycle to make sure sufficient nutrient depth is obtained to wet the media thoroughly around the roots before draining away again, without the nutrient flowing over the top of the PVC. Obviously, as the plants grow and develop and take up more space, you will have to adjust how much nutrient floods the system to prevent any overflow and the cycle will have to be increased in frequency as the small root zone area could dry out between flood cycles. However, probably the best flood and drain system are made from larger open containers that can also be scrubbed out between crops and will have plenty of depth to prevent overflow problems as the plants mature. —*L.M.*

Q: My question is on the safety issues of gardening with rockwool. I am using rockwool for hobby gardening around the house and my kids are often helping. My understanding is that the safety issues have to do with dry fibers getting into the air and being breathed in. Hence, once it is wet it is OK (though I of course try to keep the kids from too much exposure, have them wash hands, etc.). Can you comment?

A: Yes, the primary health concern with rockwool handling is breathing in small particles that could cause respiratory problems. When handling dry rockwool, it is advised that a protective inhalation mask—like a surgical mask—is worn. It's also a good idea to wear such a mask when handling bulk dry perlite and vermiculite. Also, some people can develop a skin irritation from dry rockwool when handling it without gloves. Wearing thin cotton gardening gloves should prevent any possible irritation. —*D.J.P.*

Q: I have built a box 8 feet long, 16 inches wide, and 8 inches high out of 3/4-inch pressure-treated plywood. Then I lined it with 6 mil plastic, filled the bottom 4 inches with clean lava rock and put some washed, smooth stones on top of that. Then I added a mixture of six parts peat moss and 4 parts of a mixture of perlite and vermiculite. I drilled a 1-inch hole in the bottom and fitted a drainage hose to it and about 5 inches from the bottom I drilled another 1-inch hole for the hose that is connected to a hose and then a pump. Each plant has a 0.06 gph drip—it all goes in and out of a closed 5-gallon pail. The box is elevated about 4 degrees on one end to help assure drainage.

My problem is that I'm losing about a gallon per 1/2 hour of drip. The mixture is staying very wet so I don't want to overdrip it. According to my books I should be able to use the nutrient mixture for two weeks before making new. What am I doing wrong? I hope you can help me out as I'm very excited about this project.

A: It could be that, if there aren't any leaks in the system—and it sounds like a very well thought-out and constructed system—that the missing nutrient is being used by the plants. Under warm, dry conditions, mature plants will take up a considerable amount of moisture and your nutrient levels can drop quite rapidly. For example, a mature tomato plant in summer can use 5–8 liters of water/nutrient per day (a younger plant can still use 2–3 liters per day). Your nutrient tank is a 5-gallon pail (about 18.5 liters). This means that if you have six large plants in your 8-foot box, they could potently use up all the nutrient in your pail on a warm day. Luckily, the moisture-holding capacity and large volume of media will retain additional nutrient for the plants. However, you may need a bigger pail for your nutrient solution.

Losing a gallon per 1/2 hour of drip for an actively growing crop of plants in hydroponics would be a normal uptake rate. You might want to consider installing a ball value to automatically top up the water level in the nutrient pail so that it doesn't run dry after five irrigation cycles—if using a larger pail is not an option. For your system, a nutrient reservoir that holds at least 20 gallons would be sufficient—if you're checking your system and replacing water and nutrient each day. If you only check the system once every few days, you will obviously need a much larger nutrient pail or an automated system that automatically adds water and nutrient for you. Plants taking up large volumes of nutrient is a good sign of active plant growth. —L.M.

pots, cubes, blocks, media, and even recycled materials and containers that can be adapted for use in hydroponics.

With your 2-inch PVC pipe system, the rounded base of the pipes means you really need to use something like the small rockwool seed starting cubes or the oasis foam cubes, which will absorb the nutrient and deliver it to the seedling root system while it is still developing and before it has extended out into the gully. If you obtain a few sheets of the small rockwool cubes, thoroughly wet each sheet (I think they contain 30 or so individual cubes all joined into a slab),

Perlite can certainly be used to incorporate into compost—but I would recommend it be sterilized (steam) after use, to destroy any pathogens which might be present from the last crop.

Q: I have been doing research and experimenting with hydroponics for a couple years now. Your articles in The Growing Edge have been very informative and provided many ideas to toy with. The reason I am writing is that all the books and articles I have read so far are lacking critical information, at least for me, about methods of support for the plants in some of the different systems. I've grown in rockwool without any problems but the recent NFT system I built has posed a new set of questions. My current system is constructed out of 2-inch PVC and I am considering building something similar to the system featured in The Growing Edge (in The Growing World of Hydroponics) as soon as I receive the back issues I missed, or something similar.

I guess my real question is: What are my options for starting and introducing my seedlings into an NFT system? The pipe system isn't exactly suited to the net pots as they do not sit low enough in the pipe to reach the nutrient. I am currently using small plastic cups that I cut the bottoms out and then wrap with a nylon mesh. I place the starts in the cups and fill around them with perlite. I am interested in using rockwool starter cubes . . . Would this be better? I have read several good books on the subject but they all seem to be rather vague on the actual process, showing pictures of before and after, but nothing in between. I am one of those people who learns best by both reading or lecture and by example. Any information would be greatly appreciated. I look forward to many more informative articles in the future.

A: I think you're correct. There does seem to be a general lack of information on all the different ways plants can be started and supported in various hydroponic systems—a good idea for an article perhaps! There is a huge range of

place these on a solid tray with a little water in the base, and sow your seed into the holes prepunched into the top of each individual cube. Once the seedlings have germinated, give them a dilute nutrient solution with a half strength EC until they are well developed.

Once they have four or five leaves per seedling and the root system has begun to grow out the bottom of the cubes, they can be separated by pulling the rockwool blocks apart and placed into the holes in the PVC pipe. This same system can be used for oasis foam cubes. If you can get a hold of the small coir (coconut fiber) discs, these are also very good for the type of system you have. The discs come as compressed coir. They're soaked in a tray of water to expanded the media into a cylinder of fiber usually held together with a fine net bag. After the seedlings have been sown and the young seedlings have been raised to a good size, the whole unit can be placed into the NFT system (or any other type of system) and the coir will act as a reserve of nutrient until the root system has expanded out into the gullies.

It might be a good idea to try a few of these different starter products to see which gives you the best plant establishment and growth rates. —L.M.

Q: How long can expanded clay and similar mediums like Gro Rocks be reused? What is the best way to clean and sterilize these types of mediums?

A: Expanded clay can last a very long time—almost indefinitely. In between crops, some growers just toss their expanded clay into a large bucket and spray it with a hose to remove any clinging root matter and other debris. However, if you suspect that a pathogen might be present, you might need to sterilize the clay by baking it in an oven at a temperature of at least 250°F. That should kill any pathogens that might be present. I wouldn't recommend using a diluted bleach solution to sterilize expanded clay due to its porous nature. I would be afraid that the clay would retain some of the bleach and eventually harm the next crop of plants. —D.J.P.

Q: What is the recommended watering for plants in a Dutch garden? I am running a 404 pump with two basket emitters per Dutch pot for bush beans. What would be the time and frequency of feeding? What would be the time and frequency of feeding using 4-inch rockwool cubes on a slab with 1/4-inch tubing with no emitter?

A: With any media-based container system the best indication of when and how often to feed is by the amount of leachate (or nutrient) that comes out the base of the pot. You want to aim for a 10 percent loss in nutrient form each pot at each watering with the number of waterings per day based on the environmental conditions the plants are growing under. In warmer conditions, you may need as many as 8-12 waterings per day. In cooler conditions and with a media that holds a large amount of moisture, only one watering per day may be required. Observing the plants, the media, and the drainage from each pot will give you the best indication of how much to apply and how often. —L.M.

Q: I have a homemade drip system. I'm using lava rock to grow in. I have two questions. Why does my pH always bounce around? I use bottled water and BC Hydro mix. Should I keep the pump on the whole time the lights are on?

A: Yes, when using a free straining substrate such as lava rock under lights, you should run the pump constantly to prevent heat buildup and to keep your root system from drying out. The best way to control the pH swings is to regularly adjust the pH with small amounts of "pH up" or "pH down." Sometimes, growers can use too much of these chemicals without you realizing it, causing the pH to swing in the opposite direction. If you haven't been controlling pH, some changes in the level are to be expected as the plants remove certain nutrients. As long as you keep the pH in the range of 5.0–6.8, don't be too concerned with the small changes that occur on a daily basis. —L.M.

Q: Do you know of any interesting uses for used rockwool slabs or used perlite? Can I use the used perlite with finished compost? working compost?

A: The disposal of used rockwool is a major problem for many growers and in fact many growers are changing over to more biodegradable growing media as a result. Rockwool can be sterilized and reused for a couple of seasons, and when it does finally need to be disposed of it can be shredded and used as a soil conditioner by plowing it into fields where it helps open up the soil and retain moisture for crop plants. Perlite can certainly be used to incorporate into compost—but I would recommend it be sterilized (steam) after use, to destroy any pathogens which might be present from the last crop. Perlite can also be used as soil conditioner, but it can also have a reasonably long life as a hydroponic media, with many commercial growers using it for several seasons. —L.M.

Q: I am interested in finding ways of recycling used rockwool cubes. Can they be reused? If not, how does one recycle them?

A: There has been a lot of concern about recycling rockwool for continued use over the last several years. One good way to sterilize rockwool for continued use is to steam-clean it. After you are done with a growing cycle, pull out any roots out of the rockwool that you can get. Then run it through a steamer. I would imagine that any number of contraptions could be used for this task (such as a cheap rice steamer for small cubes or you can rent a wallpaper steamer to sterilize a lot of rockwool). The steam should sterilize the rockwool at 212°F. You can usually reuse rockwool in this way two or three times.

After that point, researchers have found that rockwool can be broken down into small particles, sifted, and steamed yet again. Then it can be used by itself as a medium or combined with other substrates, such as wood chips. B. R. Jeong of the Gyeongsang National University presented a paper on the "Use of Recycled Hydroponic Rockwool Slabs for Hydroponic Production of Cut Roses" at the World Congress on Soilless Culture in Israel earlier this year. However, I don't know how feasible this is for small growers at this time.

One good resource to find information on how growers are sterilizing their rockwool would be to pose a question to the hydroponic listserv (like an e-mail discussion list), which is sponsored by the Hydroponic Society of America (hsa.hydroponics.org/lounge/mailinglist/page.html). After the rockwool is spent, toss it on your compost pile, use it for insulation, or throw it away. —D.J.P.

Q: I am a teacher of severely emotionally disturbed students, grades 9–12. We have a small greenhouse of about 10x16 feet and we would like to do some vegetable gardening using hydroponics. We would like to use 4-inch

Q: **I am doing an experiment on if plants need darkness to grow. I'm growing a set of plants with regular daily sunlight, plants with 24-7 artificial light, and plants with an automatic timer that turns a light on and off every two hours. Can someone give me information on which plants will grow better or faster?**

A: This sounds like an interesting experiment and I would suggest you use two different plant species—perhaps corn or maize, which is a C4 plant, and dwarf green beans, which is a C3 plant. Both of these plants will grow fairly quickly in your experiment. C3 and C4 plants differ in respect to their efficiency of CO_2 fixation in light and you may see differences in growth rates between the two groups of plants under the different lighting treatments (this will depend on the intensity of the light you are providing and the temperature at which the plants are grown).

Photosynthesis in plants consists of reactions that require light (called "light reactions") and those that do not require light (called "dark reactions," although they do not require darkness to be carried out). Often, plants grown for an extended length of time in 24-hour intense light will start to show starch accumulation in the leaves, which can cause distortion of the tissue and discoloration. However, most plants won't show any ill effects of being grown in 24-hour light for short periods if given "light breaks" every couple of hours. However, for some plant species, once they reach maturity, being given a long day treatment (such as continual light) or "light breaks" will act to induce or inhibit the flowering response. These treatments are often used by cut flower growers to induce or prevent flowering in their crops. —*L.M.*

Assuming we can adjust the flow of the pump to match the gravity flow from tube to tube and come up with a way to hold the plants tubes, will this work?

Are there any specific plans for such a setup? If we get plenty of air into the reservoir, will we need to run air into each tube? What would be the best way to suspend the plants? Is there a specific nutrient mix we can make or will something like fish emulsion or a mild solution of Peter's Plant Food work? Do you see any problems we would have with such a system?

A: Yes, the type of system you describe will work and has been used by many hobbyist growers with good success. However, you need to pay particular attention to the slope on the gullies to ensure that when there are mature plants in the channels, the root system does not restrict the flow too much (since these are round channels rather than rectangular ones). Being able to adjust the slope of the channels as the plants develop is useful for these types of systems.

I haven't come across any specific plans for this type of system, but the set up is simple and your description of the system sounds good. The most common type of problem with this sort of setup is making the system leak-proof. Getting the nutrient to flow from one channel down the next without leaking or dripping can be tricky. You may need to use some silicone sealant to keep this water-tight and keep a check on any leaks that might form as the plants' root systems try to grow under the sealant and between the joins in the PVC fittings.

There is actually probably no need to use an air pump at all. When the nutrient falls from the last channel back into the nutrient tank, it will introduce oxygen into the nutrient and this is usually the only form of aeration most hydroponic growers rely upon. Using the air pump to add additional oxygen into the nutrient tank won't do any harm, but it probably isn't necessary. There isn't any need to pump air into each of the channels. With this type of system, you are aiming for a flow rate of 1 liter of nutrient per minute per channel, and this needs to flow in a thin film, which isn't that easy in round channels (rectangular channels are considered by many growers to be better than round channels). You do not want a depth of nutrient any greater than 1 centimeter in the base of the channel, if possible. The plants' roots do not sit under the nutrient flow as this causes root death. The root mat should be moist with only the lower portion in the nutrient flow. The root system will wick up the nutrient by capillary action. The plants get plenty of oxygen both from within the nutrient and the air inside the channels.

How the plants are suspended in the system depends on the type of plants you want to grow. Larger plants, such as tomatoes, which will by tied up and supported anyway, can

PVC pipe in 10-foot lengths for our garden. We would like to have it set up so we can have four to six pipes with 1 to 2-inch holes in the top and plugged at each end with a 1/2-inch pipe going to the next tube. The tubes would be stepped down and filter down to each other. We have an old 100-gph pump and a very good air pump that should be able to supply all the oxygen needed. The idea is to have a reservoir (say a five-gallon bucket) that pumps the water up to tube #1, which gravity flows to tube #2 and then to #3 and so on, eventually ending up in the reservoir again.

be bare-rooted into the channels. Smaller plants, such as lettuce, herbs, and strawberries, are best raised in small, plastic tubes with a media, such as perlite or vermiculite, coconut fiber, expanded clay, etc. You can make your own small tubes with small diameter, round PVC pipe cut into 3- to 4-inch lengths, open at the base, which, when the seedlings are large enough, can be slotted into holes cut into the channels. The plants will have enough support to prevent them from slipping down into the channels and the root system will just grow out of the base of the tube or pipe. You can also use paper or peat pots to raise the seedlings and place the whole pot into the system (make sure there is a filter at the return pipe to catch any pieces of debris, etc.). You can also buy cubes of media, such as rockwool or oasis, which are used to raise seedlings and support the plant once placed into the channels.

Nutrient solutions will be essential to success of the this system. You cannot use fish emulsion or fertilizers designed for use on soil-based plants in this hydroponic system. These fertilizers are not complete—they do not feature all of the minerals required to grow plants. Hydroponic nutrients can be purchased from a large number of retailers on the Internet and these are very economical to use. Without the correct hydroponic nutrients, the plants tend to die rather quickly. Unfortunately, thus is a very common mistake make by many small growers. Fertilizers designed for soil or potted plants do not have all the essential plant nutrients required to grow plants hydroponically.

Apart from keeping a check on the leaks that might form, you might like to consider a bigger nutrient tank, if you can get one, and possibly a float value that will top up the water in the tank if it runs low and you are not there to fill it yourself. These types of systems, when full of mature plants, will remove a large volume of water, particularly under hot conditions. Having a bigger tank and/or a float value will help prevent the mishaps that always seem to occur over weekends when you can't keep an eye on the plants. A float value will also help prevent disasters from occurring should the system spring a leak. The plants will be kept alive until you can fix any problems that might occur. Smaller nutrient tanks also heat up rapidly in summer, making the nutrient solution far too warm for the plants, so having a larger tank slows the heat buildup and helps keep the plants cool for longer. —L.M.

Q: I have decided to work hydroponics into my plans. I normally have about 35 students in each class. Do you have any suggestions, about starting a small greenhouse structure? I am not sure about what type of space my principal will let me use for the hydroponics exercises, but if I can build something that is small enough for me to move if needed, that would be great. What are the important features of a greenhouse? Do you have any other advice for me?

A: Probably the best sort of greenhouse structure for your purposes would be a lean-to or partially attached type of greenhouse that is designed to be detached if you need to move it. If you can use an existing wall of a building or shed, then you can easily build a small greenhouse without the need for as much structural and foundation work as a free standing greenhouse would require. Lean-to greenhouses just require three walls, which can be clad in either plastic greenhouse (UV-resistant) film and a more rigid roof so that rainwater can be collected for the hydroponic system, if necessary. Polycarbonate sheeting (the clear, corrugated type) is reasonably inexpensive for the roof and should last many years and also prevents any ponding or pools of rainwater collecting, which often happens when the roof is covered in plastic film. Polycarbonate sheeting could also be used to clad the walls as a more permanent covering. However, this is more expensive than plastic greenhouse films. Here are some important points to keep in mind.

Ventilation: You need to have vent space (when open) that is equal to at least the equivalent of 30 percent of the floor area to prevent too much heat buildup. Not having enough ventilation is the most common factor causing plant growth problems in small greenhouses. If possible, designing some top vents in the roof that can be propped open on warm days is the best type (since warm air will naturally rise in the greenhouse, it needs to get out the top rather than accumulating inside the roof and superheating the whole structure). Also, some vents running the whole length of the side of the greenhouse and a big door that can be left open (and to get system components in and out) are all essential. Old window frames and old glass doors can sometimes be incorporated into your design if you have some you could use. You also want to consider some form of shading in summer. You may be able to stretch some shade cloth up inside the greenhouse just under the roof in summer to reduce radiation and hence light levels.

Floors: Dirt floors need to be covered to stop contamination from soil pathogens and dirt. Plastic film or woven plastic sheeting is good, preferably with a white surface to reflect back light in winter. A more expensive option is to use terra-cotta tiles or old red bricks. These act as a thermal bank to collect heat during the day and release it at night. A less expensive option that works well is to cover the floor with plastic and then place clean gravel over the top for a surface that will absorb water spills and also collect heat during the day.

Cladding: Make sure any plastic greenhouse film you select is UV-resistant (i.e., use greenhouse film, not just horticultural clear plastic, which breaks down within a year). Glass or polycarbonate sheeting is also a good cladding. However, they are more expensive and permanent and may need cleaning from time to time.

Heating and cooling: If you want to use your greenhouse year-round, you might need to consider heating and cooling. In a very small greenhouse, you could use a fan heater on a thermostat in winter to keep conditions above freezing. Good ventilation and plenty of air movement will help keep the greenhouse cool. Shading with shade cloth in summer and possibly using evaporative cooling are also options.

Other design options might include a large, cloche type of greenhouse (if you have a reasonably sheltered position or don't get high winds). These are constructed with a simple timber frame on the bottom with flexible hoops (often PVC) that slot into the frame and provide an arch, over which plastic film is stretched. The arches need to be high enough for you to walk into the structure and often need to be reinforced to prevent too much movement of the greenhouse in the wind. The problem with these sorts of structures is always ventilation. Top vents can't be built into the structure and usually the greenhouse is just left open at one or both ends to allow some airflow through the greenhouse (these are sometimes known as tunnel houses). Despite this, they get very hot in warm weather and tend to also have high humidity (not the best environment for hydroponic growing). These also aren't very resistant to wind. However, they have the advantage of being able to be put up and taken down quickly and moved to another position.

A final option would be a dome structure. These are portable and sometimes used for hydroponics. But again, heat buildup and ventilation can be a problem in these sorts of structures, even though they do look really great and are a bit different.

You could also build a bench-based outdoor hydroponic system and put a small cloche over the top for smaller plants, such as lettuce, herbs, strawberries, etc., rather than having a walk-in type of greenhouse structure.

Here are a few useful links for these sorts of greenhouses and plans for building some:

• Solar Greenhouse Plans and Information (www.hobby-greenhouse.com/FreeSolar.html)
• Shelter Systems Portable Greenhouses (www.shelter-systems.com/greenhouses.html)
• Solar Greenhouses—Horticulture Resource List (www.attra.org/attra-pub/solar-gh.html)
• Greenhouse & Hydroponic Vegetable Production Resources (www.attra.org/attra-pub/ghwebRL.html)
• Greenhouse Technology: A Step-By-Step Approach (www.crop.cri.nz/psp/broadshe/green.htm)

—*L.M.*

Q: What are the conditions influencing the rate of transpiration? Can you list the three important characteristics of xerophytes? Also, what meant by water balance?

A: The rate of transpiration in plants is influenced by numerous plant-based and environmental factors. These include the temperature, relative humidity, wind speed and direction (which influences the leaf boundary layer), radiation levels (which effect leaf temperature, the size, number and structure of the stomata where water vapor is lost), the current water status of the plant (i.e., if it is under water stress or fully turgid), the rate of transport of water from the roots to the leaves where water is lost, and the characteristics of the boundary layer close to the leaf surface.

Xerophytes grow where water is scarce, such as in deserts. Important characteristics of xerophytes are small leaves, sunken stomates, hairs on the leaves, deciduous leaves, ability to use osmoregulation to prevent desiccation, and water storage capacity in leaves and other organs.

I am not sure what you mean by "water balance" in plant physiology. The water soil-plant-air system is defined by the "water potential." Here is a definition of water potential in plants: The water potential is the chemical potential of water in a system or part of a system, expressed in units of pressure and compared to the chemical potential (also in pressure units) of pure water at atmospheric pressure and at the same temperature. The chemical potential of pure water is arbitrarily set at zero (from Plant Physiology, Third Edition, Salisbury and Ross, 1988). —*L.M.*

Q: What is the photosynthetic active radiation (PAR) needed in micromoles per meter squared for growing rice? If you were testing the growth of white rice under artificial light, what kind of light would you use?

A: The amount of radiation required to grow rice under artificial lighting depends on not only the density of the rice, but also the type or cultivar of rice being grown. However, rice plants have a high light saturation point of around 1,200 photosynthetic photon flux (PPF), which is a measure of PAR. I would suggest that to grow rice well at normal densities, you would want at least 1,000 PPF for the plants.

The type of artificial lights you will need are those that feature both the blue and red sections of the radiation spectrum since the plants will need to flower and set seed for you to obtain any crop. You can use metal halide or fluorescent lights until the plants are about to flower. At that point, you will need to add some high pressure sodium lights to provide the red spectrum for good flower formation and seed set. Alternatively, you could use full spectrum lights during all growth stages. Full spectrum lights have a similar radiation spectrum to sunlight. You will probably need a good light meter to check what radiation levels the plants are actually receiving as they grow. —*L.M.*

Q: I know that plants require a minimum level of artificial light to grow efficiently, but is it possible to have too much light? Is there a formulae for calculating the optimum light level?

A: Different plants have different recommended levels of light. For example, most lettuce varieties prefer lower levels of light and cooler weather. Conversely, most tomatoes love a lot of light and warmer temperatures. The key is to grow crops that are suited to your environment at different times of the year.

However, if you're going to be growing indoors and can control the environment somewhat through the use of artificial lighting, you can set whatever parameters you want. For example, if you want to grow lettuce, you could probably get away with using a metal halide lamp—or two or three, depending on how many plants you want to grow. Different lamps are rated to cover different size spaces. For example, a 250-watt metal halide lamp might be rated to cover 3x3 feet of direct light and 5x5 feet including indirect light. For tomatoes and similar plants, you would probably want to use a wider-spectrum lamp, such as a high-pressure sodium lamp or something similar.

Just make sure to find out what the type of plants you will be growing prefer in the way of temperature, humidity, light level, etc. For more on artificial lighting, see www.growingedge.com/community/archive/search.php3?query=light&c=all. —*D.J.P.*

Q: In regard to specific vegetables and plants, is a vegetative light cycle a standard 18-hour on/6-hour off, and a flowering light cycle a 12/12? Or are there varying cycles to trigger the change? I ask this intending to have a separate greenhouse for growth and one for fruit-producing and moving plants that are ready to flower from the vegetative greenhouse to the 12/12 one.

This seems to me to be key information to someone who wants to control what a plant does even throughout the winter season.

A: You are correct, in that there are different cycles to trigger the flowering response in some plants, but this is very species dependent. Some plants will flower, irrespective of how long the day length is, provided they have reached a certain physiological stage of development and are ready to flower. Other plants are triggered into flowering by being exposed to short days, long days, short days combined with chilling, or just by changes in temperature, such as the warming that occurs outdoors in spring.

Triggering of flowering (or prevention of flowering) will depend entirely on what plant you are growing. For example, a tomato crop could be grown under the same cycle of 16 hours on 8 off, right from germination, changing the light duration will not advance flowering. The plant will be triggered to initiate flowering when it has developed sufficiently and when conditions are right for development (i.e. warm enough), irrespective of what light duration you provide. On the other hand chrysanthemums can be triggered into flowering by providing a short day length (less than 13 hours of light in every 24 hours). Some other crops are also manipulated in this way to promote or delay flowering—strawberries have varieties that can differ in their day length requirement—some require short days to trigger flower initiation, some long days, and some are "day neutral" where the length of the light period has no effect on flowering. It would probably be a good idea to find out the flowering requirements of the particular species you are growing before you invest in separate flowering greenhouses and lighting systems. —*L.M.*

Q: I have heard that you can use a six hours on six hours off cycle. Is this true & are there any benefits to using this—i.e., is it possible that the plants' metabolism is speeded up?

A: I can't really see how a six hour on six hour off cycle would speed up plant metabolism. Most plant species grow best under a 12–18 hour day followed by a night break of at least 6 hours of darkness. Plants have evolved under these types of day/night conditions. However, I don't think the

6 hours on, 6 hours off will seriously harm the plants—although it could disrupt flower initiation in some species. Anyway the plants would probably adapt to this type of schedule. If it saves electricity cost for you, then by all means, give it a go. —L.M.

Q: How close should I keep the light to the plants? The plants are two weeks old and seem to be a little leggy.

A: Different lights should be kept at different minimum distances from plants. The main consideration is heat. If your lights give off heat, they should be kept a little further away from the plants to avoid any scorching. Otherwise, you want your lights pretty close to the plants—within a few feet. If your plants look leggy, it might mean that they are not receiving enough light. You might want to purchase a light reflector to place around your plants. One cheap way to perform this task is with aluminum foil and cardboard. Just wrap the foil around cardboard supports with the shiny side out. Place the reflector around your plants (ideally, on all sides) so that it sits at about a 45 degree angle. If you wish to purchase a reflector, many hydroponic suppliers carry them and they aren't very expensive. If you are looking to learn more about how to supply the best light possible to your plants, I would recommend George Van Patten's "Gardening Indoors with H.I.D. Lights." It covers all of the basics growers need to know in this area. —D.J.P.

Q: In a sealed room growing environment, what would be the symptom I should look for on my plant's leaves if I had CO_2 levels set too high? Would I even see any symptoms in this situation?

A: Yes, excessive levels of CO_2 from CO_2 enrichment in a sealed environment will indeed cause crop damage. This problem is not often seen in greenhouses—mostly because it is not economical to enrich past 1,000 ppm for most crops and because leakage from the greenhouse and the need for ventilation always lowers CO_2 below the danger point. However, in growth cabinet trials and in a sealed growing environment it is not difficult to enrich to levels that will damage plants, although the level at which damage will occur depends on a number of factors such as the type of plant, rate of CO_2 uptake, temperature, rate of enrichment, and timing of enrichment.

Just as with most other plant nutrients, too much CO_2 is detrimental to plant growth and the initial symptoms you might see would be visible leaf injuries such as chlorosis (yellowing), necrosis (dead spots or areas of tissue), and curling of the leaves. In some cases, growth reductions can occur at high CO_2 concentrations without any visible injuries. The injury caused by high CO_2 levels have been explained as being:

• Too high leaf temperatures at high light levels as affected by reduced transpiration at high CO_2 concentrations
• Accumulation of starch, which breaks down chlorophyll promoted by high light (in this case you might see thick and twisted leaves that turn a purple color from starch accumulation)
• Reduced nutrient uptake because of reduced transpiration, particularly at high air humidity

Also, if CO_2 enrichment is being carried out by the burning of hydrocarbon fuels, several air pollutants can be produced via this process, which causes their own problems and set of symptoms. —L.M.

Q: I have been using three hydroponic systems in my classrooms for three years now. I get flowers but never any fruit. I have tried tomatoes, chiles, and cucumbers. I am positive that the reason for this is the light sources—I have all fluorescent.

Are there any funding sources that you know of who will support indoor growing ventures in schools?

A: Fluorescent lights can be used to grow a variety of ornamentals, herbs, and salad greens in hydroponic systems indoors. However, you will need better lighting in order to grow fruiting plants indoors (without any help from a bright, sunny window).

There are a few ways educators can source capital for a hydroponic project. One of the best ways is to write a grant for the project. Educational grants are available throughout the United States. You can inquire through your union (if the teachers are unionized in your area) and local and state boards of education for a list of grants that are available every year. Some grants are also available on the national level—check with the National Education Association and National Gardening Association.

Another way to source supplies would be through local businesses. You could draw up a proposal for what you need and then see if you can get donations from relevant businesses in the area. I have heard about many school greenhouses that have been entirely funded by a local corporation (then the corporation gets a little plaque on the greenhouse that says "funded by . . ."). Ideally, the corporation would be interested in horticulture in some way or another. It's good PR for them.

I've also heard about groups that have organized to push regional law enforcement departments to donate confiscated equipment for use in schools. You could also push your local school district to provide the funding. Of all of these options, your best bet is probably to find a applicable grant to write for your needed equipment.

I don't know if you are familiar with our Educational Outreach program, but we routinely send out free copies of our magazine to schools around the country for use in the classroom (enough copies so each student can have their own, if they want). If you are interested in this offer, just let us know and we'll put you on the list. Every issue of the magazine has something in it that is useful to educators. —D.J.P.

Q: I have a small flood system (5-gallon reservoir). I have a problem with algae growth in the trays where the plants reside. The water does not drain completely out of the trays after the pump turns off. The algae is starting to cover the roots. I have heard that peroxide is the answer but I am concerned about how the plants will react. Also, if peroxide is the answer, what kind of concentration should I use and will it hurt to keep flooding the plants with the peroxide?

A: The only real long-term effective solution to algae control is to exclude as much light as possible from the root system and try to cover the top of the media where algae is growing. Algae is a form of plant life and most of the chemical products used to kill algae have the potential to also affect the plant roots, particularly of young, sensitive plants.

Hydrogen peroxide (H_2O_2) will indeed kill algae. However, getting the dose just right so that it is enough to kill the algae but not attack the plant roots (which are all organic tissues and H_2O_2 does not discriminate between algae cells and plant root cells), is very difficult. The problem also exists that even if you kill the algae in your system and not damage the plant root systems, the algae will rapidly regrow in a matter of days and you would need to add higher and higher doses of an algaecide on a regular basis to keep the problem under control. You can use high levels of H_2O_2 to clean out your system between crops when no plants are in it and then rinse well with plain water and replant.

The best solution is to take whatever measures are necessary to exclude light from the root system since algae covering the roots will soon suffocate the root system of oxygen and start to have a negative effect on plant growth. —L.M.

Q: Some of my new bean shoots are coming up with yellow leaves or yellow edges to the leaves. Can you help?

A: This is a common occurrence with many large seeds such as beans. Usually, it is caused by conditions that are too cold for rapid and normal germination and the green chlorophyll pigments are much slower to develop in the cotyledons (seedling leaves). It can also be caused by old seed that has lost some viability during storage and, while it may still germinate, cellular damage has occurred, which causes the yellowing or slow development of green pigmentation in the seedling leaves. Another option could be that there is some chemical residue in the media or soil that is causing the yellowing. Certain herbicide residues will cause this problem even if only tiny amounts are present in the soil. Finally, if there is insufficient light for the young seedlings, then green chlorophyll development is inhibited and the leaves will be yellow or very pale. —L.M.

Q: I live in the sunny south right dab in the middle of Georgia and Alabama. I am considering a greenhouse but would like to know if there is any type of plastic covering that is low emission or is shade cloth the only option? Also, is there any information available on selective tinting of greenhouse coverings?

A: There is a huge range of greenhouse cladding films available these days that will give you many options when it comes to lowering the emission and increasing shading of your growing structure, so shade cloth certainly isn't the only option. There are also products that can be sprayed onto the inner or outer surface of greenhouse film to provide shading when required.

With plastic films there are a number to choose from, including low-density polyethylene, polyvinyl chloride, and ethylene vinyl acetate copolymer—but polyethylene is the most commonly used film. It is now possible to get coextruded plastics, which include multiple layers of plastics that can create an infrared barrier, reduce condensation, and reduce disease or insect pressure to regulate plant growth with wavelength-selective plastics or simply to provide some specified degree of shading.

If you simply want shading on your greenhouse, but don't want to use a pull over shade cloth cover, there are plastics that are white instead of clear with different levels of shading. A 60 percent white 6 mil plastic will give you good shade without cutting out too much light for most plants. Below are a couple of good Websites with information on the various cover films for greenhouses and tunnels, their properties, and benefits for plant production.

www.greenhouses-etc.net/glazing/polyfilm.htm
www.kpmagencies.com/map.asp

—L.M.

Q: Our school has a DRF hydroponic system where the medium for growth is purely liquid. Recently, we have been interested in growing different kinds of flowers, such as daisies, zinnias, petunias, aster powderpuffs, carnations, and chrysanthemums. The instructions given for the growth of these flowers are damp soil but not wet. Will our system be able to allow the plants to grow? Will adding an air pump in the system that aerates the nutrient solution help? If not, what adaptations can be carried out to encourage growth?

Also, our Singapore weather is hot (77–86°F) and humid. Will such conditions be suitable for promoting flowering? If not, is there any possible nutrient ratio that can promote flowering?

A: Yes, your system will allow these plants to grow hydroponically—provided the nutrient solution does not become too warm in your climate and you pay particular attention to keeping the oxygen levels high in the nutrient. Under warm conditions, the nutrient holds much less dissolved oxygen and at the same time the plants' requirement for oxygen in the root zone increases due to a rapid growth rate. So you will need continual oxygenation of the hydroponic nutrients with a large air stone and air pump—or possibly more of these depending on how large the system is and how many plants are growing in it.

The plants you mention should flower when they are large enough. However, some flowering plants, such as chrysanthemums, may have to meet a day length requirement to induce them to flower. Chrysanthemums have a requirement for short day lengths to induce flowers—a critical day length shorter than 14.5 hours. There isn't a nutrient ratio that promotes flowering in these plants. The formulation of the nutrient does not affect whether a plant is switched to flowering or bud production. Flowering is a physiological process that can be influenced by the environment but, in most plants, occurs when the plant is mature enough to flower. —*L.M.*

Q: I am converting an old cow pen, about 10,000 square feet, to grow tomatoes in rockwool. The structure itself has very thick and high walls, thereby protecting the crop from wind. I would like to avoid having to roof the structure, which means my crop would be subjected to occasional showers. Is this something I should be worried about?

A: Hydroponic crops are grown outdoors (without an overhead structure) successfully in many situations. However, with your particular system, there could a be a couple of potential problems. While occasional showers (provided they are not heavy) will not physically harm the plants, they can provide conditions that will predispose the plants to attack by fungal and bacterial pathogens. Generally, some gentle air movement through and under a crop such as tomatoes is required to keep the atmosphere dry and humidity levels below 90 percent. This prevents many diseases from developing. With solid, high walls around the crop and showers wetting the foliage and growing structure, humid-

ity levels have the potential to become very high and, under warm conditions, plant disease problems will most likely occur very quickly.

You may be able to modify the environment by installing air movement fans at ground level to move warm, humid air up and out of the crop after rainfall but, depending on how often it rains, humidity levels inside such a structure are likely to be very high. Many greenhouse designs in warm, humid climates have side and bottom vents so that fresh air can be drawn up and through the crop, removing high humidity levels and drying the foliage if it becomes wet. If you are able to introduce a few ventilation gaps in the cow pen walls, this may also help with moisture removal and disease prevention. —*L.M.*

Q: In terms of plant transpiration, what is the difference between fluorescent light, home light, and sunlight?

A: Plant transpiration, which is the loss or evaporation of water from the plant's leaves, is more affected by the heat produced by different light sources than the radiation levels and types of wavelengths themselves. Fluorescent lights produce very little heat and therefore won't have much effect in terms of increasing plant water loss through evaporation. Home lights, such as the normal incandescent bulb, do give off heat and if placed too close to plants can heat the environment thereby increasing the rates of water loss through transpiration. However, incandescent bulbs aren't usually used in horticultural applications. Sunlight can be the most intense of all light sources and can heat the environment in a greenhouse to fairly high levels resulting in rapid plant transpiration.

However, once temperature levels become too high in the plant's environment, transpiration actually becomes reduced as the plant closes it stomata to prevent excessive water loss. For most crops, this will occur in the 79–104°F range, although a few plants can tolerate warmer temperatures before shutting down transpiration completely. —*L.M.*

Q: Will ceramic tile work as thermal mass? If so, can it be ordinary ceramic tile?

A: Thermal mass is ideally a darker color, which will heat up quicker and hold more warmth than lighter colors that tend to reflect radiation. However, plain, unglazed terra-cotta tiles also work well as an attractive heat sink. The thicker the tile the better, as it will hold more heat and be a more efficient thermal mass. An even better material would be terra-cotta or clay bricks that have a greater mass than tiles. Such materials have been used for centuries as heat sinks for crops (as greenhouse walls, floors, etc).

Generally, shiny, white, or pale-colored surfaces reflect back heat and light and are not as good for storing thermal heat. If you have an option, look for naturally darker-colored tile materials for a heat sink. Failing all else, a bank of gravel or stones can also work well to store heat during the day and release it at night. —L.M.

Q: I'd like to know if I can be successful in growing vegetables in my basement in South Dakota. I can't erect a hydroponic setup due to space constraints. If I keep the humidity up around 80 percent, can I grow in normal soil and will grow lights be sufficient? I'd like to grow tomatoes, green onions, and bell peppers.

A: As long as you keep the environmental conditions at levels that are acceptable for the crops you want to grow and provide sufficient light, you shouldn't have any trouble growing crops in your basement. Since you want to grow fruiting plants, your lights need to provide good levels of red and far red light. A good choice would be high pressure sodium lamps. A relative humidity level of 80 percent is fine. You will need to facilitate a good air exchange in the growing area. This means that you need to provide ventilation and regularly introduce fresh air into the growing area. One way to do this would be to use fans to pull stale air out of the growing area and introduce fresh air into the growing area. A temperature level of around 70°F. should be maintained for optimal growth. Try to not let the temperature drop much below this level at night. If temperatures drop below 60°F. at night you might start to experience problems—especially during flowering, fruit set, and fruiting. During flowering, you should gently shake the trusses every day to help facilitate good pollination and fruit set.

Growing in soil is fine, but you should know that hydroponic systems come in all sizes. Many systems can be built in a matter of a few hours out of readily available materials. Also, there are many good commercial systems that have been designed to fit into small spaces. One of the easiest ways to grow hydroponically is to simply grow the plants in pots filled with a mixture of perlite and vermiculite (or another soilless growing medium) and feed them regularly with hydroponic nutrient solution. You could even automate the process with a Dutch pot type of setup. Many commercial growers operate their greenhouses in this manner with the use of drip irrigation or drip emitters. If you're interested in the variety of hydroponic systems you could use, take a look through the following links:

www.growingedge.com/basics/tutorial/03_systems.html
www.growingedge.com/basics/easyplans/plans.html
www.growingedge.com/community/archive/
read.php3?c=ED&q=144

These simple systems are just the tip of the iceberg. If you're interested in finding out more about hydroponics, you might want to visit a some hydroponic retailer Websites to check out some of the systems they carry. Visiting stores in person is a great way to experience these systems firsthand. I don't know of any hydroponic retailers in South Dakota although I know of one in Nebraska (see www.growingedge.com/magazine/retailers/index.php3?country=USA&stateprov=NE) and a few in Colorado (see www.growingedge.com/magazine/retailers/index.php3?country=USA&stateprov=CO) if you ever travel to those areas. A beneficial aspect of many hydroponic systems is that they can be automated so that you don't have to worry about turning on and off the lights or watering the plants when they need it (which is particularly nice if you're away for a few days). —D.J.P.

Q: When growing plants in aeroponics, what are the necessary nutrients needed? Is it possible that the system's chamber can be made of metal? How many times do I have to spray the nutrients in one day?

A: When growing plants using an aeroponic system, you need all the essential elements plants require for growth and development: nitrogen, potassium, phosphorus, calcium, magnesium, sulfur, iron, manganese, zinc, boron, copper, molybdate, and chloride. These must be provided in the correct form (i.e. greenhouse or laboratory grade fertilizer salts of high solubility and iron in the chelate form), in the correct ratio for the crop you are growing, and at the correct concentration (EC).

Yes, the chamber can be made of metal, so long as it is painted or lined with a plastic material or film so that the nutrient does not come into contact with the metal surface itself.

How often the nutrients are misted onto the root system depends on the temperature, size of the root system, design of the system, capacity of the pump, and a number of other variables. Spraying can be carried out continually in warm climates or for a period of 15 seconds every 3-5 minutes, so long as the root system never dries out between mistings. —L.M.

Q: How would you do hydroponics in an outdoor greenhouse in Kodiak, Alaska? The climate is similar to Vancouver Island—some heat available and lots of sun for a short growing season.

A: The type of hydroponic system that would suit this type of climate largely depends on the types of crops you want to grow. Lettuce and salad greens could be grown in small diameter nutrient film technique (NFT) gullies with minimal heating. Larger, fruiting crops would require either a media-based system or larger NFT channels and would certainly require a good heating system, particularly to maintain night temperatures and prevent disease infection.

I would suggest that you start small with an experimental unit in the outdoor greenhouse to determine what cropping factors are going to be most limiting in your climate and how long the growing season will actually be. Often, this is the only way to really determine if light, temperature, and other variables are suitable for the types of plants you want to grow and whether you are going to need additional equipment for heating/cooling, lighting, venation etc.

For a short growing season, you may like to consider "alternative" cropping techniques such as the single truss system of tomato production. This is where tomato plants have the growing point removed three leaves above the first flower truss so that only one bunch of fruit per plant is permitted to develop (or sometimes two, depending on the length of the growing season). This speeds up the development of the fruit so that tomatoes can be obtained much quicker than they would under a normal, multi truss cropping system.

sick, aren't setting fruit properly, and the flower buds abort. White spots occur on leaves, but it isn't mildew.

If, in fact, this is due to salt accumulation, what is the correct flushing procedure? If you feel there may be another cause, please advise.

A: The best way to avoid salt accumulation is to obtain a good electrical conductivity (EC) meter and check the strength of the nutrient solution going into the system and then coming out. What you are aiming for is an EC that drops slightly as it flows through the system. If the EC of the solution draining out of the system is substantially higher than that going in, salt accumulation is likely. With fruiting crops, flushing with water is only really a good idea between crops since it can cause fruit splitting and other problems.

The problem of white spots on the leaves could describe any of a number of nutritional, physiological, or other problems. Zinc, potassium, and calcium deficiency can sometimes result in pale or white patches on the leaf surface. Also, mites cause a yellow speckling followed by a pale bronzed appearance of the foliage. Leaf scorch—which can result in white, papery patches on the upper leaves—isn't uncommon under lights. Plants that are sickly looking with floral abortion could be troubled by mites, an environment that is too hot and dry, or could be the result of nutritional problems.

Salt accumulation tends to result in plants that are small, dark, and stunted. The leaves may take on a leathery appearance with browning at the leaf margins. This may also cause flower drop. You may also notice salt crusting on top of the media—particularly in flood and drain sys-

---

The trick is to irrigate frequently enough so that the growing media doesn't completely dry out between cycles and not so often that the media always stays soaking wet.

You also might want to read about John Harmon, a semi-commercial gardener who has been growing hydroponically in greenhouses outside of Whitehorse, Yukon. He who wrote an article for The Growing Edge in Volume 12, Number 1. —L.M.

Q: This is my first year growing hydroponically and I've been experiencing some problems that I feel may be caused by the accumulation of salts. I'm growing in PermaTill (expanded slate) and originally was using a one-part premixed powder nutrient solution. I've since changed to a three-part solution. Many plants are beginning to look

tems—or around the sides of the growing bed, on pumps, and on other equipment. If you suspect that salt buildup is the problem, flushing with a dilute nutrient solution (one-quarter strength) is better for the plants than flushing with plain water. Flushing should only be undertaken once every couple of weeks. —L.M.

Q: I would like to know how long, in seconds, the sprayer must be on and off in an aeroponic system.

A: For young plants with a small root system, you need to mist for short periods of time on a very frequent basis since there isn't any media to hold moisture around the root zone.

How often and for how long you mist may need to be evaluated by you as it also depends on things like the pressure of the spray, volume sprayed over a certain time, type of spray nozzle, droplet size of the spray, design of the system, number of nozzles, temperature of the air in the root zone, and so on. I would suggest you initially try 15 seconds in every three to four minutes and see if the root system stays sufficiently moist between mistings. This should be increased with longer misting periods as the root system gets larger. —L.M.

Q: We have just started growing hydroponically. We grow all our own herbs as well as other vegetables. Currently, we grow each plant in different containers. My question is which plants use which minerals (i.e. if tomatoes use more nitrogen and basil uses very little nitrogen)? Everywhere I have asked, I get the same reply—more or less, "plant it and it will grow," which it has. I am growing sweet basil, oregano, thyme, sage, mint, rosemary, corn, tomatoes, lettuce, and carrots. But I would like to grow more and I looking for references to something along the lines of "companion growing" for hydroponics or aquaponics.

A: This is a very valid question! You are correct in that different plants and even different herbs have very different requirements in regard to their mineral ratio requirements. As a very general grouping, many smaller growers will have one system for leafy salad greens and succulent herbs and another system for fruiting crops, such as tomatoes, corn, etc. These two separate cropping groups would have not only different recommended electrical conductivity (EC) levels (higher for the fruiting plants) but also a different nutrient formulas.

If you are looking for the ideal in plant nutrition, then there is pretty much a specific optimal nutrient formula for each plant species and this is what commercial growers who are "monocropping" aim to use. Therefore, every crop would have their own nutrient solution. Hobbyists rarely get this sophisticated.

In general, fruiting crops, such as tomatoes and corn, have a higher potassium and phosphate requirement for good fruit growth, quality, and flavor when compared to the vegetative only crops that use a higher nitrogen to potassium ratio. This ratio can vary widely depending on the crop's state of growth and a number of other factors. Even amongst your herbs, there is a wide range of different "optimal" nutrient ratios and formulas that give the best growth, flavor, and yields. For example, basil is an unusual herb nutritionally since it has a high potassium requirement compared to other herbs that have a higher nitrogen requirement. Various other herbs, such as chives and garlic chives, prefer more sulfur in the nutrient, while iron levels need to be kept higher for other plants, such as mint.

Many of the guides to "companion growing" exits for general, soil-based gardening. These can be applied to hydroponics if you are simply after information on what plants produce well next to each other and which seem to inhibit each other, those that attract beneficial insects, and so on. One good source is at www.gardenguides.com/TipsandTechniques/vcomp.htm. This has a good list of combinations of plants for planting. There is also a book called "Carrots Love Tomatoes" that has much information along the same lines. —L.M.

Q: Is there a design criteria for aerating deep pools? For example, how much aeration should be designed into a system for each square foot of plants? I plan on using diffusers to create bubbles in the reservoir.

A: The problem with this type of calculation is that you need to take a few other variables into account. First of all, you need to consider the temperature. If the deep pools are being heated or the environment is warmed, more oxygenation will be required in the system than if the nutrient was cool. This is because warmer solution holds less oxygen and the plant root requirement for oxygen increases as temperatures rise. Thus, a tropical deep pool system would need a much greater degree of aeration than one in a cooler climate. Secondly, you need to take your crop into account. Larger plants, such as fruiting tomatoes, require more dissolved oxygen (DO) than smaller seedling plants, such as lettuce or herbs.

Probably the best way to find out how much DO is enough would be to start by installing one diffuser per square foot of plants. Then get yourself some DO test strips (available from Hanna Instruments, www.hannainst.com/, and other companies). Take DO readings as the crop progresses, temperatures changes, and so on. You would want to achieve a DO level of at least 5 parts per million (ppm) in warmer conditions (68°F and above), which would probably be around 7 ppm in cooler conditions. Saturation occurs at about 12–13 ppm, which would be the ideal level, but you will probably need to balance out the cost of the diffusers versus the amount of oxygen you can keep in the solution. Oxygen diffuses very quickly out of the solution and plant oxygen uptake can often surprise growers. Running a trial is the best way to obtain exact figures. —L.M.

Q: What is the optimal amount of time that it should take to flood a ebb-and-flow system? What is the optimal time to drain? My system floods in 5 minutes and drains in about 3. Is this too fast? too slow? I thank you in advance for your help and look forward to hearing from you soon.

A: Your flood and drain times are a bit on the fast side, but I doubt that it is something to be concerned about. What is more important is the frequency of the irrigations. The frequency of irrigation for ebb-and-flow (also called flood-and-drain) systems varies for a number of reasons. Mainly, the frequency depends on the type of media being used (different growing media, such as rockwool and expanded clay, have different water-retention properties) and the environmental conditions of the growing area (how much light there is, the relative humidity, the temperature, and the amount of air movement present).

The goal is to let the growing media dry slightly—but never completely—between irrigations. You also don't want the media to be soaking wet all of the time. Too much water can drown the roots. Also, keep in mind that as the plants grow, they will begin using more water. Therefore, younger plants need fewer irrigations and as they get older, the frequency might need to be increased a bit.

I have heard so many different recommendations for irrigation cycles that it's pointless for me to relay them to you. They vary from once an hour to once every six hours to once every twelve hours. I would recommend that you try to devise your own cycling times for your particular environment and different types of media. Just keep an eye on your plants and see how they react to your irrigation cycles. If they're happy, you're doing something right! —D.J.P.

Q: Other than tomatoes and bean plants, are there any other types of fruits or vegetables that are suitable for hydroponics? What advantages can there be if hydroponics is grown in a city like Singapore?

A: Yes, there is a very wide variety of crops that have been properly tested for hydroponic cultivation. Practically any plant can be grown in a hydroponic system. The most popular commercial hydroponic crops are tomatoes, lettuce, salad greens, cucumbers, herbs, and bell peppers. But more crops are tested every year. Commercial hydroponic growing can be lucrative.

Many people in large cities such as Singapore cultivate hydroponic gardens. In fact, I happen to know that Singapore has a well developed hydroponic community. Some people have small greenhouses for their hydroponic crops. Others grow on rooftops. And still other hydroponic gardeners simply grow plants next to sunny windows, on their balconies, or under artificial light indoors.

Some of the advantages of such hobbyist cultivation are the same as with any other type of home gardening—namely, enjoying the process and the fruits of your labor. But hydroponics also conserves space and water better than other types of gardening. Hydroponic gardeners can grow more

food in a smaller amount of space as traditional, soil-based gardeners. And under good conditions, hydroponic growth rates and yields can be higher than traditional gardening. So you can see how hydroponics is well suited to a crowded city where space is limited. —D.J.P.

Q: I am very new to hydroponics so I don't know the answer to this question. I have a spaghetti squash plant on the go. It is still a little one with only six true leaves right now. When putting some support on it (a string attached to my ceiling), I noticed that there is a split in the main stem. Will my plant be alright or do I need to give up on it and start a new one?

I use the flood and drain method and, up until now, the plant has been doing great. I am not sure what could have happened to make a split in the plant but I am sure that it has only happened within the last day. I am anxiously waiting for your reply. Thanks for your time.

A: If you don't have any, go buy some green horticultural tape. This type of tape is usually used to join stem grafts for propagation purposes and should be available at your local garden center. It's a cloth type of tape. Use this tape to join your split stem. Don't use any other type of tape since the glue or plastic could be phytotoxic (poisonous to plants). I can't make any guarantees, but this is probably your best chance at saving your plant.

Over the next several days, make sure you handle your plant with extra care. Also, make sure that the support string you have attached isn't pulling too much on the plant. It should be just firm enough to support the plant—maybe even just a little bit slack for the next several days. If the plant survives, don't remove the tape. It won't hurt to leave the tape on throughout the life of the plant.

If the split in the main stem isn't too low on the plant and you have some lateral leaves or shoots below the split, another option would be to trim off the main stem at the spilt and let the plant regenerate below the injury. —D.J.P.

Q: There is definitely a knack for being a good green thumb. I have spent a lot of money on all of the finest indoor growing supplies on the market today. I would like to know from germination to harvest the best nutrients, solutions ebb and flow nutrient release times (for 24 hour period), general tips on timing (when to use all high tech products)—pretty much the whole enchilada—so I don't spin my wheels and waste any more money. As far as grow guides it seems to me that a lot of authors from different books contradict each other. Please help to send me down the right road with a no nonsense list of helpful tips (moronic version please).

A: You're correct in noting that there are many different ways to achieve success in hydroponic growing. This is largely due to the fact that different growers use different types of systems, media, and plants. Also, every growing environment—amount and type of light, temperature, humidity, etc.—is different. Therefore, it is a good idea to tailor your particular growing situation to your environment. But here are some general tips to help get you started.

Hydroponic retailers carry many different kinds of all-purpose hydroponic nutrient solution—including both inorganic and organic varieties and those that come in liquid and powdered form. There will usually be two different solutions for the two different stages of plant growth: growth and blooming. Many of these products will work well in a variety of growing systems and with many different crops on a hobbyist level. If you want to, when you are shopping for a nutrient solution, just mention the types of plants you will be growing and the type of system they will be growing in. Chances are, the store employee might be able to recommend a particular nutrient solution for your situation.

The number of times a grower will irrigate their plants in an ebb-and-flow system varies depending on the type of media used, the stage of growth the plants are in, and the environmental conditions. The trick is to irrigate frequently enough so that the growing media doesn't completely dry out between cycles and not so often that the media always stays soaking wet. Recommended guidelines vary from once every hour to once every six hours. Try some different timed cycles in your growing environment and see what works best for you. Keep in mind that younger plants take up less nutrient solution than older, mature plants. Also, warmer, drier conditions will require more frequent irrigations than cooler, humid conditions.

Our Hydroponic Q & A Archive might be a good resource for you as you begin growing (see www.growingedge.com/community/archive/topics.html). Chances are, many of the questions you might have to ask have already been posed by other folks. Browse around the archive and see if you can learn anything. Just remember that what works for one grower in their particular growing situation may not work for every grower—but it might be worth a try.

Also, learn as much as you can about what the plants you are growing need in regard to light levels, humidity, temperature, and so on. Different crops have different requirements, so it's best to be as informed as possible before you begin growing. —D.J.P.

Q: What is the proper method for topping plants? How much should be cut off, how often?

A: Some plants can be trimmed (also called "pinching back") in order to create a shorter and bushier—instead of taller and skinnier—plant. Without knowing what type of plant you are referring to, I cannot make any specific suggestions. However, here are a few general rules.

Gardeners usually trim plants while they are in vigorous vegetative growth (usually spring when growing in uncontrolled conditions). Cut off the top part of any side shoot that will still have a few (three or so) growth nodes left after taking the cutting. Doing so will encourage the plant to develop more side shoots.

If the plant doesn't have any side shoots, it is possible that you can cut the top off it to encourage new growth. However, the plant should be established, sturdy, and in a good stage of growth when such a cutting is made. If the plant is too young and weak, such a cut may not encourage growth, but rather shock it and cause trouble.

Make sure you always use a sterile knife or scissors (a knife is better—like an "exacto" knife or utility blade) to make cuttings. Fresh cuttings in plants are susceptible to disease. If the stems aren't too thick, sometimes you can just pinch the ends off with your fingers.

You can then root the cuttings (if they are of a decent size) you have taken and grow more plants from them (to grow yourself or give away). —D.J.P.

Q: Do you know of any wholesale or retail U.S. growers of soilless plants that can be potted in the Luwasa hydroculture pot systems?

A: Not many nurseries specifically raise "soilless" plants. However, most ornamental and houseplants are raised in media that doesn't contain soil but is composed of other organic and inorganic (inert) matter, such as peat, bark, sawdust, pumice, sand, expanded clay, perlite, vermiculite, etc.—all of which are compatible with hydroculture systems since they are not usually contaminated with soil.

It's a fairly simple operation to shake off the excess soilless media from most plants, soak them in a bucket of water (with some dilute fungicide product added if you are worried about root diseases), then plant them into your hydroculture pot system. Local nurseries and garden centers should have a good selection of plants that have been raised in soilless potting media. Whenever possible, use young plants or seedlings as these will establish more rapidly in your new system. —L.M.

Q: I have made an "aguafarm" that consists of a bucket with nutrients and another bucket with the growing media and plants and an air system that pumps the nutrients up to the top and drips down through the growing media and back to the nutrient tank. My question is: How long should I run the drip system or what should the on/off cycle time be?

A: Sounds like you have the start of a nice system going! How frequently you irrigate your plants can be based on a few factors—mainly the temperature, amount of light the plants receive, type of media being used, and the stage of growth of your crop.

Every time you irrigate your plants, you want to be sure they get a good watering. The media should be evenly wetted. Evenly feeding the plants can take anywhere from 5–15 minutes, depending on the size of your bed and the ability of your media to retain water. Then, when you irrigate again will depend on when the media dries out. If your media is very free-draining and dries out quickly, your temperature is normal to high, and the plants are exposed to a good amount of sunlight, you might want to irrigate a few times a day—maybe every two hours for five minutes each time. If the media retains water well, irrigating twice a day might be enough. Every system and situation may be different. Just keep an eye on how long it takes for your media to dry out and how your plants are going. Also keep in mind that younger plants don't take up as much water as mature, established plants.

I grow some pepper plants in an ebb-and-flow system in expanded clay pellets. Since the clay holds water well, I only irrigate the plants once a day when they are just getting started. Then, when the plants are established and mature, I irrigate twice a day. It's best to keep an eye on your plants to see how they behave in relation to your irrigation schedule. Never let the media dry out too much. Try a system of irrigation that wets the media, lets it dry somewhat, and then feeds again.

Also keep in mind that you will need to flush your media with dilute nutrient solution every so often to remove any excess salt buildup. Maybe once every few weeks, flush your media with plain water or dilute nutrient solution to remove the buildup. This will help keep your plants healthy. —D.J.P.

Q: Firstly, I'll describe my setup. I have a tank of nutrient solution with an air pump into it and air stones on the end to increase the solubility of the air into the water. I also have another tray that sits partly into the nutrient tank (with drain holes so the solution returns to the bottom tank) and in that tray are the lattice pots and the plants in them with expanded clay medium. So that means the plants are always about an inch into the solution. I use a water pump in the solution in the bottom tank to drip feed the plants from above at the base of the exposed plant every 2 hours for about 30 minutes. The top tank fills to the base of the plants of the course of that 30 minutes. Also I use a Son T Agro lamp, exhaust fan, and cooling fan onto the plants. I use Optimum Growth solution with Monstabud solution and root accelerant. I use pH upper/downer to get the right levels.

Now the questions: The bottom leaves are turning yellow, why? Is this too much feeding? Are there ways to improve my setup?

I've heard that the roots at the top are the feeding ones and the bottom roots are just drinkers, is this true? If so, what is the best way of watering each type of roots and which ones take in oxygen?

A: There are a number (actually quite a number) of problems that can cause the yellowing of the bottom leaves on plants. Many nutrient deficiencies (such as nitrogen and magnesium), a number of diseases, and a number of physiological conditions cause these type of symptoms. Without knowing the exact composition of your nutrient solution, I can't comment on whether this is a nutritional problem or not. It is likely that since your plants are always about an inch into the solution that this is a lack of oxygen. Despite you having air stones in the nutrient, the roots should not be constantly submerged at the bottom of the pot. This can

lead to stagnation and oxygen starvation. If you can arrange the system so that the bottom of the plant pots are not sitting in any nutrient, that will help the situation.

Yes, your plants are being fed too often. Your plants are in an expanded clay medium, which will retain enough moisture for them between feedings and also allow oxygen to penetrate—where the plants are not sitting in nutrient constantly. Feeding every 2 hours is fine, but 30 minutes is a bit excessive. You might just want to drip (or flood and drain) to replenish the nutrient in the media—not wash it all through for 30 minutes. Perhaps 3–5 minutes every 2 hours would be sufficient—or 1–2 minutes every hour under warmer conditions.

There are a number of strange theories about "root specialization," but it is not true that the roots at the top are the feeders and the bottom ones are the drinkers. All live roots actively absorb minerals and water. There is some degree of root specialization in the plant kingdom—mangroves, for example, have aerial roots that can absorb oxygen from the air—but this is generally not the case with most of our cropping plants. The best idea is to ensure all roots have access to sufficient moisture, nutrients, and oxygen for maximum growth and yields. I hope this helps you to improve your system a little. —L.M.

Q: What type of temperature and humidity levels should I keep my grow area at for maximum carbon dioxide (CO_2) absorption?

A: The temperature level for maximum CO_2 absorption and growth is largely species dependent—for example a tomato plant will have a maximum uptake of CO_2 (provided there is sufficient light) at about 75–79°F but a lettuce plant has a lower temperature requirement of about 53–60°F. Humidity levels play a lesser role with respect to CO_2 uptake, provided they are not excessively high or low—the ideal range for a grow room would be between 70–85 percent humidity, which can be difficult to achieve if you have a lot of large, actively transpiring plant in an enclosed space. Often, if ventilation is not sufficient and space is limited, the humidity can reach 100 percent very quickly (due to water loss from the plants, media, nutrient etc), so measuring humidity levels can be important. High humidity levels also predispose your plants to many fungal pathogens, so trying to keep the levels down is a good idea. —L.M.

Q: Do plants use CO_2 during the day or during the night or both? I am wondering when I should supply extra CO_2.

A: Plants use CO_2 during the day, in the presence of light, and give off oxygen as a by-product. At night, when it is dark, no photosynthesis takes place, so the plants don't take up CO_2, but use oxygen in the process of respiration instead. So, applying CO_2 at night would be pointless. Generally, growers will start to enrich the plants' atmosphere with CO_2 about one hour after dawn when ambient levels of CO_2 start to decline as the CO_2 that has accumulated at night is absorbed by the plants and CO_2 levels in the air start to drop to a point whereby photosynthesis is affected and reduced.

CO_2 enrichment is most beneficial where it is combined with light levels high enough to give a good stimulation of photosynthesis and hence accelerate plant growth. The temperature also needs to be warm enough to keep the whole process of photosynthesis ticking along at maximum speed. CO_2 enrichment is also most efficient where the growing area is not constantly venting to the outside as the CO_2 you supply can all be lost through ventilation before the plants get a chance to use it. At the same time, some ventilation is also required to remove excess moisture, which the plants are continually producing, from the air and to give some degree of temperature reduction if required. For this reason, the use of CO_2 enrichment and ventilation is a process of compromise. —L.M.

Q: With any successful grow room, what is the best procedure for exhaust blower operation—its duration, the best time to enrich with CO_2, and the best time to operate the inlet blower?

A: The amount of time necessary to operate an exhaust fan to facilitate good air exchange rates depends on several factors, including how much artificial lighting is being used, how large the grow room is, the stage of plant growth, how many plants are being cultivated, and the effectiveness of the ventilation setup. A rule of thumb is that you want a complete air exchange every hour. However, this is not always possible in an indoor setting.

Your best bet will be to gauge your required level of ventilation according to how warm and humid the growing area gets during the day. You want to keep temperatures and humidity levels at close to optimum levels for the crops you are growing. Exhaust fans are usually rated based on the amount of air (usually cubic feet) they can move in one minute. So, once you have calculated how large the grow room is, you can figure out how long it will take to exhaust the entire area. Try to keep the venting fan (or fan connected to ductwork, whatever your system is) high in the room, if possible. That will permit more humid air to be vented. At the same time, you want to have another fan that will be introducing fresh air (or at least an opening that will passively pull fresh air into the area while the exhaust fan is working). Then, once your venting time is complete, the openings to the outside (vent and fresh air introduction windows or ductwork—everything) need to be closed. Then you can introduce the desired level of CO_2 during the day to aid the crop until the time of the next venting. You should also have good air movement within the room at all times with the use of fans. Some sophisticated indoor garden set-ups can facilitate these functions automatically with the use of sensors and timers. You will want to keep an eye on your plants as much as possible in the early stages of implementing your ventilation setup to see how they react and how the environmental conditions in your room develop. —*D.J.P.*

Q: Is it safe to have a worm composter in my hydroponic grow room or would there be a risk of disease or pests transferring to my plants? I'm thinking that it might be a low-tech way to add CO_2.

A: Generally, a vermicast system would not produce sufficient CO_2 to increase levels in your growing area to numbers that would benefit plant growth. CO_2 levels in the air are about 360 parts per million (ppm). To get a significant increase in plant growth, the atmosphere needs to be enriched to at least 800 ppm, but preferably over 1,000 ppm. Given that you need to have some form of venting in your growing area (which removes CO_2) and that the plants remove reasonably large quantities of CO_2 when exposed to light, the vermicast system would not provide CO_2 fast enough to improve plant growth (unless you have a very large worm farm and very little ventilation in your growing area).

There are other low-tech ways of providing CO_2 that don't have the associated pest and diseases risks of having compost or vermicast in your growing area. These include fermentation (although this also doesn't provide a great deal of CO_2 and is a slow method of production), dry ice, burning various fuels, and compressed CO_2 cylinders.

Generally, it is not recommended to have composting or a worm farm in the same area as your plants unless it is isolated from the growing area so that there is no transfer of pests and diseases. While the finished vermicast is usually OK, the material you may put into the system could contain fungal spores, bacteria, and pathogens that could be transferred over to your plants. Also, composting and vermicast systems tend to attract fungus gnats and some other pests that could carry disease over to your plants in addition to becoming pests in their own right. Your worm farm would be better sited away from the plants—somewhere that you can safety compost your crop residues and other materials without the possibility of contaminating your crop. —*L.M.*

Q: In a tightly sealed grow room with CO_2 controlled at 1,500 ppm and the temperature controlled with air conditioning, is it still necessary to exhaust the room and bring in fresh air on a regular basis?

A: It is possible to run a grow room without venting at all, provided you keep CO_2 levels up during the day and return CO_2 levels to ambient during the dark or night period when plants don't have any need for CO_2 (but need O_2) and if you control the temperature within the correct rate for plant growth. However, you also need to have control over relative humidity levels within the grow room. Without venting moist air to the outside and bringing in fresh, dryer air, humidity within the grow room will rapidly increase to very high levels as the plants give off water vapor via the process of transpiration. This high humidity level then not only provides the ideal conditions for pathogens to attack, but also slows plant growth. If humidity levels become so high that they prevent the plants from transpiring (and they will very quickly in a warm grow room), nutrient uptake and photosynthesis will be negatively affected and plant growth will slow. Physiological disorder conditions may also develop and the plants could even develop a condition called "edema," which occurs when excess water is in the plant cells under high humidity conditions. If you control and remove excess humidity as the plants release water into the air then, in theory, there isn't a need to vent and bring fresh air into the grow room. You will need to monitor humidity levels and scrub excess moisture from the air with a dehumidifier unit to maintain a level around 75–85 percent. —*L.M.*

Q: Where can I find some real data (actual data, not theory) concerning the correlation between the uptake and absorption of CO_2, light (lux, PAR), nutrient EC (and each element), pH, RH, and temperature?

A: This type of data is crop specific. Data for CO_2, nutrients, pH, relative humidity, and temperature will vary considerably depending on a number of factors and will also be very different for each type of greenhouse crop. However, there is a very good book that details these factors:

Carbon Dioxide Enrichment of Greenhouse Crops, Volume II—Physiology, Yield, and Economics, M. Z. Enoch and B. A. Kimball, (CRC Press, Boca Raton, Florida 1986). (Volume 1 might be of use as well.)

There are also a number of individual references to studies that have been carried out on various aspects of the data you are looking for:

"An Analysis of Some Effects of Humidity on Photosynthesis by a Tomato Canopy Under Winter Light Conditions and a Range of Carbon Dioxide Concentrations," B. Acock, et al, Journal of Experimental Botany, Volume 27 (1976), pages 933–941.

"Effect of Light Intensity, Carbon Dioxide, and Leaf Temperature on Gas Exchange of Carnation Plants," H. Z. Enoch and R. G. Hurd, Journal of Experimental Botany, Volume 28, page 84–95.

There is also a review article that has some links to the studies you are after:

Review: "CO_2 Enrichment in Greenhouses, Crop Responses," by L. M. Mortensen, Scientia Horticulturae, Volume 33 (1987), pages 1–25.

Also, here are some Websites that have some information and reports on crop CO_2 enrichment:

www.co2science.org
www.fao.org ("The Effects of Elevated CO_2 and Temperature Change on Transpiration and Crop Water Use")

These sources should provide much of the data you are searching for and also lead you on to some other sources of information. —L.M.

Q: Does CO_2 build up naturally from the plants in a greenhouse during no-light periods? I'm just wondering if I should stop ventilation part-way through the night and leave it off for the first half-hour or so of light in order to make use of this extra CO_2. Does this make sense?

A: Some—but not all—plants do release a blast of CO_2 after dark. This is directly related to photosynthesis. And yes, most plants need good supplies of CO_2 during the day in order to grow vigorously. Commercial growers frequently invest extra capital into CO_2 enhancement devices.

any stored supplies of CO_2 will quickly disperse. I would imagine that this is a nonissue. Good ventilation during the day is the key.

This process of supplying different levels of CO_2 to different plants at different stages of growth can get pretty involved. I wouldn't worry about it unless you notice slowed growth in your plants. If that occurs, it is possible that you have lower levels of CO_2 in your atmosphere in your area (however, that is rare these days…). —D.J.P.

Q: I am a new grower in hydroponics and have just bought a ppm meter. I was wondering: What is the best reading to have in my solution for flowering plants? I have been having a lot of problems with my plants wilting and leaves turning yellow and burning—very little growth and I have lost some plants. That is why I bought a tester but am not sure what the best reading should be.

Also, I was thinking of getting a CO_2 enhancer. What would be your suggestion (for the least amount of money)? I have a small garden around 8x8 feet.

A: Although knowing the parts per million (ppm) of your nutrient solution is worthwhile when you mix it, after that point, it really doesn't do you much good. The best way to measure the strength of your nutrient solution is with an electrical conductivity (EC) meter. Different crops have different EC ranges that they should be grown within. For example, roses should be grown at an EC between 1.8 and 2.6. Please see www.growingedge.com/community/calc_conv.html for a more thorough explanation of ppm measurements vs. EC.

Room cooling, in an enclosed space, is best carried out by extractor fans to remove the warm, humid air from the growing area and bring in cooler, drier air from outside.

However, one of the best ways to cheaply supply good levels of CO_2 to your plants is to have good ventilation in the greenhouse during the day (when the plants can use the CO_2 during photosynthesis). Studies have shown that as the level of turbulence over the leaf's surface increases, the more CO_2 the plant takes in. That's why it's a good idea to have a fan in the greenhouse.

I doubt that trapping the CO_2 that your plants give off will be a better supply than can be obtained through good ventilation. Many growers routinely close the greenhouse off at night in order to retain heat. However, when the greenhouse is opened and ventilation begins the next day,

You should also be monitoring the pH of your nutrient solution. Most plants grow well at a pH between 6.0 and 6.5, which is a slightly acidic solution (a pH of 7 is neutral; above 7 is alkaline). Most hydroponic retailers sell premixed pH up and down solutions to help you maintain the proper pH. Many manufactures sell combination EC and pH meters. It is possible that you could trade in your ppm meter for such an instrument. The pH of the nutrient solution can also be determined with litmus paper and a color guide (commonly used with swimming pools), which is very affordable. However, an electronic pH meter is much more accurate.

Some indoor growers use carbon dioxide (CO_2) generators when they do not have a good source of fresh, outdoor air. However, for the size of your garden, I wouldn't think that it would be necessary (unless the growing area is completely closed off from outside air). I would recommend that you simply set up a small fan on a timer to turn on and gently blow air across the garden (maybe for a few hours each day). Ideally, this fan would be able to draw air from another room or from outside (if the temperature is OK). That way, fresh air will be blowing across the plants giving them CO_2 and increasing transpiration (the uptake of water). It is a good idea to regularly introduce fresh air into your growing area. —D.J.P.

Q: Can dry ice cool down a room that is too hot? Are there any other methods besides air conditioning that could provide cooling?

A: Yes, dry ice can be used to cool a small enclosed space. However, whether or not this is economically sound depends on a number of factors, such as the level of heat in the room, the desired temperature you want to maintain, and the cost of the dry ice, which is difficult to store for any length of time and needs to be continually purchased. Dry ice (solidified carbon dioxide) has 15 times more cooling capacity than wet ice of the same weight and lasts about five times longer. Dry ice has a temperature of -108.4°F, so you need to be careful when handling or working around it as it can cause burns to the skin from direct contact.

The major advantage of dry ice is that when it "melts" it doesn't produce water like wet ice, but rather carbon dioxide (CO_2) gas, which accelerates plant growth. In fact, dry ice is sometimes used in grow rooms purely for the CO_2 it releases as it melts, enriching the atmosphere to promote growth and plant development. You may need to experiment to determine just how much dry ice is required to get the cooling effect you require and how often this needs to be replaced.

Another effective method of temperature reduction might be evaporate cooling—depending on the humidity of the air. This involves drawing air over or through a screen over which water is flowing. As the water evaporates, it cools the air coming into the growing environment. However, it also increases the humidity of the air. This may or may not be beneficial depending on your current humidity levels.

In some situations, simply increasing the rate of air exchange in the grow room with the outside environment (depending on the ambient air temperature outside) is sufficient to cool the crop. At least one complete air change per minute is required for this type of cooling. —L.M.

Q: I am looking for an economical cooling solution for growing lettuce in NFT. My question is, do you know anything about an electronic system of cooling known as an electrostatic sprayer? I have heard of a unit comprising a small circuit with a high voltage (15,000-volt) output that is used with a small sprayer. Water or nutrient passes through this high voltage field and out of the sprayer; inlet temperature of almost 90°F and outlet temperature is about 70°F. An advantage of this system is that it consumes very little power—only 1 or 2 watts. Is such a device on sale?

A: Electrostatic charging is not generally used to reduce solution temperatures. In fact, there isn't any reason why electrostatic charging of the solution should lower solution temperatures.

The reason why the sprayer is "allegedly" lowering temperatures may solely be due to the evaporative effect of producing a fine mist, which is a characteristic of electrostatic sprayers. This would also be true of any device that produces small droplet sizes. As the droplets leave the sprayer, evaporation reduces their temperature. This effect is not due to electrostatic charging.

Electrostatic sprayers are widely used by large commercial growers in the United States (see www.spectrumsprayers.com/ for more information). The real advantage is the superior spray coverage achieved by imparting a positive charge to the spray droplets. This attracts the droplets (at a size of 50 μm) into the crop canopy and results in superior coverage—even in areas of the crop that are hidden from the spray.

If you require a system to lower solution temperature, a simple misting device—with or without a electrostatic component—will be sufficient. —L.M.

Q: I want to drop the temperature in a small 6x16-foot greenhouse from approximately 98°F to around 80°F. I have a good exhaust fan and vent but cannot get the temperature down. The outside temperature is about 90°F. Would a misting system accomplish this task?

A: Provided the outside humidity isn't too high, an effective method for reducing air temperature is to cool the air entering the greenhouse by way of evaporative cooling. A simple system for achieving this involves constructing panels covered with several layers of shade cloth over which a slow stream of water is trickled and recirculated. These evaporative coolers can be about 6 1/2 feet wide by the height of the greenhouse wall and placed every 6 1/2–10 feet along one wall of the greenhouse.

As air is forced through the evaporative coolers, it is reduced in temperature. On the opposite wall, extractor fans are placed at regular intervals, say about every 13 feet. Using your existing system, just recirculating water over screens covering the vents you have, while running the exhaust fan, may help considerably. —L.M.

Q: What do you think is best for room cooling? Water supply is a major problem.

A: Room cooling, in an enclosed space, is best carried out by extractor fans to remove the warm, humid air from the growing area and bring in cooler, drier air from outside. In areas where the outside air is too warm to be of much use in cooling, extractor fans are still required since carbon dioxide (CO_2) must be continually introduced. However, an additional chiller (refrigeration unit) or air conditioner unit may be required. For very small areas, dry ice can be used on a regular basis to both bring the air temperature down and introduce some additional CO_2 for plant growth. If water supply wasn't a problem, evaporative cooling units also works well—although they can increase the humidity of the air and this doesn't work so well when humidity levels are already high.—L.M.

Q: Where can I find plans for an inexpensive evaporative cooling unit for cooling nutrient solution? I live in a tropical area.

A: There is a good Website that explains how evaporative cooling works and gives a simple plan that could be used to cool the nutrient solution (see www.coolmax.mx.com.au/evapcool/evapopn.htm). —L.M.

Q: I live in Phoenix, Arizona. In past years, I have shut my hydroponic garden down when solution temps reached 95°F or higher. This year, I finally set up a cooler for my solution. So far, it has been able to drop the solution temps from 90°F to 75°F. I was very excited until I remembered reading an article by Rob Smith in "The Best of The Growing Edge, Volume 2" on pH and temperature. It mentioned that "A problem can occur when the air temperatures are 5–10 degrees higher than the root temperatures."

What is this problem? Does it pertain to all species?

A: In your situation, where solution temperatures were reaching 95°F, you have no option but to cool the nutrient if you want to produce successful crops. At 95°F in the root zone, just about all plant species become extremely stressed and the incidence of root death and pathogen attack would be very high and the roots would be "cooking." Dropping the solution temperature down to 75°F will greatly enhance plant growth, provided you have some air movement and shading to try and keep temperature levels around the upper part of the plant down as much as possible.

I think what Rob Smith was referring to might have been a different situation. In more temperate climates, solution warming is often used in winter to keep temperatures up in the root zone and around the plants. What can occur in certain situations is, during the morning, the aerial greenhouse environment can warm up rapidly while the nutrient solution is still fairly cool. The nutrient solution takes much longer to warm up than the air in the greenhouse, so a situation can develop where the plants are sitting in a warm atmosphere with their roots in cold nutrients. This often results in wilting since the cold plant roots cannot take up sufficient water to be transported to the top of the plant, which is warm and rapidly transpiring moisture. Obviously, different plant species have different optimal temperature levels both within the root zone and in the aerial environment.

Under your particular conditions, cooling of the nutrient is a good option. In other hot climates, such as Singapore, this method of nutrient cooling is being successfully used to grow aeroponic lettuce in conditions that would otherwise make production of cool-season crops difficult. It appears that the effect of a cool nutrient solution affects the physiology of the plant even through the aerial environment may not be optimal for production and high quality lettuce and other plants are produced. In fact, hydroponics is probably the only way many of these cool-season vegetables can be produced under difficult conditions in hot climates as control can be achieved with regard to solution and root zone temperature in a way that would be very difficult in soil. So I don't see any potential problems with cooling of the nutrient in your hydroponic garden, provided you can protect the aerial portion of the plants from direct sunlight and provide some air movement to help the plants cool through transpiration. I would be very interested to hear how well your hydroponic plants respond to the nutrient cooling. —L.M.

Q: We have high humidity virtually all year and high temperatures after May and usually through October (75–104°F). If heating the nutrient solution helps in the colder months to warm greenhouse, can chilled solution help in the heat? I wonder if a cooled nutrient solution would work as well as a cooling system in the hot months. Is the root ball more susceptible to high heat than the foliage and flowers?

A: Chilling of the nutrient solution can assist a great deal with plant growth under warmer-than-optimal conditions. However, this effect depends on the type of plants being grown, the system used, and the how high ambient temperatures are. For example, in Singapore and other warm climates, cool-season lettuce and other greens are being successfully grown aeroponically using solution chilling—although the environment is shaded to provide some control over temperature. For a small, short-term plant, such as lettuce, chilling the nutrient solution affects the plant's physiology so that crops of cool season plants can be grown where normally they could not. Chilling of the nutrient in this case improves quality, yield, and reduces problems such as premature flowering and other disorders that occur under warm conditions.

However, for larger plants, such as tomatoes, the result is not as significant and often cooling of the air is required as well. If you have continual high humidity, evaporative cooling may not be the answer in your climate. However, shading the crop during time of the year when higher light levels exist will assist greatly with keeping temperatures down. Tomatoes do benefit somewhat from solution cooling since under warm conditions the nutrient tends to heat up and retain this heat long after dark—and warm temperatures in the root zone cause growth problems. When the solution temperature becomes too high (over 77°F for tomatoes), the plants start to suffer from a lack of oxygen. Little dissolved oxygen is held by the nutrient at this temperature and the rates of respiration by the roots that use oxygen increase dramatically under warm conditions. This reduces the uptake of water and nutrients and predisposes the plant roots to pathogen attack. Root morphology also changes when the nutrient solution becomes too warm—the roots become thinner and browner in color.

Cooling the nutrient will assist with all these problems but, at the top end of your temperature range, you will need some form of environmental cooling as well. This is because with plants such as tomatoes and peppers, some parts of the plant, including the flowers and pollen, are more prone to high temperature damage than the foliage. Fruit can also be damaged by high temperatures, causing a number of physiological disorders and the only way to prevent this is to chill the environment. Pollination problems in most fruiting plants will occur at the higher end of the temperatures you encounter (above 86°F). However, there are some new cultivars that have been developed that appear to be much more heat tolerant than others.

The combination of high temperatures and high humidity can be particularly damaging in many crop plants since they are not able to transpire to cool themselves, so having some air movement within the crop becomes essential. Probably a combination of nutrient cooling, some form of environmental cooling (only during the hottest months of the year), selection of heat-tolerant cultivars, shading, ventilation, and air movement within the crop will allow you to produce many of the commonly grown fruiting plants in your system. —L.M.

Q: My temperature in the grow room reaches 100°+ during the day. I came up with the idea of extending a duct from one of the main air conditioning ducts in the attic. Now the problem that I'm facing is that the thermostat is not in this room so I have no control of the temperature. I'm trying to built some kind of device like a thermostat up there in the room that, in this case, will close this duct every time the temperature reaches a certain level.

Do you think you could give me some ideas on how to do it? I'm in a testing process and this is my major concern right now. Do you think that I will have problems with a lack of humidity after accomplishing this? Will it be too dry? How can I compensate for this? Your help is much appreciated.

A: Instead of just trying to pipe cool air into your grow room, I would recommend that you draw the hot air out of the area and try to reduce your growing temperature. If you are using HID lights, you can use water-cooled jackets to reduce and nearly eliminate the amount of heat they put out. If you are growing hydroponically, cooling the nutrient solution will help keep the temperature of the plants down.

If you don't have a fresh air source in the grow room (such as a window), piping conditioned air (or at least some outside air) might be a good idea. However, you should also have a fan that is blowing air out of the growing area so that the room has proper circulation. Set the air conditioning on a low setting, put an air temperature thermometer in your grow room, and see how it works. If your plants get too dry and the relative humidity (RH) is low, just mist the plants with water on a regular basis. Also, if the plants are getting too dry, make sure you aren't blowing the air directly on the plants. Indirect air movement would be better if the RH is too low.

If you want to automate the control of the air conditioning, you could have an electrician install a thermostat in your grow room (I would never recommend that anybody work with electricity without the proper training). However, I would first strongly recommend that you attempt to reduce your grow room temperature by other means, such as by using water-cooled jackets and facilitating proper circulation. —D.J.P.

Q: I just built an aeroponic system and have an important question. How can I keep the temperature of the nutrient solution down? I grow under a 1,000-watt lamp and the temperature of the nutrient solution seems too high. So far, everything I've read on this topic just makes suggestions for raising the temperature.

A: The heat produced by lamps in an enclosed environment does tend to increase the temperature of the nutrient solution. This can be a particularly severe problem in aeroponics where the nutrient is delivered in a mist or fine droplets, which when exposed to the warm environment are quickly heated.

One of the simplest ways to slow down heat accumulation in the nutrient is to have as large of a reservoir tank as possible. The greater the volume of the nutrient, the longer it takes to heat to damaging levels. Also, the tank should be kept as far away from the lamps as possible. And—if this is an option—try to insulate the tank. It's also possible that your pump is increasing the nutrient's temperature since larger pumps are usually required for aeroponic systems.

A more complicated—and expensive—method of keeping the nutrient cool would be to install a refrigeration unit. Some smaller growers can get away with dropping blocks of ice into the nutrient tank when temperatures begin to get to high. But the success of this method depends on the grower being on-hand to notice that the nutrient solution is getting warmer so they can add the ice. And ice quickly melts—and dilutes the nutrient.

Another method to consider is evaporative cooling. This process pipes the warm nutrient returning from the root zone to run over an evaporative cooling plate that has a large surface area. As the nutrient runs over this plate, a fan blows air over it. As the water evaporates, it cools the nutrient solution, which is then returned to the nutrient reservoir. However, keep a close eye on the electrical conductivity of the nutrient solution since it can rise as water evaporates from the solution.

Finally, cooling the general growing environment can help keep the nutrient solution cool. Using heat extractor fans to bringing more fresh air into the area and using water-cooled jackets on your lamps are good options. —L.M.

Q: My nutrient solution is getting hot. Here is a list of the important aspects of my setup:

• 10-gallon Rubbermaid container
• 4 gallons of nutrient solution
• PVC & 2-liter coke bottle setup; two plants per container
• Powerhead aquarium pump #420
• 15 minutes on and 30 minutes off, 24/7

Initially I had a heavy duty, chemical-resistant submersible pump but the nutrients were really cooking them. Only 4 gallons of nutrients to conserve. This pumps better but still kind of hot. I'm a total newbie. Any suggestions?

A: Yes submersible pumps do produce heat and with such a small volume of nutrient, heat buildup will be a problem. One option would be to use a different type of pump that isn't submersible (one that sits outside the nutrient container and sucks up the nutrient) and won't add to heat buildup in the nutrient tank. Perhaps a less costly option is use more nutrient solution and thus slow the rate of heat buildup. If you have a 10-gallon tank, putting 10 gallons of nutrient solution in it will slow the heat buildup. Obtaining a larger tank than this

would be even better. Also, make sure that your nutrient delivery lines and return pipes are covered and not exposed to your lights. The nutrient tank should be kept covered—again, away from any heat that might be generated by artificial lighting or sunlight. Finally, if the problem still persists after trying all these options, you may need to rig up an evaporative cooling unit for the nutrient solution. This involves allowing the nutrient to flow over an open surface on which air is directed by a fan. The evaporation of water from the nutrient will cool the solution. —L.M.

Q: I am just starting with hydroponics and will be growing hot peppers and tomatoes in my basement for the most part. I intend on having only one grow light to begin with and have a room that I built that is insulated with pink house insulating foam sheets that is 6 feet tall, 10 feet wide, and 6 feet deep. I built this insulated room before I decided to step up to a hydroponics system with high powered lights, so ventilation will have to be added to the room when I start.

I have been doing quite a bit of reading and have determined that I definitely want to build my own system that does the watering automatically with a timer and pump. I am not sure what the exact setup should be but either a drip system or a flooding type system seem to be the most appealing for what I am trying to do. I have found lots of information on these types of system but none of it completely answers all of my questions on how the things are set up and which would necessarily be the best. How can get all of these questions answered so I can simply go out and buy the equipment that I need and get to work! I do not want to buy a kit—I want to build this thing. Therefore, I need to know all of the particulars on exactly what kind and size of fittings to get, what material they should be made of, how to find the right timer that that I will need, etc.

I am wanting to grow tomatoes and hot peppers in my basement in an automated hydroponic system that will water automatically and be dependable, efficient, and pretty much fuss-proof. What would be the best system? The NFT concept seems appealing to me, but I'm not sure I understand all of the principles of it.

A: Probably the best and easiest system to build would be one that involves some media that would retain moisture and nutrients should something go wrong with the irrigation when you are not there. On the other hand, nutrient film technique (NFT) systems have some benefits in that if they are designed well with sufficient slope, they will not overwater and saturate the media. Flood-and-drain systems are particularly good in an indoor growing situation since they lessen the chance of leaks occurring and eliminate the recollection of nutrient that is necessary with drip systems.

Q: I want to grow tomatoes hydroponically for my 6th grade science project. I want to know where I can obtain the start up kit. What different variables can I keep? I have just four weeks in hand. Can I finish the project by then?

A: You would need more time to grow tomatoes. Most types require around two or three months to grow to harvest. Some crops that grow to maturity faster include some herbs, salad greens, and lettuce. You might consider growing one of these crops instead.

Many hydroponic manufacturers carry start-up kits, which might include a system, nutrients, seeds, and a light, for educators. I would recommend that you check to see if a hydroponic retailer exists in your area (see www.hydromall.com/stores/index.html for a listing of stores). If a retailer isn't based in your area, you can always shop for supplies online (see www.carbon.org/GlobalClassroom1/kits.htm for some examples of start-up kits that are available). Most retailers, both online and in person, are eager to help educators get started on a hydroponic project.

Once the hydroponic system is up and running, many different aspects of growth can be measured and evaluated. Students can take data on germination rates, growth rates, electrical conductivity and pH levels, problems encountered, time to harvest, etc. One popular experiment is to grow the same types of plants in both a hydroponic system and in good soil and then compare and contrast plant performance. To get a better idea of what other educators are doing with hydroponics in the classroom, see www.growingedge.com/kids/educators/links.html. —D.J.P.

There are a couple of good hydroponic system plans at the following Websites that should help you with your system. These include the materials you need to buy and how they are put together (using equipment and materials you can get from a hardware store).

• www.simplyhydro.com/freesys.htm (good plans for simple hydroponic systems, including water culture and ebb-and-flow)

• www.hort.cornell.edu/Gardening/fctsheet/growflow/ (some very well laid out plans for a horizontal hydroponic system, including an extensive list of materials, step-by-step assembly instructions, and operation of the system)

—L.M.

Q: I am building a small, 10x12-foot greenhouse. It will contain three homemade Dutch pot systems growing peppers, tomatoes, cucumbers, and cantaloupes. I also plan to have a 'Bibb' lettuce crop, also in a homemade system. I was planning to use a small raft system with Styrofoam sheets and small 2-inch cups of perlite to hold the plants in the holes in the Styrofoam. Also, I have been thinking about using 2-inch PVC for an NFT system. I have built NFT systems before, using 3-inch vinyl rain gutter downspouts.

My question is: Would it be better for a hobbyist grower, such as myself, to use the raft system or the 2-inch PVC NFT system? I would be growing less than 50 plants at a time. Also, keep in mind that any system I end up using will be homemade with nothing purchased from specialty hydroponic stores.

A: If you want a small, easy-care way to grow 'Bibb' lettuce for personal use, I would recommend the raft system. We currently have a number of both raft and NFT systems of various types operating in our greenhouse and by far the easiest way to produce lettuce is on the rafts. While NFT systems can be used to grow perfectly good lettuce, there is always maintenance involved with these systems—pumps, delivery systems, and filters must be cleaned out and blockages in the nutrient delivery tend to occur regularly basis (particularly when you're away for the weekend . . .). Pumps need to be replaced from time to time and plants in NFT will die rapidly if the power is cut for more than 30 minutes on a warm day.

Your can make your own raft system for very little cost. A plastic children's pool works well. The pond can also be made out of timber and lined with a couple of layers of thick black plastic or pond liner film. The floats can be cut to size from sheets of polystyrene, which is commonly sold in hardware stores. Holes for the plants can be burned into the sheets with a piece of hot metal pipe. These homemade raft systems should last several seasons and will require very little maintenance.

We've found that raft systems take care of themselves. After making up the nutrient to a depth of about 1 foot and putting in the floats, outfitted with young seedlings, any further nutrient adjustment is unnecessary for short-term crops. Having a long, thin air stone attached to an air pump, such as those used in aquariums, aerating the nutrient may increase production quality—but it isn't really necessary for short-term crops.

A small raft system of this sort will hold 30–60 'Bibb' lettuces. You might want to stagger planting dates in order to have a continual supply of lettuce ready for harvest. Once a plant is harvested from a float, just put in another seedling. Other small plants, such as some herbs, could also be grown with the lettuce in the float system. Provided your pond doesn't spring a leak, you can leave the system unattended for weeks at a time. This is a great way for new growers to experiment with hydroponics without the need for expensive systems—or even electricity. —L.M.

Q: I would like to grow tomatoes and cucumbers in a hot country like Pakistan. In summer, the daytime temperature goes up to over 104°F and during the nighttime it's around 77–82°F. In winter (November to February), daytime temperatures are around a maximum of 80°F and at times dips down to 28°F. However, sunshine is plentiful, throughout the year. Electricity is the most expensive in the world.

I am sorry I haven't come up with anything that should encourage you to guide me through. However, land is cheap. Labor costs are very low, the local demand is high, and the export market is also very good there.

A: Given the extremes of temperature—both high and low—year-round in such a climate, the only way to grow the crops you want would be with a well designed, fairly high-tech, environmentally controlled greenhouse complex. This would require chiller units to handle conditions of 104°F and heaters to deal with 28°F. There is the advantage of high light levels year round, which will enhance cropping. However, you may need to consider the use of thermal screens or shading since high radiation levels can lead to excessive heat buildup inside the greenhouse and cause crop damage. Since electricity is expensive, you might need to consider gas or solid fuel for heaters and gas-powered chiller units. Either way, it will be an expensive greenhouse to keep at the correct temperature levels for the crops you want to grow, which would be in the 64–82°F range year-round.

There was a two-article series I wrote on this subject in The Growing Edge magazine, Volume 12, Number 3, (January/February 2001) called "Greenhouse Extremes, Part One: Minimizing the Effects of High Temperatures," and in Volume 12, Number 4 (March/April 2001) called "Greenhouse Extremes, Part Two: Minimizing the Effects of Low Temperatures," which deals with controlling overly warm or cold conditions. These should provide a lot of the information you are after in more detail than I can give here. —L.M.

Q: I'm interested in knowing the recommended planting density for tomatoes in the tropics. I have been advised to plant 10 plants per square meter. However, there are people here that say that number is too high.

A: Ten plants per square meter for multi-truss tomatoes is definitely very high—even for the tropics! The average density of a commercial long term crop of tomatoes is 2.5 plants per square meter. This can vary depending on season. When light levels are high, three plants per square meter is an acceptable density. When light levels are low (such as in the rainy season in the tropics), a better density is two plants per square meter.

If a long term crop of tomatoes was grown at a density of ten plants per square meter, not only would the crop be impossible to manage, prune, train, pollinate, and harvest, there would be little in the way of yield as the plants would not have sufficient light for good development. Also high densities, particularly in the tropics where humidity levels are usually high, predisposes the plants to fungal pathogen attack and getting spray penetration into plants at this density would be impossible.

The only way you can grow tomatoes at a density of ten plants per square meter would be to use a "single truss" system where each plant is only permitted to develop one truss of plant and then the growing point is removed—and ten plants per square meter is even on the high side for that method. —L.M.

Q: I am trying to crop tomatoes in Puerto Rico. Our temperature and humidity are high so I want to know how to build a cooling system.

A: There are two types of cooling systems you could use: evaporative cooling (see www.growingedge.com/community/archive/read.php3?s=yes&q=378) or a chiller unit for either the air or nutrient solution or both. The nutrient solution can be cooled using evaporation before it is pumped out to the crop. You might also need to consider using thermal screens or shade covers over the greenhouse or crop to help reduce air temperatures by lowering the amount of radiation that enters the cropping area. This method—unlike evaporative cooling—doesn't have an effect on humidity levels. —L.M.

Q: Can anyone help me with my tomato? The heat is terrible, low of 71°F, high of 107°F. I do not prune down the leaves anymore to provide more protection.

I use aeroponics and I feed them well—ratio is 1.5 minutes spray and 7 minutes of waiting till next spray . . . 6 A.M. to 6 P.M. cycle. I change my fertilizer strength mid-day because that is when I find time to do that activity. I try to keep my N down and my K really high—ratio is about 1:1.5.

However, I get shoulder crack . . . can't do anything about the temperature, but could this be a case where I have too much nitrogen? Is transpiration too fast causing the skin to crack? If I change the fertilizer mix late in the day, could this reduce the transpiration rate till temperature is cooler?

A: I'm not sure what you mean by "change the fertilizer strength mid day." If you are suddenly increasing the EC or strength of the nutrient (whether it as at mid day or any other time), this can induce the fruit splitting you are encountering. If you are simply adjusting the EC slightly (by adding more water or a small amount of nutrient stock solution so that the EC only changes by a small amount (0.2–0.4 EC), than this is fine. If, however, you are increasing or decreasing the EC by a larger amount, than this will induce fruiting splitting. Any changes in fertilizer strength need to be made gradually, in small increments. The reason for this is that the tomato plant "adjusts" to the EC or fertilizer strength. If this level is suddenly decreased, the plant reacts by taking up a large volume of water before it has time to adjust to the new level. If the fertilizer strength is suddenly increased too much, the plant goes into "osmotic shock" and loses water from its cells back into the nutrient solution. When the EC then drops again, it takes up large amounts of water and this can be rapidly transported into the fruit causing the fruit to swell, crack, and eventually split. This problem also occurs in media-grown crops where there is infrequent watering and is particularly worse under warm conditions where these things all happen much faster. So, if your plants roots are drying slightly between irrigations, this could contribute to the problem.

Some fruit varieties are also more prone to shoulder cracking and splitting than others, so trying a less susceptible cultivar might assist the problem. Shading the plants and fruit will also assist this problem by reducing temperature of both the air and the fruit flesh. If direct sunlight is falling on exposed fruit, the flesh temperature can increase to very high levels and cause a number of ripening problems including fruit splitting. Your N to K ratio of 1:1.5 is good, but you could increase this to 1:2 or even 1:2.5 when the plants have a heavy crop load. I suggest you try a couple of split-resistant cultivars with your next crop. Your seed company should be able to recommend a variety that is less susceptible and more heat-resistant. Also avoid any sudden changes in fertilizer strength, keep the potassium level high with an EC level in the range 2.5–3.5, and shade the plants and fruit. Hopefully the problem will not be so severe with the next crop.—*L.M.*

Q: What type of watering system would be good for tomato plants? I have built a planter and I want to eventually plant either tomatoes or some other vegetables. Should I install a sprinkler or a soaker-bubbler type watering system?

A: One of the most precise methods of watering plants—whether they're being grown in soil or not—is via drip irrigation. This method has a minimum of water wastage and barring equipment problems, ensures accurate and regular delivery of water. You can set your drippers to water precisely the amount you want to deliver at regular intervals and each plant will have an irrigation hose leading the plant with one emitter or dripper per plant. For more information about drip irrigation, see:

www.google.com/search?q=drip+irrigation
www.growingedge.com/dgssearch/search.php?q=drip+irrigation&r=10

—*D.J.P.*

Q: What is the growth rate for tomato plants per day? For example, how many centimeters does the tomato plant grow in one day?

A: The growth rate of tomatoes per day depends on a number of factors, such as cultivar, the environment (light, temperature, relative humidity, CO_2 levels, etc.), nutrition, moisture levels, presence of pests and diseases, general plant health, and the stage of plant development. Actual rate of growth in terms of centimeters per day can range from zero to several, depending on the growing conditions.

However, centimeters in height isn't a good measure of the actual or "relative" growth rates in tomatoes (and most other plants) since a plant may be growing quite rapidly in terms of fruit expansion and dry matter accumulation while not increasing in height at all. Also, a plant in crowded conditions that doesn't have sufficient light may stretch several centimeters upward, but not actually be gaining anything in terms of plant weight or assimilate production. —*L.M.*

Q: I am doing a science project on hydroponic tomatoes for a science fair at my school. There are four red and yellow pear tomato plants in a 3-gallon container filled with perlite. There is also a battery operated pump to circulate the water. Could you please tell me what type fertilizer I should use? I am currently using 15-30-15 Miracle-Gro fertilizer but lots of algae has started to grow on the perlite and the tomato plants look sickly. I am afraid I might be using the wrong type of fertilizer. Is there anything I should also know about growing hydroponic tomatoes?

A: Unfortunately, your tomato plants will be deficient in calcium and magnesium using the Miracle-Gro fertilizer—and both of these are minerals are essential for plant growth. Miracle-Gro is an excellent fertilizer for container plants, lawns, indoor houseplants growing in potting mix, and for general crop growth. However, it is not a complete

hydroponic nutrient, meaning it does not contain all the elements necessary for plant growth. In a potting or container mix, the plants can receive their needed calcium and magnesium from the lime or dolomite in the mix and/or from slow-release fertilizers such as osmocote—or whatever was initially added to the potting mix. Therefore, a liquid fertilizer, such as Miracle-Gro, applied to such plants does not need to feature calcium or magnesium. From memory, I think Miracle-Gro has nitrogen (15), phosphorus (30), potassium (15), iron, and all the other necessary trace elements. So, in order to be able to use this to grow a hydro-

ponic plant, you need to mix in calcium and magnesium in the form of calcium nitrate and magnesium sulfate (commonly called Epsom salts). Perlite is a good hydroponic media, but it's inert and doesn't contain any mineral elements in the way that soil or potting mix might, so you have to use a complete hydroponic nutrient to successfully grow your plant. I would suggest you contact one of the hydroponic suppliers on the Internet and get a good general purpose hydroponic nutrient that will contain all the mineral elements the plants need.

The algae growing on top of the perlite is a common problem in most hydroponic systems. Algae is a form of plant life and will grow wherever there are nutrients and a light source. The best way to solve this problem is to make some media covers out of thick plastic (black plastic that won't let the light through). Cut a circle in the middle and a slit so the cover can be wrapped around the plant stem. The objective is to prevent light from falling on the surface of the perlite. If light isn't hitting the surface of the perlite, algae can't grow. Although the algae may look ugly, it generally won't harm the plant.

Apart from changing your fertilizer to a good hydroponic nutrient (check the label to make sure it contains all necessary nutrient elements: N, P, K, S, Ca, Mg, Fe, Mn, B, Cu, Zn, Mo) to mix with water and then use to feed your plant, there are a few other things to note when growing tomatoes.

Tomatoes need fairly high light levels for good growth and development so make sure they are in a well lit position. Also, tomatoes require warm temperatures—in the range of

www.hydro4u.com/resource_centre/faq.htm
www.oardc.ohio-state.edu/hydroponics/tomatoes
www.ag.arizona.edu/hydroponictomatoes/
—L.M.

Q: Last year, I started a hydroponic garden in my classroom. It's a recirculating drip system using a medium of a brownish rock mixed with shredded coconut shell. We keep the pH as close to 6.0 as we can. I was changing my reservoir about every two to three weeks. But recently I read something that said to change the solution every week. Is this necessary? We grew tomatoes, strawberries, basil, and peas under metal halide growth and fruiting bulbs. The garden grew fine for three months but never produced anything. The strawberries flowered but never fruited. The cherry tomato plant gave us one tomato. We were using 1/4 to 1/2 teaspoon of nutrient for every gallon of water in the reservoir. The drip system is on a timer that waters the system for about 15 minutes 5 times every 24 hours. There

---

The best way to tell if you are providing enough flooding or nutrient to your plants is to check that between the flood cycles the plants don't start to wilt indicating they are not receiving enough moisture.

60–80°F. Make sure the temperatures at night don't drop too low, or the plant can really suffer. Warm temperatures over 83°F will stress the plants, can induce many root pathogens, and can reduce fruit quality. Once you have open flowers on the plants, you'll need to pollinate these by generally tapping or shaking the plants to releaser the pollen from the flowers. The flowers will then pollinate and the fruit will set (bees do this job outside). The tomato plants will also need some support—either tying the stems to a strong stake or using strings to tie them up to an overhead wire or support structure. The lateral branches (small shoots that form in the axils of the main leaves) need to be removed so the plant is grown as a single stem. Otherwise, the plants can rapidly turn into a tangled mess. Finally, you may need to space your plants out a bit. Only grow one or two tomato plants per 3-gallon container so that the mature plants, which will get quite large within a few months, have enough room to grow and develop.

There are also some good Internet sites on growing hydroponic tomatoes and the following links might help out with your project.

is no "pooling" of water except in the very bottom (below the drain hole) of our growing containers. The medium is kept damp. In our fourth month, we got an infestation of whitefly and lost everything. But I felt we should have had some fruit before that even happened. Is there something we can use to stop whitefly on vegetables and fruits? With the system setup I described, do you have any suggestions to improve our results?

A: You don't need to change your nutrient solution every week. If you keep an eye on your electrical conductivity, pH, and nutrient levels—and amend the solution as necessary to keep it within your desired parameters—you shouldn't experience any problems with your nutrient. It's possible that if the strawberries and tomatoes produced flowers, but no or very little fruit, that they did not receive sufficient pollination for fruit set. This is assuming there weren't any other causes, such as insufficient or incorrect lighting, temperature, nutritional problems, and so on. Make sure that you provide the proper conditions and nutrient solutions for your crops. Both strawberries and tomatoes need some help with pollination when they are growing in an enclosed environment. Commercially, this is carried out by either introducing bumblebees into the greenhouse or by artificial means. Tomatoes can be pollinated by "truss vibration"—using a mechanical device that vibrates the flower truss so that the pollen is released to fertilize the flowers and provide a good level of fruit set. You can get the same effect by gently shaking the plants or tapping on the stem opposite where the flower truss has formed. When pollination has occurred, the fruit will set and begin to grow. Strawberries also will benefit from pollination help. In commercial situations, they use bees or big air blowers (like a giant hair drier). You can carry out this process using a mild, cool air blast from a hair drier onto the flowers. Or simply use a clean, dry, soft paint brush to spread the pollen from flower to flower.

The infestation of whitefly could also effect fruit set and development. You will need to use a safe method of control for these insects in your classroom. There a few natural traps and insecticides that may help. For very small whitefly populations, you could try hanging up the yellow sticky cards, which are sometimes used by home gardeners. The whiteflies are attracted to the yellow color and become stuck to the cards. However, this is unlikely to control all of the insects. Some other options you might like to try are mixtures of dishwashing detergent and water or vegetable oil and water. These solutions will smother the insects, but you need to get good coverage of all the whiteflies. Another safe method is to use an "insect growth regulator," which will break the insect's life cycle. A natural, botanical insect growth regulator is neem oil, which is nontoxic and doesn't involve using any complicated safety equipment. Several products exist that contain natural neem oil. —*L.M.*

Q: We have just built a hobby greenhouse and are building an aeroponic system using 18-gallon containers using two spray nozzles per container and 8-inch grow pots with coco fiber and expanded clay. We plan to grow heirloom tomatoes from seed.

We have read that the tomatoes will grow 12 to 15 feet . . . we only have a 7-foot, 6-inch greenhouse . . . What is the proper nutrient timing cycle, i.e., on time and off time? Do we need to add hydrogen peroxide to the mix? If so how much, what strength, and how often?

A: The height that tomatoes will grow depends on what type of tomato cultivar you are planning to produce. With tomatoes, there are determinate and indeterminate varieties. Determine varieties are largely used as outdoor processing types and are also known as "bush" tomatoes. These produce a short plant that naturally "stops" and bushes out. The fruit are produced all at once over a reasonably short season. The indeterminate types are usually grown in greenhouses and in hydroponics. Indeterminate tomatoes will continue to grow in height indefinitely, to whatever height you require, until you remove the central growing point at the top of the plant, which will stop any further growth in height.

Many greenhouse growers will "layer" tomato crops. The plant continues to grow upward until it reaches a predetermined height (5–6 feet is an average since this is as tall as the average person can harvest without outside help). Then the plant is "dropped." The whole plant is lowered down and moved forward along the row, the leaves are removed from the lower portion of the stem, and the bare stems then are tried together at the base of the plant. By continually lowering the plants and layering in this way, many growers will end up with a plant stem that's over 25 feet long with only the top 5 feet of stem featuring leaves and fruit trained upward. The rest of the stem, which has finished production, is simply neatly tucked away against the grow bags or troughs of the system. Other growers prefer to grow shorter term crops and won't let the plants grow beyond whatever height they can manage. This might be 5–6 feet in your greenhouse. Once they have grown to the desired height, remove the growing point and let the plant finish fruiting before removing the whole crop and replanting.

In a true aeroponic system where the plant roots aren't surrounded by any growing media and are misted inside a chamber, the misting should be continuous for a large plant such as tomatoes. This is mainly because it is very difficult to maintain a cycle of misting and not misting that won't cause the root system to dry out. Also, a large, mature tomato plant can take up large volumes of water in warm conditions and any moisture stress will affect yields and fruit quality. Also, temperatures inside an aeroponic chamber can rapidly build up to damaging levels when the misting is turned off on a regular basis.

However, in a modified aeroponic system where you have a reasonably large volume of media around the roots, the media will retain moisture and nutrients between mistings and provide a degree of temperature buffering. In such a setup, you can probably have a cycle of a few minutes of misting followed by a few minutes of draining. The exact cycle would have to be determined by you when the system is up and running as it will depend on a number of other factors, including the environmental conditions, stage of plant growth, and moisture holding capacity of the media. You should aim to keep the media moist—but not saturated—and provide sufficient time for the media to drain any excess nutrient off between mistings. You will need to increase the frequency and duration of the misting cycles as the plants grow and develop.

Unless your system is particularly "dirty" (i.e., full of unwanted organic matter), adding hydrogen peroxide (H_2O_2) to the nutrient solution isn't recommended. The problem with H_2O_2 is calculating the exact dose to use is difficult. H_2O_2 is highly reactive and oxidizes organic matter—pathogens, old roots, etc.—in the nutrient. However, if there isn't any organic matter to react with, the H_2O_2 will damage healthy root systems. If necessary, it's better to treat your source water with H_2O_2, let it react and dissipate (to a level of no greater than 6 ppm), and then use this to make up your nutrient in the system. Good luck with your tomato operation. —L.M.

Q: How often do you need to increase the size of your pots before your plants become root-bound? I have six tomato plants in individual containers in a flood-and-drain system with a clay pebble and coco-fiber medium. One plant is yellowing and wilted looking toward the bottom. Since this is the oldest plant, I'm assuming that it may be root-bound. Is this a possibility?

A: I'm not sure what the size of the pots your plants are currently in . . . However, in a flood-and-drain system, the best idea is to have the plants in open-weave or plastic lattice pots that allow the roots to grow out and into the flood and drain tray. Tomatoes can actually produce fairly well in a small volume of media provided they are supplied with all the oxygen, moisture, and nutrients they require for growth.

The problem is likely to be not so much that the plants are root-bound, but the small rooting volume is restricting the amount of oxygen available for the plants, which is becoming rapidly depleted between cycles. If the plants are flooded too often and the media is overly damp, oxygen is

excluded from the root zone and conditions become anaerobic. You then start to see plant wilting and gradual decline. On the other hand, if the plants are not irrigated often enough, then the electrical conductivity (EC) can increase in the media and salt buildup occurs between irrigations. The other cause of the symptoms you describe are a number of root pathogens that destroy the root tissue. As a result, the plant starts to wilt since it can't take up water and oxygen and the leaves begin to yellow and fall off.

The best media for a system that uses a frequent flood-and-drain cycle is just the clay pebbles by themselves without any additions since they drain freely between irrigations and don't hold excess moisture, thus providing high oxygen levels for the plant. Coconut fiber is better used where there are limited flood cycles (perhaps only once a day or even less frequent) as it holds and retains moisture between irrigations very effectively. —L.M.

Q: I want to put together a drip system for hydroponic tomatoes using rockwool bags. Do I need to have drains on the bags and return the waste water to a holding tank?

A: Yes, the rockwool bags should have slits cut into the bottom in various spots so that excess nutrient solution can drain away. And it is a good idea to have the runoff drain back into your nutrient solution holding tank. Any stagnant water could cause mold to form leading to root rot and a number of other problems.

One popular way to do this is to situate the rockwool bags in a large plastic tray that has been outfitted with a drain hole. Make sure the drainage hole is at the lowest spot in the tray so that gravity will naturally drain the excess nutrient solution. Run a length of plastic hose from the drain hole back to your tank. Hydroponic retailers should have a variety of trays that are already outfitted with return hoses to choose from. If you don't have a hydroponic retailer in your area, you could shop online or see what your local garden center has to offer. I have built similar setups on my own from plastic gardening troughs, a drill, some plastic hose, and silicone caulk. —D.J.P.

Q: My tomatoes are in 1/2 gallon pots with holes the size of the tip of ones pinky. The pots are filled with grow rocks, and are in an ebb and flow. The roots of my tomatoes plants are starting to come through the holes, and I am wondering if I stick the pots into larger pots filled with rocks if the roots will get strangled by the pinky sized holes as they penetrate to get to the new rocks?

A: If your tomato plants are starting to outgrow their containers, you have two choices. You could just let the plants take their course and let the roots grow out of the drain holes and see how the plants behave. Or, you could transplant them. Tomato plants can develop some pretty large root systems. I usually recommend one or two tomato plants per gallon container depending on the variety being grown.

If the plants still have a ways to go before reaching maturity, I would recommend transplanting them. Remember to keep the roots of the plants moist while out of the pots during the transplanting process.

However, if the plants are close to maturity, you could probably get away with just leaving them as they are. Don't worry too much about the roots poking through the holes are sold for use with house plants and container plants), but a visual inspection is just as good.

Unfortunately I can't give you an accurate and definite figure for the maximum amount of high pressure sodium light that tomatoes can use per square foot, it is very dependent on such factors as the size and stage of development of the plants, the density of the plants, the distance of your lights from the plants, reflectors, other sources of lighting in the area and the type and size of the bulbs you are using. The best idea is to check with the manufacturer of your particular lighting system and see what they would recommend for their equipment. —L.M.

The primary cause of small tomato size in nutrient film technique (NFT) systems is not usually due to the system itself, but to the growing environment or the way the crop is managed.

---

in the bottom of the container. When the roots don't find any nutrients outside of the container, chances are, they won't grow too much further out of the holes.

Sticking the existing pot into a larger pot probably wouldn't be a good idea. Then the roots would be encouraged to grow further out of the drain holes and—as you guessed—they would probably not develop healthy growth. —D.J.P.

Q: I have an ebb-and-flow system featuring 1/2-gallon pots. The pots are filled with grow rocks. My tomatoes are flooded for 30 minutes four times a day while in vegetative growth. What is the best way to tell how often I should flood to achieve optimal growth? Also what is the maximum amount of HPS light that tomatoes can use per square foot?

A: The best way to tell if you are providing enough flooding or nutrient to your plants is to check that between the flood cycles the plants don't start to wilt indicating they are not receiving enough moisture. Make sure you carry out these checks under warmer conditions just to be safe. With your system using grow rocks, which not only drain well, but hold a supply of nutrient between waterings, it is safe to flood the system more often then is required to ensure the plants receive sufficient moisture under all conditions. As the plants grow and increase in size, you need to gradually increase the number of waterings per day and you also need to take into account the temperatures. If the temperature increases over time then you also need to increase the number of waterings per day. There are a number of small watering devices which can be pushed into the media and will indicate when the root zone is becoming to dry (many of these

Q: I am a first-time hydroponic gardener. I have a passive system (Emily's garden) with 6 pots. How often should I be changing the nutrient solution/water mixture? As the water seems to evaporate quickly, what should I be adding between water changes?

My plants started out very well but now are not setting any new fruits. The tomatoes have very large and full foliage and the first tomatoes to come on are growing and looking good. However, no new ones are setting. In fact, the flowers seem to be drying up. The same thing is happening with the green peppers. The new flowers have tiny peppers but they are not developing.

A: Most people monitor the characteristics of their nutrient solution with pH and electrical conductivity (EC) meters. The pH is a measure of the solution's acidity or alkalinity. The EC is a measure of the solution's strength. When the solution's pH goes higher or lower than is required for quality growth (6.3 pH is considered ideal for hydroponics), the grower can add pH up or down solutions (diluted acid or alkaline solutions) for adjustment. Likewise, when the EC of the solution goes down, some growers will add concentrated nutrient to the system to raise the EC to appropriate levels (2.2–2.8 EC for tomatoes; 2.0–2.7 EC for bell peppers). However, effective, ongoing nutrient solution management can become fairly scientifically involved. Some growers just use the meters to let them know when their levels have changed. Then, instead of fooling around with amendments and so forth, they just make a wholesale change of their nutrient solution at that point. On the other hand, some growers just routinely change their system's nutrient solution about every two weeks and don't even bother with meters. When dealing with hobbyist growing methods, advice can run the gamut.

Personally, I would recommend a combination of techniques. I would advise that you purchase either a pH testing kit (litmus paper and indication guide; very inexpensive and available at swimming pool supply stores) or pH meter (more accurate; also more expensive). I would also recommend that you buy "pH up" and "pH down" solutions and adjust your pH as necessary.

I would also recommend that you purchase an EC meter (some meters come as a combination device that will read your EC and pH in one device). However, with a simple system like the Emily's Garden, I would recommend that you simply use the EC meter as a reference guide. When the EC level drops too low for your plants, simply change the entire nutrient solution and add fresh. This will probably occur every two weeks or so. You can use spent nutrient solution on sturdy houseplants and garden plants.

As your nutrient solution level drops, add dilute nutrient solution (around two parts regular nutrient solution to one part water) to the system to raise the level. This will also raise your EC a bit, effectively extending the life of your nutrient solution.

Tomatoes and bell peppers need a certain level of humidity and pollination to set fruit. Mist your plants with plain water every so often. Also, when the flowers appear, shake the trusses every so often (like, maybe once a day when you check on the garden). This will help increase pollination and fruit set. —D.J.P.

Q: What are the optimum lumens needed for 120 dwarf beefsteak tomatoes in a 32x24-ft. area with use of 1000 watt metal halide bulbs? How many bulbs?

A: You might like to contact a lighting retailer or manufacturer to check these details, as lighting is not my area of specialty and these are only rough calculations. The actual number of bulbs will be determined by plant size, density, stage of growth, and the setup of the grow room. As an estimate, you will need about one 1,000-watt metal halide bulb per 8x8 foot area to provide about 108,000 lumens. So in your grow room (if you have no other sources of lighting), you will need a minimum of 12 bulbs for the 120 plants. With this many bulbs in the grow room you will have to ensure that they are either cooled or that adequate ventilation and cooling is installed—this will produce a lot of heat. Finally, I understand that halide lamps provide a bluish-white light that is excellent for plants that grow mostly in the vegetative stage, such as lettuce or herbs. You may need to consider another source of lamps to get good flowering and fruiting on your tomatoes. —L.M.

Q: This was my first year with trying hydroponics and I am growing outdoors. I had a fair results with my tomatoes, but would like to know which varieties are best for hydroponics in Colorado.

A: With tomato varieties, the system of production doesn't make that much difference. What you really want to match up is the particular climate and environment where the plants will be grown. The best varieties that are well suited to Colorado are listed as being 'Big Boy,' 'Good-n-Early,' 'Lemon Boy,' 'Spirit,' and 'Yellow Stuffer.' The Colorado State University Cooperative Extension Website lists suitable vegetable varieties for Colorado (see www.ext.colostate.edu/pubs/columngw/grvegvar.html). —L.M.

Q: In a drip system, is perlite OK as the sole medium or is it best mixed? What would the other media be? What is the ideal can size for greenhouse tomatoes in a perlite drip system?

A: Yes, perlite is an excellent medium and can be used alone in a drip system. I would suggest you make sure you select a grade of perlite which has had the finer particles screened out (2–5 mm granules are best) for drip systems. Also perlite is a relatively free draining medium, so you will need to make sure your drip system supplies sufficient nutrient so that the media does not dry out excessively. On the other hand, the free-draining nature helps guard against oxygen starvation and root rot diseases. Perlite is also often mixed with vermiculite to increase the water holding and retention capacity of the mix, but this is not essential and often whether or not perlite is mixed with another substrate is a personal preference of the grower.

The ideal size for an individual tomato planter would be between 12–15 liters. Most commercial crops would be grown in planter bags containing about 15 liters. This volume of media ensures that sufficient moisture will be held within the media between irrigations and that the root system has sufficient space to expand into. If the plants are going to be stopped or only permitted to produce a few trusses then a smaller volume planter can be used. —L.M.

Q: I have a few questions. I originally used geolite as my medium for an ebb and flood system. Then the only change I made was switching to Hydroton, that stuff that looks like small round gum. Since my change I noticed a slower growth rate. Do you have any information on how to make the Hydroton perform more like the Geolite or is the Hydroton just inferior for the ebb and flood system?

I also am wondering about using bat guano to make a tea for my tomatoes. How much bat guano per gallon of water should I use? I found a high P as well as a high N guano for the different stages. Should I mix any other organic amendments with the guano? Lastly is bat guano "safe" to work with?

A: I suspect that with the new media you might need to change the frequency of the flood and drain cycle. If the Hydroton has a lower water holding capacity than the geolite, you will need to flood more frequency so that the plants have sufficient moisture held within the media for maximum growth.

With the bat guano, I don't recommend you use it to make a tea for your tomatoes—unless it is first processed via composting or through a vermiculture (worm farm) system. Although bat guano tends to be sold as a "ready-to-use" fertilizer (which is fine for soil crops), it needs to be broken down for use in hydroponics. The guano, like other manure, needs to be broken down by microbes and bacteria before the minerals can be released into a plant-available form. One example is the ammonium content in the guano, which needs to be converted to nitrate for plant use. Otherwise it will damage your plants. Also, mixing bat guano with water and putting it into your system will cause an explosion in the growth of microbes, which will rapidly deplete all the dissolved oxygen in your system. The solution will then turn anaerobic, start to stink, and kill of the plants' root system (if the ammonium content hasn't already done so).

On the other hand, if processed correctly, bat guano does have a useful (but not completely balanced) nutrient content. You will need to compost the guano (or use a worm farm) over a period of weeks to turn it into a substance, from which you can make a compost tea. Using this method you can also add in some other organic materials to help balance out the nutrients—things like blood and bone, other animal manure, seaweed meal, fish meal, etc. Using this method will result in a tea solution that will cause less problems than a straight guano and water (unprocessed) solution. When you make up the tea, soak a bag full of the guano compost in water overnight; then check the EC of the solution to make it up to the strength you require.

Also, although there is guano with different N-P-K levels, none of these can be used as a standalone nutrient for tomatoes. Most guano will have an N-P-K of 8-4-1 or perhaps 3-10-1. The first example has a higher nitrogen content, the second the higher P content. This is fine, but if you are growing tomatoes, when it come to fruiting, its not the higher P you want, but a nutrient solution with a much higher potassium ratio (K). The K content of most guano tends to be quite low and a fruiting tomato requires high levels of K (higher than even N when in fruit). Using guano as a standalone nutrient will not give a very good tomato crop.

Yes, you should mix other organic amendments with the guano, especially to boost the K levels, but they all need to go through the composting process before you make the tea. On the other hand if you wanted to use a complete organic nutrient solution to grow you plants, you might like to consider some of the ones which have been developed for hydroponic use such as Earth Juice, Pure Blend, or the Meta Naturals range of organic nutrients for hydroponics. These have been correctly processed to get around the problems encountered with products like guano.

Bat guano is fairly safe for you to work with. Make sure if you are using a dry product that you don't inhale any of the fine dust that might be in the bag. Most health problems with organic raw materials come from unprocessed and often fresh manure that may harbor bacteria. Standard hygiene measures will prevent any problems. —*L.M.*

Q: My tomatoes keep splitting on the vine. What causes that and what can I do about it?

A: The most common cause of tomato fruit splitting is uneven watering of the plants. If the plants become a little dry and are then watered or irrigated heavily, the plants take up a large amount of water all at once. This is transported into the developing fruit and the fruit cells expand faster than the skin can stretch and it splits open.

Tomato plants, when carrying a heavy fruit load, need constant drip irrigation, not heavy watering to restore a dry soil. This is most common where the plants may have dried out during a warm, sunny day and are then watered heavily in the evening when conditions are cooler and water is taken up by the plants faster. Mulching the soil, installing drip irrigation, or using automated hydroponic techniques are all ways of preventing sudden changes in the moisture levels of the soil or other growing media. Also, preventing the plants from becoming too hot with the use of overhead shading also helps prevent splitting.

If your plants are in a hydroponic system, avoid sudden changes in the electrical conductivity (EC) level. An EC drop will also cause the plants to suck up large volumes of water and split the fruit. —*L.M.*

Q: What would be the primary cause of small tomato size in NFT systems. The tomatoes also have streaks running down the shoulders of the fruit.

A: The primary cause of small tomato size in nutrient film technique (NFT) systems is not usually due to the system itself, but to the growing environment or the way the crop is managed. Small fruit size can be a characteristic of certain tomato varieties. It is also most common where the tomato plant is carrying a heavy crop load and has many fruit that are of a smaller-than-average fruit size. In this case, thinning the number of fruit per truss will increase fruit size. Small fruit size is also common where light levels are limiting (such as in winter, in many areas) or where temperatures are above or below optimal (61–79°F). A lack of potassium, low electrical conductivity (EC) that is below 2.5, or other nutrient deficiencies can also lead to small fruit size.

Sometimes, disease in the plants or root system can lower yields and fruit size if they don't kill the plant outright. Virus diseases in particular, of which a great many can affect tomato plants, can lead to small fruit that never fully develop their full size potential.

The streaks down the shoulders of the tomatoes could be just an effect of the variety. There are cultivars (e.g., 'Mr. Stripy') that naturally have stripes on the fruit. If this is not the case, than the most likely cause is a virus infection of the plants. Tomato mosaic virus can cause stripes to develop on the fruit, but you most likely would also notice strange symptoms on the plant as well. Sometimes, exposure of the fruit to direct sunlight and high temperatures causes color disorders, including unusual coloration, blotches, or stripes. In that case, shading the crop will prevent the problem. Good luck with your tomato plants. —L.M.

Q: This is my first time I've tried hydroponics. I'm growing tomatoes and cucumbers in the same system in my greenhouse. Tomato vines grow very high but produce tiny tomatoes that don't seem to ripen. My English cucumbers are doing great, long and slim like their supposed to be, except for some reason the last few inches of the cucumber gets very large in diameter.

A: It sounds like there are pollination problems with both your tomato and cucumber plants. Tomato plants grown indoors need pollination assistance. Outdoors, insects (mostly bees) would pollinate the flowers, but in your greenhouse you need to carry this out yourself. The best way to pollinate tomato vines is to wait until the flowers are fully open and then gently tap behind each flower truss to release the pollinate and create fruit set. If pollination does not occur, or is inadequate, you may get small fruitlets that don't contain any seeds and therefore will not swell, develop, and get any larger. The other cause of tall vines with small fruit that do not appear to grow are a lack of nutrients, such as running the electrical conductivity (EC) too low. Tomatoes need an EC level of at least 2.2–2.4 for good plant growth in a mixed cropping system. Some varieties also naturally have tall vines and small fruit (such as cherry tomatoes). Low light levels will also cause the vine to stretch and the fruit to be small.

The "bulging" of the ends of the cucumbers is again a pollination problem. When growing the long European (or 'Telegraph') cucumber, which is normally seedless, you want to prevent pollination (and hence the formation of seeds). If a 'Telegraph' cucumber type gets pollinated, it will develop seeds, usually at only one end of the fruit and these will made an area of the fruit grow large (and the fruit will be misshapen).

So, you need to pollinate the tomato vines in the greenhouse yourself and prevent any bees or other insects from pollinating your English cucumbers so they remain seedless and long, thin, and uniform in shape. Enclosing the cucumber flower with a paper bag while it is setting fruit will help, as will removing any male flowers that sometimes occur on normally "totally female" English cucumber varieties under certain growing conditions. If there aren't any male flowers present (which have a stamen with pollen on it inside the flower), the female fruiting flowers cannot be pollinated and cause the misshapen fruit. But watch out for insects flying into the greenhouse, which may be carrying pollen from outdoor cucumbers in the area as well. —L.M.

Q: Our tomato plants seem to be healthy. They have many green tomatoes already. They are planted in an old bathtub filled with sandy loam and several bags of Miracle-Gro Garden Soil (about half and half). They get full sun. The weather is hot and dry most of the time. Lately, the leaves have started to curl up around the edges. What should we do?

A: The tomatoes sound like they are suffering from some heat stress. The problem with the bathtub planter system is that it is likely that the soil and root systems are really heating up during the day (particularly with a light, sandy loam mixture) due to high radiation and air temperature levels and possibly moisture stress. All of these factors could be causing the leaves to curl up.

Tomato plant foliage has the ability to curl upward during times of high light levels to try and protect itself from the damage high radiation levels can cause and to try and prevent excess moisture loss under dry conditions. I suggest that you keep the bathtub well irrigated (drip irrigation during the day would be a good idea) and also install a shade cloth cover over the top of the plants to reduce the amount of light and heat falling on them. Stapling some 30–55 percent shade cloth material to a wooden frame over the plants will probably give them a much better growing environment during summer and would also help ensure that you get larger, better quality fruit and less problems with sunscald and blossom end rot. —L.M.

Q: I have been growing eight tomato plants from seed over the past three months. I put the plants outside for the second time on a warm 75°F day. Some of the leaves turned a dusty white and now two of the plants have sagged flat and may die. What is happening to my plants and how can I help them live?

A: It sounds like your plants, which had been in a protected environment, have suffered from sun scorch or damage when placed outside on a warm day. Tomato plants that have been growing in a protected environment tend to develop thin leaves with a thin cuticle (the layer that protects the leaf surface) and, when suddenly exposed to full sun and warm conditions, the leaves can suffer scorch or burn damage, which results in white, papery patches or large spots on the leaves. Under these conditions, plants that have not been sufficiently hardened off have difficulty in taking up sufficient water to prevent wilting and can end up become very wilted. The plants need to be given some protection when placed outside for the first few times. Overhead shading works well to keep direct sun of the plants while they adapt to the new environmental conditions. This shade can be removed after a week or so when the plants have hardened off enough to be able to survive the new conditions. —*L.M.*

Q: My 5-month-old tomato plant is 6 feet tall and has 20+ green fruit on it. The tomatoes are small for what is called a beefsteak variety, 'Trust,' and they don't show any sign of ripening. Some of the fruit are over 60 days old and the plant continues to put out new blooms. It's grown in Hydroton, under a 400-watt HID, the pH is in line, humidity is between 50 and 60 percent, and the temperature is 60–70°F.

A: The fact that the plant is actively flowering, growing more leaves, and getting quite tall will be slowing the expansion and ripening of the green fruit on the lower trusses. If you "stop" the plant at this stage by pinching out the growing tip and preventing further leaf and flower formation, you will force the plant to put all of its energy into developing and ripening up those green fruit. At the moment, the plant is focusing on producing more flowers at the expense of fruit expansion. This is a common problem under low levels of artificial lighting. The plant has limited assimilates and tends to put these reserves into foliage and flower production at the top of the plant rather than into rapidly filling out the fruit that have already been formed.

Also, you need to remove any lateral growth that has occurred. Laterals are those small shoots that form in the leaf axils on the main stem. Many people think they should leave these laterals to develop and produce flowers and more stems, but this is certainly not a good idea as the plant will

do this at the expense of the fruit that have already formed and you will end up with a number of very small, green fruit rather then well formed, large, ripe fruit.

The second problem is that the temperatures you are running, 60–70°F, are at the low end for good tomato production. In this range, plant growth—particularly fruit expansion, development, and ripening—is being restricted. Tomato plants have a temperature optimum of 70–80°F for best growth, yields, and fruit development. Your humidity levels are also low—70–80 percent would be a better range. You can increase this with the use of "evaporative" pans of water, which will bring relative humidity levels up in your growing area.

The nutrient solution you are using could also potentially be a problem. Tomato plants need high levels of potassium for good fruit growth and quality, so using a fruiting formula at this stage is required. The green fruit will eventually ripen, the slowness of this process is a combination of plant and environment factors which can easily be changed. —*L.M.*

Q: I want to grow tomatoes in my Megagarden system. It is 2x2 feet and has 15 rock baskets in it. I'm using a 400 MH. I would like to know how to keep all the plants around 1-2 feet high—as short as possible—since I have such a tight area. Can this be done? Will it help make the tomatoes bigger and better? Also, if I did 12 hours on and 12 hours off on the light cycle, would I get better results than if I had a 16–18 hour cycle of light?

A: Yes, you can easily keep you tomato plants at a height of about 2 feet if you have limited space. And yes, there is much evidence to suggest the fruit will be not only larger but of better quality. This type of system of tomato production is called "single- or double-truss cropping." This means you let the plant develop only one (or two) flower trusses, the plant has its growing point removed after the development of two or three leaves above this one truss so it doesn't grow any taller. All the plant's energy will then be forced into producing this one (or maybe two) trusses of fruit and hence the fruit will be larger than normal and should have a higher quality (higher sugar content, dry weight, and flavor). This type of short-term tomato cropping has been extensively studied and while it involves more work—that is, after you harvest your one truss of fruit, a new plant has to be propagated and started in the system—the yields and quality more than make up for this in your type of situation.

This type of system also makes the maximum amount of use of your lights. With the normal "tall" tomato plants, sometimes not enough light reaches the lower leaves of the plant where the fruit are developing and fruit size and quality often suffers.

If you chose to grow these single-truss, short term plants, you can also plant them at a much higher density than you would with a tall plant (often densities are 4-6 times that used for large plants). It also means there is less hassle with tying the plant up and supporting its weight.

The best day length for tomatoes is 16–18 hours on and 6-8 off. This is because tomato plants do better in terms of yield under longer day lengths. The greater the number of hours in which they can photosynthesize and produce assimilates (sugars) for fruit growth, the better—realizing of course that they do still need some "dark period" for other important plant process to occur. You will still produce acceptable fruit under a 12 on and 12 off program, but plant growth and fruit development is likely to be slower and it will take longer to get your fruit. —L.M.

Q: I am experiencing yellowing and brittle roots in my lettuce but the arugula, basil, and tomatoes that share the same hydroponic bed and nutrient tank do not manifest such tendencies. What do you think this is? The yellowing roots causes slow growth. Also, do you have a nutrient solution recipe for tomatoes? I am in the Philippines.

A: In your climate you will be constantly battling with temperatures which are much higher than optimal for the growth of lettuce, which is essentially a cool season crop. I suspect the yellowing and brittle growth of your lettuce roots is caused by nutrient solution temperatures which are too warm (there may also be some pathogen infection, such as Pythium), but it is difficult to diagnose a problem like this since the same symptoms can be caused by a wide range of factors, pathogens and conditions. Ideal root zone temperature for lettuce would be between 50–70°F. Lettuce will grow at warmer temperatures, but often there are growth problems in these types of climates.

Boron deficiency on lettuce plants will show as tip burn on the leaves and a puckering or crumpling of the leaf edges, the growing point may eventually become blackened. On the root systems, the symptoms are less severe but often there the growing points of the roots die back, resulting in a branched root system which is also smaller and shorter than usual.

Providing a boron level of 1 ppm to the nutrient solution should not under normal growing conditions induce boron deficiency—a level of 0.70 ppm is recommended for lettuce crops. However if you suspect boron deficiency based on the appearance of the plants it would be a good idea to get a nutrient solution analysis carried out to confirm this.

In a commercial situation it is not ideal to have both lettuce and tomato crops using the same nutrient or planted in the same bed. The reason being that these two crops are at different ends of the scale when it comes to their nutrient

requirements. Lettuce prefers a low EC, with a very different nitrogen to potassium ratio than a fruiting tomato plant. Tomato plants need a much higher EC for maximum yields and fruit quality as well as a completely different nutrient formula when they are fruiting (one that is higher in potassium, calcium and some of the other elements). It is difficult to achieve good yields of both crops and produce high quality produce from the one nutrient solution (nutrient formula). However it is possibly to successfully mix similar crops such as lettuce and salad greens with herbs using the same nutrient and a different nutrient mix and system for fruiting plants such as tomatoes, cucumbers, eggplant, peppers, etc.

Below is a standard nutrient mix formula for tomatoes (in tropical climates). While this can be used for a high quality water source (i.e. one with few dissolved salts) if your water contains any minerals, this will need to be adapted to allow for these.

Hydroponic Tomato Nutrient Formula

(Grams of Nutrient Salts to Be Dissolved Into Two Separate 40-liter Stock Solution Tanks)

Part A

Calcium nitrate	5,890
Potassium nitrate	2,073
Iron EDTA	200

Part B

Potassium nitrate	2,071
Monopotassium phosphate	1,696
Magnesium sulfate	3,125
Manganese sulfate	32
Zinc sulfate	4.4
Boric acid	15.6
Copper sulfate	1.2
Sodium molybdate	0.406

This will give an EC of 3.5 and a pH of 5.98 and results in N=363 ppm, P=89 ppm, K=510 ppm, Mg=77 ppm, Ca=295 ppm, S=102 ppm, Fe=4.9 ppm, Mn=1.97 ppm, Zn=0.25 ppm, B=0.7 ppm, Cu=0.068 ppm, Mo=0.05 ppm. —L.M.

Q: I have tomato seedlings growing outdoors. I want to bring them inside because it does frost every now and then in San Diego in the winter time. Would changing sunlight to indoor fluorescent light stress the plant very bad? Should I slowly change sunlight into indoor lighting? Also once frost is over and there is more daylight hours I plan to put them back outside, will this cause too much stress and greatly affect the plant?

A: Yes, it would be a good idea to slowly expose your plants to their new environment. The ideal situation would be to bring your plants in for a few hours at a time—making

Q: What causes tomatoes to be floury and soft? I am growing Roma tomatoes and they are disappointing. I know they should be better than they are.

A: Soft, floury tomatoes are very disappointing to grow and eat! But this problem can be solved since these attributes in tomato fruit are largely due to the genetic potential of the plant or cultivar and the growing conditions—both of which can be controlled.

First, the main cause of floury, tasteless, soft tomato fruit is a lack of potassium during fruit development. If you are growing your plants in soil, cut back on the nitrogen fertilizer at the time of fruit set and side dress heavily with potassium (potash). In hydroponics, you need to switch from a vegetative formula to a bloom or fruit formula that has a higher level of potassium. Tomato plants take up huge amounts of potassium when fruiting (when compared to non-fruiting plants) and it is easy for the fruit to be deficient in this element. Also, make sure the plants have sufficient calcium. A lack of calcium in the fruit will result in cell breakdown and that floury texture you are experiencing.

Tomato plants also tend to produce soft fruit when given too much water. The best textured and flavored tomato fruit are grown on plants that are slightly water stressed—when growing in soil. In hydroponics, the same effect is achieved by increasing the electrical conductivity (EC) of the nutrient solution. This acts to increase the sugars and acids in the fruit and to also lend a greater degree of firmness to the flesh. Overly warm conditions (above 80°F) also results in soft, mealy tomato fruit, so your plants may need some shading temperatures are too high.

You could also try some different cultivars. Many different varieties have different fruit characteristics and there may be some other types that are more suited to your climate and growing conditions and will produce the fruit quality you are after. Check with some of the seed companies and see what they are recommending for your climate, growing season, and taste preference. —*L.M.*

---

sure that when the plants are outside that they are safe from frost—each day. Start by moving the plants inside for two hours a day. Then, after a few days, move that number up to four. Then move the time inside up to six hours a day. If the plants don't show any signs of stress, you can probably keep them inside all of the time after that point.

Ideally, it would be best to place your seedlings by a sunny window and then supplement the sunlight with fluorescent lights. The best setup for this would be to use two different lights, one "warm" lamp (which provides more red light) and one "cool" lamp (which provides more blue light). Each setup should cost around $15.

If the nights are getting cold, make sure the window you place your seedlings by is insulated; keep your tomato starts warm. Tomato plants are unable to take up sufficient phosphorous when they are exposed to cold conditions. This deficiency will be seen as a purple tinting on the undersides of the leaves and on the stems.

After the threat of frosts has ended, repeat the gradual reintroduction process when you move the plants back outside. That way, you won't stress your plants. —*D.J.P.*

Q: The air coming out of my fan jet tube causes the tops of my hydroponic tomatoes to shake quite a bit. Can these windy conditions cause any physiological disorders?

A: Exposing your crops to strong winds can cause a variety of problems. Although good circulation is key to good crops, too much wind will reduce the humidity to undesirable levels and increase flower abscission, thereby reducing fruit set.

The best way to avoid this is to have your fan blowing out instead of in. Most greenhouses use exhaust fans to remove the old, stale air inside and draw fresh air from passive vents on the other side of the structure. Then, if further circulation is necessary in the greenhouse, they use smaller fans to move the air around.

Keep an eye on your plants to determine if your conditions are too windy. If the leave seem dry and you are having trouble with flowers falling off and fruit setting, you might want to look into ventilation alternatives. Here is a good link to many online resources for hydroponic greenhouse gardeners: www.attra.org/attra-pub/ghwebRL.html. —*D.J.P.*

Q: I plan on growing tomatoes hydroponically in a small greenhouse (16x8). Since I live in Las Vegas where the average temperature is over 100° in the summer, I will have a evaporative cooler running to keep the temperature down. My question is, should I be concerned about the CO_2 levels for proper growth?

A: In answer to your question regarding CO_2 levels for growth, this will depend on whether you keep your greenhouse entirely closed (almost airtight) to prevent the loss of your cooled air. Plants require CO_2 for photosynthesis and the levels can rapidly be depleted during the daylight

hours if there is no exchange of air or enrichment with CO_2 gas. This tends to happen in winter, where the greenhouse vents are kept shut to prevent the loss of heated air. But at the same time, the plants are using up the ambient levels of CO_2, causing a drop to very low levels. CO_2 in the atmosphere is present at a level of around 360–450 ppm. However, tomato plants have been shown to benefit from enrichment to levels of 1,000 ppm and higher, which increases crop yields. This is why commercial growers will often have CO_2 enrichment systems.

I think the objective in your case would be to prevent the CO_2 levels dropping off in a closed environment, so you will need to have fresh air constantly coming in. This is particularly important in a warmer climate such as yours were the plants will naturally be photosynthesizing at a faster rate and therefore will have a higher CO_2 requirement. Provided there is sufficient ventilation to allow fresh air to come into the greenhouse and replenish the CO_2 levels, you don't need to be concerned about levels for proper growth. —L.M.

Q: I am trying to grow tomatoes hydroponically for the first time. The plants are outside and seem to have a very low tolerance to daytime temperatures over the mid 80s. The soil-grown plants in the same vicinity do not suffer the same sensitivity. What I can I do to keep the hydroponic plants alive and producing?

A: I suspect it's not that your hydroponic plants have a lower heat tolerance, but that even though the air temperature is in the mid 80s, the temperatures around the root zone of your hydroponic plants may be considerably higher. Soil acts as a buffer zone to temperature change—simply because of its large volume. That means it takes a long time to heat up, and tends to stay considerably cooler than a smaller volume of media out in the open would. If your tomatoes are growing in black media containers—or even white NFT channels—the temperature inside this smaller root zone might tend to heat up very rapidly when exposed to sunlight and warm air. When the temperature in the hydroponic plant's root zone builds up—and if the plants are in direct sunlight, the temperature can be double or even higher than the air temperature—the plant comes under considerable stress, can't take up water or minerals, and will start to wilt. The temperature of the nutrient solution you apply could also be playing a major role here. Cooler nutrient means cooler roots. I would suggest that if you think this is the case, you will need to give some form of shading to the plants. Also, it might be a good idea to cover or bury exposed nutrient pipes to make sure they aren't super-heating the nutrient solution. Hopefully this will solve the temperature problems. —L.M.

Q: I could really use your help regarding an improvised hydroponic system I made. I filled a 3-liter, dark, glass bowl with drinking water. I placed a little aquarium fish air pump at the bottom center of it, which takes air form the outside and causes bubbles that cover the most of the bowl's inside area. On top I placed the plant's medium, a kind of a small stretcher with a hole in it. I placed a tomato plant through the hole, letting its root system drift over and above the air bubbles.

The plant survived this vicious assembling, although yellow coloring started to appear rapidly from the bottom of the plant and upward. The leaves are dying one after another, bottom to top. My question is: What do you think may have caused this?

Please note that at first I thought too much nutrient solution was added so I changed the water. I waited a little while without adding further nutrients. So far, no change.

A: While your system should work since you are providing dissolved oxygen into the nutrient solution, it appears that the tomato plant was damaged or diseased in some way, perhaps during the transplanting process. I would suggest that you start off with a butterhead or looseleaf lettuce seedling to trial your new system as they are much more forgiving of handling damage and also are much more suited to the type of "raft" or "float" system you have designed.

Tomato plant root systems don't seem to be well adapted to totally submerged conditions. They have a very high oxygen requirement and sometimes this is not met in this type of system, despite the introduction of oxygen. Also, tomato plants do not like the roots being moved by the air bubbles.

It also sounds as if the roots were damaged at some stage and a root disease may be the cause of the leaves gradually dying. Trying a different type of plant—lettuce, watercress, mint, or something similar—should get a much better result from your system. —*L.M.*

Q: I have a yellow pear tomato plant that is doing extremely well. However, the stem have developed small, white, thorny "daggers" growing on them. Do you have any idea what these daggers are?

A: The "daggers" are most likely small root initials on the stem of your tomato plant. Tomatoes, particularly some varieties, have a habit of forming these white or pale bumps that can grow outward a few millimeters on the lower portion of the stem. If the stem was buried, these root initials would grow into new roots to anchor the plant more firmly into the soil or to replace the old root system should it become diseased or damaged. Don't worry about them. If the plant is doing well, they won't cause any problems, although they can become numerous under certain conditions. —*L.M.*

Q: I have several tomato plants that are just now getting tomatoes. I've noticed that some of them kind of have ridges around the sides instead of being perfectly smooth. The tomatoes are about the size of a cherry. Do you have any idea what could be causing this?

A: This is a common problem with certain tomato varieties (particularly many of the older, heirloom types) and it is due to problems with pollination and fruit set. If conditions were not optimum for pollination (usually too hot or too cold), or there was a lack of pollination for some reason, the fruit may still set but will be misshapen, often with ridges, deformities, and strange outgrowths. The fruit will also usually be of a small size.

However, there are some varieties of tomato that have fruit that are naturally ridged or fluted and these are grown as a specialty item. However, assuming this is not the case and most of the fruit are round and smooth, I suggest you remove the misshapen fruit. Later trusses of fruit further up the plant should pollinate and set better as growing conditions improve. —*L.M.*

Q: While visiting Disney World, Epcot Center, I observed an unusual method of growing tomatoes at an attraction in The Land Pavilion. They were rooted in what appeared to be a white plastic tube about 10 inches in diameter. A tomato plant was growing about every 24 inches. All were hanging from above with several strings. I think I saw drip irrigation tubing going to each plant.

I would like to try growing some peppers and tomatoes this way but need some help with what to use. I haven't had any response from Disney. Can anyone give me some hints? By the way, I live near the Twin Cities in Minnesota.

A: What you were seeing was some sort of tiered drip irrigation hydroponic system. Epcot is always experimenting with different types of hydroponic systems to mostly serve as demonstration units. Most of The Land's hydroponic systems and greenhouses were designed by Dr. Merle Jensen, a professor in the Life Sciences Department at the University of Arizona and an occasional contributor to our magazine.

Hydroponics is a method of agriculture that doesn't use any soil. Plants are fed with nutrient solution that contains all the minerals they need for growth. Hydroponic systems can be either media-based, with some sort of inert media supporting the roots, or water culture, which don't feature any media at all. Hydroponics is commonly used on Space Shuttle missions and on space stations to supply some fresh food. Since soil doesn't exist in space, researchers believe that hydroponics is the way to go in the future for long-term stays on space stations or on long orbiting missions and NASA is always experimenting with new setups. We ran a profile of The Land in Volume 8, Number 1 (Fall 1996) of our magazine, The Growing Edge. We continually run new articles that cover NASA's hydroponic work.

Hydroponics is also used by commercial greenhouses to grow a lot of the fresh vegetables you eat. Tomatoes, peppers, cucumbers, and lettuce are popular hydroponic crops. The reason hydroponics is gaining popularity is due to the fact that soilless growers can avoid a lot of the pests and diseases that are commonly associated with soil. Also, they can provide very precise nutrition for their plants since they know exactly what they put into the nutrient solution. Commercial growers make custom nutrient solutions for different crops in order to provide exactly what the plant needs at different stages of growth. Hydroponic systems can be easily automated so many more plants can be grown with less human input. Also, hydroponics permits a higher planting density so harvested yields are dramatically higher than soil-based gardening.

Many hobbyist growers also employ hydroponic techniques. A lot of hobbyist hydroponic gardeners like to build their own systems to put in the yard during the summer, out in the greenhouse, in a sun room at home, in front of a sunny window, or in the basement or garage, supplemented with artificial lights, in order to have fresh, homegrown food all year round. Our magazine runs profiles of hobbyist growers and their systems all the time. Most major cities now feature hydroponic retail stores where prefabricated systems, nutrient solutions, and other essential hydroponic gardening tools can be purchased. Many of these stores also have hydroponic systems set up as demonstration units. One store in your area is Interior Gardens (2817 Lyndale Ave. S, Minneapolis; (612) 870-9077). Retailers can also provide some good advice for beginning hydroponic growers.

Hydroponics may seem kind of otherworldly and complicated at first, but it really isn't very different from other forms of gardening. The main differences are that soil isn't used and the water used to feed the plants always has fertilizer in it. If you're new to hydroponics—and interested in giving it a try to grow some vegetables at home—I would recommend that you browse around our Website and learn a few of the basics (try www.growingedge.com/basics/start.html and www.growingedge.com/community/archive/topics.html; search in the archives for "tomatoes" and "peppers"). Then, getting going at home won't take any more effort than planting a regular garden. A hydroponic "system" can be as simple as a few large gardening containers (the type usually used to grow plants) filled with a mixture of inert media, such as a 2:1 mixture of perlite and vermiculite (commonly available at gardening stores everywhere), and fed with a good hydroponic nutrient solution (available at your local hydroponic retailer or over the Internet). Tomatoes and peppers are popular choices for home gardeners. Once you get growing, our Website can be a great free resource for hints and tips for hydroponic gardening success. —D.J.P.

Q: I'm growing determinate patio tomatoes under a 1,000-watt lamp indoors. How should I prune these, if at all? It seems like everyone has their own opinion. Some say to remove only the bottom couple of suckers, some say don't prune at all, some say to remove all of the suckers, and some say to leave one sucker below the first flower cluster and remove all of those below it! Which is the right way?

A: Determinate patio tomatoes are often confused with standard indeterminate greenhouse tomatoes that always have the laterals (side shoots) removed and are grown upward on a long stem system. Determinate tomatoes are different and the growth habit will naturally form a short bush without pruning. However, what does tend to happen under lights is the plants form a dense bush and the light source cannot penetrate into the lower layers of the plant, causing the leaves

to become thin and yellow, eventually dying back. Humidity levels will also increase in the thick foliage where airflow is restricted. This encourages disease pathogens to invade.

In your case, growing indoors and under a light, I would suggest that you perform some light pruning of the side shoots around the base of the plant to allow some airflow into this area since these leaves won't be carrying out much photosynthesis anyway. At that point, the plant shouldn't require any further pruning—it will form its own "determinate" shape. Remove any discolored, diseased, or damaged stems or foliage that you notice throughout the life of the plant. Also, the plant will likely need some form of support to prevent it from collapsing from the weight of the developing fruit. This can be facilitated by tying the plant to a stake driven into the growing media when the plant is young and the root system hasn't fully developed yet (to prevent any damage to the roots) or to an overhead support. If you find the fruit size is too small, removing some of the additional flower trusses or thinning to four or five fruit per truss will help increase size. —L.M.

Q: How do you prune roma tomatoes in a greenhouse for maximum yield?

A: Roma tomatoes are a type of determine tomato plant that does not require pruning. Determine tomato plants naturally form a short bush type of growth so they don't require that the lateral or side branches be removed.

On the other hand, indeterminate tomatoes, which are the normal type grown under cover or in greenhouses, continue to grow upward indefinitely and eventually need to be "stopped" and have the growing point removed. Indeterminate tomato types also require any laterals or side shoots to be removed so that fruit only form from the main stem (otherwise the plant becomes difficult to manage and fruit size is compromised).

Roma and other determinate tomato types are traditionally grown out in the field as processing crops because their growth habit means they don't require any pruning or support (although they are sometimes grown in greenhouses as well). The only pruning you might need to do is to remove diseased shoots or any shoots that are very thin and weak and may become diseased. You might like to remove any old leaves or shoots at the base of the plant if they start to become yellowed. The plants, might also benefit from some plant support with stakes or by tying it to an overhead wire to maintain fruit quality and make the crop easier to manage. If you are aiming for a large fruit size, you might need to "truss prune"—that is, remove excess flowers from the end of the flower truss so that only six or seven fruitlets

Q: **When growing plants in a closed greenhouse, do you need bees for pollination? If so, for which plants? tomatoes? bell peppers? cucumbers?**

A: You are correct that when growing in an enclosed area, you'll need to help your plants with pollination. However, unless you are growing a lot of plants, you can perform this task yourself without the help of hired insects.

When your pepper and tomato plants are in flower, tap or gently shake the branches once every day to help distribute the pollen. Gently shaking the plants also helps ensure good fruit set. Pepper and tomato flowers have "perfect" flowers that have both male and female sexual characteristics in the same flower, so they're pretty easy to pollinate.

Cucumbers and other members of Cucumis (some gourds and melons) produce both male and female flowers, so you will have to transfer the pollen from the male flower to the female. If you grow this type of plant, you will have to be diligent about your artificial pollination duties in order to get good fruit. But some cucumber cultivars exist these days that only produce female flowers. These are called "gynoecious" cultivars and don't require pollination. These are seedless varieties.

Growers who have a lot of plants usually purchase boxes of bees that take care of their pollination demands. Or, I've heard about some greenhouse growers simply leaving a window open in the greenhouse hoping that bees will be attracted to the plants and will fly into the greenhouse and pollinate the plants. However, if you leave a window open in the greenhouse, you never know what other bugs will get in. —*D.J.P.*

---

form, ensuring they are all of good size. Sometimes, if fruit numbers of 10 or more fruit form on any one flower truss, the fruit size on average will be much smaller than if only 6 fruit were allowed to set on the truss. This will give you high yields of fruit of a larger size. —*L.M.*

Q: How long does it usually take for a tomato bloom to become a ripe tomato? I have roma and 'Better Boy' plants.

A: Once the flower has been properly pollinated, it should develop a small fruit within a week or two. The trick to good fruit set is to make sure the flowers are pollinated well. If you're growing in an enclosed environment, such as a greenhouse, you will need to assist with this process by gently shaking the plants every day during pollination. Insects perform this job outside. You also need to make sure your temperatures and humidity levels are at the proper levels to help facilitate fruit set. A dry, overly hot or cold environment can prompt blossom or fruitlet drop. For more information on growing tomatoes, see:

www.growingedge.com/community/archive/search.php3?query=tomato&c=all
ag.arizona.edu/hydroponictomatoes/
ohioline.osu.edu/hyg-fact/1000/1624.html
www.ces.ncsu.edu/hil/hil-8107.html
www.msue.msu.edu/msue/imp/mod03/03900103.html
www.wvu.edu/~agexten/hortcult/homegard/tomatoes.htm

There are many more resources on the Web on this topic. This is just a sampling. —*D.J.P.*

Q: I am growing tomato in the highlands and I have a problem regarding fruit size. The first cluster of fruit to fifth the fruit size OK. After the fifth cluster, the fruit size becomes small. What is the cause?

A: The falloff in fruit size from the first fruit truss in tomatoes is normal to a certain extent. The first fruit truss will always be the largest and highest quality since the fruit in this truss aren't completing for assimilates as much as latter trusses when the plant is carrying a heavy fruit load. By the time you get to the fifth truss, the plant has a high fruit loading (many trusses) and so all fruit developed at that time can be smaller than normal. If the plant is not able to produce sufficient assimilate—either due to light, temperature, water, or nutrition conditions—trusses further up the plant will suffer. Also, if the nutrient solution is not providing sufficient levels of certain elements—or if potassium in particular is in short supply (as often occurs at this stage of development)—fruit size will also be affected.

At the fifth truss stage, the plant is trying to continue the development of sufficient foliage to support the plant and fruit development, while at the same time expand many fruit. This competition often results in fruit size falling away. You can increase fruit size by thinning the number of fruitlets on the fifth and subsequent trusses. Too many fruit will give a small fruit size, but by thinning to four or five fruit per truss, fruit size can be increased. Another solution is to grow a short term crop with only three to four trusses per plant. Then, remove the growing point three leaves above the top truss. That way, all fruit will be of a maximum size. Short term cropping techniques like these are often used where fruit size, under certain less than optimal growing conditions, is being compromised. —*L.M.*

Q: I'm growing hydroponic tomatoes under eight 48-inch fluorescent tubes positioned directly above plants. The plants are doing very well. How can I support the vines? The light blocks me from hanging lines from the ceiling. Is there anything commercially available that I can buy? I can't use things like chicken wire because I need access underneath the plants. Are there any sites or books that describe possible solutions?

A: There are a couple of workable solutions for floor-based support of your plants. The first one involves using some of those plastic, outdoor market umbrella stands that are filled with sand or water. These can be used to hold up a plant support pole or thick stake. Since tying a large tomato plant to a pole can be a little tricky, there are also a number of good products that can be used that are designed for outdoor plants (i.e., they're usually pushed into the soil). The following Website has a plant support system you could use in this way (the "Garden Buddy"): www.thebuddycompany/com/index.html.

The other method is a bit more involved but is better suited to large, heavy plants that may topple a single pole system. This involves either constructing or buying a "wigwam" or "tepee" for each plant or group of plants. By using 6-10 thick, bamboo or plastic stakes or poles tied together at the top, you can still access your plants from the floor and the system should be free standing. If you don't want to construct your own, many garden outlets sell outdoor plant support systems based on the wigwam concept. Here is a good site that shows what can be done with this system and where you can get a wigwam kit for your plants ("Panda Stix Wigwam Kits"): www.ericthepanda.co.uk/pandastix/wigwam.html. —*L.M.*

Q: I'm in the process of preparing my tomato lineup card for my hobby hydroponic garden next spring and it would be wonderful to include some heirloom varieties, such as the famed 'Brandywine.'

I miss all the great-tasting, sandwich-size tomatoes that my grandmother and mother used to grow years ago. Everyone I know concurs that heirloom tomatoes are very palatable with a memorable, distinctive, old-fashioned tomato taste when compared to most modern hybrid counterparts. I'm not putting down hybrids—I've enjoyed growing them in the past.

Are there any obstacles that would prevent me from growing heirloom tomatoes hydroponically? People often say that heirlooms are best grown in soil. I realize that the yield of heirloom tomatoes might be less consistent than modern varieties and would appreciate hearing from someone who had some experience growing heirloom tomatoes hydroponically.

A: There isn't a problem in growing older, heirloom tomatoes in hydroponic systems. In fact, they often perform better in terms of getting some flavor back into tomato fruit. The down side is that yields and resistance to some diseases can be lost with certain cultivars.

We've grown a number of heirloom varieties in hydroponic systems and there are a couple of points to note. First of all, that great-tasting tomato flavor we remember from the old varieties was most likely a result of being grown in soil with a high salt content, under moisture stress in full sun, and during the long days of summer. They were probably ripened on the vine and eaten immediately after harvest. These are all factors that act to concentrate the sugars and flavor in the fruit. Many heirloom types grown in hydroponic systems can have poor flavor if they aren't grown correctly—just as they can when grown improperly in soil. Tomato flavor is a combination of genetics and environment, so it's important to get both right if you want to grow tasty fruit.

Once the plants start to set fruit, growing them at a reasonably high electrical conductivity (EC) level (above 3.5) with a high potassium nutrient mix will give good flavor without compromising much in the way of yield. Make sure good light levels are reaching the plants, that the plants are spaced so that air movement can be achieved, and that the right temperature levels are maintained. Make sure sufficient leaves are left on the plant to produce sugars. Don't remove the lower leaves until the truss of fruit above them has been completely harvested.

Some heirloom varieties are more prone to root pathogens and virus diseases, so keep a close eye on the plants and remove any diseased seedlings or foliage and burn the matter away from the greenhouse. I would suggest that you try two or three different heirloom cultivars in your hydroponic system to see which performs the best and has the flavor profile you're seeking. Some varieties naturally have more sugars and/or acids than others. Some of the better-tasting heirloom varieties we've tried are 'Rose,' '`German,' and 'Moskvich'; 'Brandywine' and 'Yellow Brandywine' are also good. 'Potentate' and 'Moneymaker' are worth a try. An old-fashioned, tasty cherry tomato is 'Principe Borghese.' Seeds should be available from Johnny's Selected Seeds at www.johnnyseeds.com.

As with all tomatoes, letting the fruit ripen on the vine will ensure the best flavor. After harvest, the fruit must be stored at room temperature. Tomatoes that are stored in the refrigerator or at temperatures lower than 44.6°F will rapidly lose their hard-won flavor, become watery, and develop a mealy texture. This common mistake has done much to ruin formerly good tomato fruit! —L.M.

now over 2 feet high. I recently had to move the plant from the center of the tray to the row along the outside wall of the tray. After I moved it, I noticed that some of the leaves began to curl and there are yellow spots on some of the older leaves. It has blooms and is still growing at the same rate but now it has these little nodules along the base of the stem. Is this a virus? Did I put the plant in some kind of shock by moving it? Is this spider mites? I have not seen any webs.

A: Moving a 2-foot-high plant should not cause too many problems for a tomato. However, the root system was disturbed. As a result, the plant will now attempt to initiate new roots and re-establish itself and it is likely that the little nodules along the base of the stem are root initials. Tomato plants commonly try to initiate roots on the lower stem when they have had some sort of root stress such as transplanting or root death due to other causes (such as water logging). Leaves that are beginning to curl and dis-

Growers who choose to make their own nutrient solutions need to have a good understanding of hydroponics, botany, mathematics, and chemistry. Most hobbyist growers simply buy premixed liquid or dry nutrients that they then mix with a good quality water to make their nutrient solution.

Q: I run a nutrient film technique (NFT) system with tomatoes. I run the water every one-half hour. I'm new at growing hydroponically. Should I leave the water on more or less? I test my pH regularly and the system runs fine.

A: NFT systems are usually run continuously, provided that a thin film of nutrient is maintained so that the root system isn't flooded. However, some systems are run for only a few minutes at a time. Since most NFT systems don't feature media that could hold moisture between irrigations, the frequency of nutrient application needs to be carefully monitored. No more than a few minutes should pass between irrigations to ensure the root system doesn't become water stressed between applications. If there's sufficient media around the root system to hold moisture then you can increase the period between irrigations. As long as you keep an eye on the root system and the plants to ensure they aren't in danger of drying out between nutrient applications the system should continue to work well. —L.M.

Q: I installed a hydroponic system in my basement this past February. I have a tomato plant that I started from a pack of seeds my boss got in the mail. The plant is

color could also be a result of the root disturbance. These leaves may in fact eventually need to be removed. As long as the top portion of the plant is growing well, don't be too concerned at this stage. The yellow spots you describe could also be magnesium deficiency, which is common in tomatoes. The plant will most likely take some time to recover from its transplanting shock, but tomatoes are very adaptable. Provided there aren't other cause for these symptoms and the root mat remains healthy, you should still get many more flowers and fruit. —L.M.

Q: What is the recommended growing method for hydroponic tomatoes and bell peppers? Will a plant survive root-bound in a 4-inch pot being grown hydroponically? What size container is recommended for mature plants?

A: There are many different ways to grow hydroponic tomato and bell pepper plants. Two of the most popular methods are the nutrient film technique (NFT) and media-based pots. NFT is quite a bit more complicated than just using pots. For more information on NFT, see www.growingedge.com/basics/tutorial/03_water_culture.html.

Growing hydroponic plants in soilless media is quite similar to growing in soil. However, instead of using soil to hold the plants in place, growers use perlite, coconut fiber, rockwool, peat moss, or another soilless media. A good, simple mix for peppers and tomatoes would be three parts perlite to one part peat moss. Some growers just use perlite.

After the seedlings have grown out in propagation trays, and then smaller pots, transplant juvenile plants that are about 6-inches tall into large pots. Be very careful to not disturb the roots too much when transplanting. Tomatoes have a larger root system than bell peppers and should go two plants per 5-gallon (12-inch diameter) pot at the least. They can go into smaller pots than this, but the plants won't grow as large or produce as much fruit. Pepper plants can go into smaller pots—around two plants per 3-gallon (8-inch diameter) pot. Since different gardening supply manufacturers create different sized pots that are available in different areas, these gallon and inch figures are approximate. Just try to find something close to these guidelines. Make sure the pots you use are sterile and do not have any traces of soil in them.

As your plants grow large, you will need to provide some method of support, such as a trellis. If all goes well, the plants will become heavy with fruit and will need to be held upright. Some growers use string tied to the growing plant in a safe, sturdy place that is then connected to an overhead structure. Then they keep the string taught with a slipknot as the plants continue to grow.

Make sure you use a good hydroponic nutrient solution suitable for peppers and tomatoes—both "grow," for vegetative growth and "bloom," for when flowers and fruit form. These crops are frequently grown together by hobbyists with the same nutrient solution formulation. A hydroponic retailer can help you find a good nutrient solution to use. To find a retailer near you, see www.hydromall.com/stores/index.html. Flush the media every few weeks with clean, plain water to remove any accumulated mineral salts. Make sure the plants receive quality pollination by gently tapping or shaking the flowers every day when they form. This procedure will also help ensure good fruit set. Also, make sure you provide the necessary environmental conditions for your tomatoes and peppers, including plenty of light. —D.J.P.

Q: What is the best variety of tomato for hydroponics? We have a room that is roughly 400 square feet and covered with Mylar. What would the best light readings and combinations of lights be? We are interested in growing flowers, herbs, and hydroponic tomatoes.

A: There is no one "best" variety of tomatoes for hydroponics. Actually, there is a huge range of cultivars that do well in hydroponics and the choice is usually determined by what the grower wants to end up eating or what the market requires in terms of size, shape, color, and flavor. I would suggest that you contact a quality seed supplier—such as Johnny's Selected Seeds—and check their selection to see what appeals to you.

The light reading you are after would be about 18–20 watts per square meter (Wm2) for young seedlings and then increased to 24–32 Wm2 for more mature plants. The combination of lights you will need for fruiting plants is either a combination light—that provides an adequate spectrum for both vegetative growth and fruiting—or a mixture of high-pressure sodium (HPS) and metal halide (MH) bulbs. You could also have a few fluorescent tubes along the sides of the crop to increase light intensity as much as possible. In an enclosed grow room without much outside ventilation, you might want to consider outfitting the bulbs with water-cooled jackets to reduce heat buildup and plant scorch. Johnny's Selected Seeds (www.johnnyseeds.com/) —L.M.

Q: I've been reading about hydroponics and some of the techniques used in this work. I'd like to know something about a technique called NFT (nutrient film technique). How does it work? How can I set up a inexpensive NFT system? I want to cultivate tomatoes and hot peppers. I have a liquid nutrient called: DYNA-GRO and the formula is: 7-9-5. Is this more or less the appropriate mix for the plants?

A: The nutrient film technique (NFT) is a system that pumps a very thin film of nutrient solution down growing troughs that support the plants. NFT systems are usually closed-loop and recirculating. NFT systems are frequently built out of food-grade PVC plastic pipes (flat-bottomed is favored over round). Many people build their own NFT systems so that they can efficiently grow their own herbs and vegetables. Hot peppers and tomatoes are commonly grown in NFT systems.

I would recommend that you read up on the basics of NFT before attempting to build and operate your own system. There are several texts on the market that will help teach you what you need to know, including The ABC of NFT (by Dr. Allen Cooper), Hydroponic Crop Production (by Rob Smith & Lon Dalton), and Hydroponic Food Production (by Dr. Howard Resh). The latter two texts ably cover the basics of NFT and also provide a lot of other hydroponic information.

Also, Rob Smith is a regular columnist for our magazine, The Growing Edge. In his column called "The Growing World of Hydroponics" he has instructed readers how to build their own NFT system, step by step. Each issue of the magazine provides another step in the process. This series on the NFT system began in Volume 12, Number 3 (January/February 2001) and continued through Volume 13, Number 5 (May/June 2002). Having someone like Rob—who is an expert in hydroponic cultivation—instruct how to build an NFT system really helps prevent problems in design and operation (he still writes a column in every issue of The Growing Edge but the topics vary).

Since I do not know all of the proportions of nutrients in your Dyna-Gro mix (you only supplied the N-P-K), I cannot comment as to whether it is suitable for peppers and tomatoes. If your fertilizer mix has been specifically formulated for general hydroponic growing, you should be fine. Just make sure that you're not using fertilizer created for use with soil-based plants, since such a mix would not provide all of the minerals soilless plants need. Again, a good textual guide to hydroponics would help you understand these issues.

Serious hobbyist and commercial growers sometimes create their own nutrient solutions. For your reference, here is a suggested formula for growing hydroponic tomatoes

(provided by Dr. Lynette Morgan). You could also compare the list of nutrients on the packaging of your Dyna-Gro fertilizer to the list below to see if the same types of minerals are represented.

The salts listed below should be dissolved into two separate 5 gallon stock solution tanks. Add small quantities of the stock solution to the nutrient tank until you get an electrical conductivity (EC) reading of around 3.5. Every couple of days, check the EC and add more stock solution or water as required to maintain this level.

Tomato Nutrient Formula
(Ounces of Nutrient Salts to Mix Into Two 5-Gallon Stock Solutions; Dilution of 1:100 Will Give an EC of 3.5)

Part A
Calcium nitrate 98
Potassium nitrate 34
Iron EDTA 2.4

Part B
Potassium nitrate 34
Monopotassium phosphate 28
Magnesium sulfate 52
Manganese sulfate 0.53
Zinc sulfate 0.07
Boric acid 0.26
Copper sulfate 0.02
Ammonium molybdate 0.007

When dissolved and diluted 1:100, an EC of 3.5 and a pH of 5.98 will result (TDS=2995).

Growers who choose to make their own nutrient solutions need to have a good understanding of hydroponics, botany, mathematics, and chemistry. Most hobbyist growers simply buy premixed liquid or dry nutrients that they then mix with a good quality water to make their nutrient solution. —D.J.P.

Q: Can I remove the soil from around the tomato plants that are about 12 inches high and put them in a support media of Styrofoam cups held up in foamcore board in an aquarium with nutrients dissolved in water and air stone around the roots of the plants? Do I need to add nutrients to the water every week or two? I want to do this ASAP so the plants will produce tomatoes before school is out. Do I need to hand pollinate the flowers and with each other or other plants? In the past I had problems with the flowers falling off so no tomatoes were ever made.

A: Luckily, tomato plants (even ones that are 12 inches high), tend to transplant well and will recover quickly and produce new roots, so there should be no problem with what you are planning. I would suggest you immediately give the plants some support in their new system by tying them up to a wire or something similar above cropping height—they will get fairly heavy when carrying the fruit. The nutrients in the aquarium with an air stone is fine, but you don't want any light falling on the nutrient, so the aquarium needs to be wrapped with light proof material to prevent this. If you use a sheet of black plastic or cardboard a few layers think this should stop light from causing algae growth in the nutrient—and allow you to take this off to view the roots every now and then.

With tomato plants, which are fairly heavy feeders, you will need to add nutrients probably every second day and completely dump and change the nutrient once a week. If you have an EC meter, this is easy. Just maintain the EC at about 2.5–3.0 and add more nutrient stock solution as this drops. If you don't have an EC meter, completely change the nutrient once a week and replacing with a fresh batch should keep the plants growing well.

Tomato flowers do need artificial pollination for good fruit set. Tomato flowers are self fertile, so just gently tapping or flicking the flower truss will release the pollen and fertilization will occur (you can also use a paint brush if you like). In other words, you don't need to cross pollinate flowers with other flowers or between plants—just shaking the flower truss to make the pollen release is sufficient. Without this pollination assistance, many of the flowers and even very small fruitlets will drop off early on and the plants won't develop many fruit. Carrying out pollination every second day is a good idea to ensure all flowers are covered. Also, make sure the plants are getting sufficient light. Low light and temperature are another reason for a lack of fruit or flowers falling off, since tomatoes have a fairly high light requirement. —L.M.

Q: I have some interest in growing "hanging tomato plants." Could I get more info? Is it hydroponic? What type of watering system? If my customers wanted to set this up on the eaves of their home, how would they go about it? I may set one up at the store with a copy of the article.

A: The photo you mentioned in your question was taken by Rob Smith. The upside-down tomato plant in the picture was grown as an isolated experiment to see how much fruit a hydroponically grown plant could really put out (this one produced over 100 lbs. of tomatoes). The plant is simply allowed to flop over the sides of the planter. The media is probably perlite or a mixture of perlite and peat moss. In this case, it looks like the plant was simply fed by hand with nutrient. In order to produce such a large amount of fruit, I would imagine that the nutrient was painstakingly evaluated and that the plant was given optimum growing conditions.

I would think that a self-watering pot (wick) or just a setup with drip emitters could work in this situation to reduce the amount of active care needed by the plant. —D.J.P.

Q: I grow cucumbers and many other plants from seed four to six weeks before hardening them off outside. From the first day they are outside, the cucumbers seem to have had problems. It seems as though the leaves are drying up. The bigger, lower leaves, 2–3 inches across, turn white and eventually disintegrate while the rest of the plant stays green. Since this is a repeat of what took place last year, in about four weeks or so the plants will die after being planted in the garden. We've had 70°F days and 50°F nights with rain every three to four days. All the other plants in the garden seem to be OK. What's going on with the cucumbers?

A: The problem your young cucumber plants are having when put outside is called "photoinhibition." This means that although light levels are good for maximum photosynthesis, the temperatures are too cold for the process to complete itself correctly. Thus, you get damage caused when the processes inside the leaf are inhibited because of cool temperatures that "freeze up" the cell membranes while light levels are at the same time inducing photosynthesis. The products of photosynthesis cannot then be processed by the plant and they begin to build up and cause cell damage. This cell damage appears as the whitening on the bigger, lower leaves that you are seeing, which eventually causes the leaf tissue to disintegrate. The temperatures the plants receive outdoors are low (particularly the night temperature and most probably the soil temperature) and you can prevent this damage by increasing these temperatures with use of a cloche, heating pad, or solar sink to radiate heat back to the plants. Temperatures need to be about 75°F by day and at least 65°F at night—minimum—to prevent this damage from occurring on the cucumber plants when they are placed outside to harden off. Cucumbers never really harden off to low temperatures such as those you mentioned. If they do continue to grow, they will be stressed and will not grow well until conditions warm up. I hope this information helps with your next lot of cucumber plants. —L.M.

Q: I have a cucumber plant that is blooming right now, but there aren't any male flowers, just female. I'm using Ionic Bloom nutrient with a continuous flow system and 16 hours of artificial light (a 400-watt HPS and a 400-watt MH).

I was also wondering if there was a nutrient more suited to assorted plants (tomato, peppers, herbs, lettuce, and cucumbers) in one system. Will there be any problems with bolting or younger plants?

A: I suspect that you are growing a variety of cucumber that only produces female flowers—a gynoecious hybrid. There are many types of cucumbers. The American types of greenhouse cucumbers (pickling cucumbers) are monoecious plants—that is, they have both male and female flowers on the same plant and require pollination to produce good fruit. These fruit tend to have seeds in them, which isn't desirable for many markets. For this reason, the female-only gynoecious types were developed. These types don't require pollination and therefore don't need male flowers.

If you think that you have a monoecious plant that should have male and female flowers, there are a couple of conditions that can inhibit male flowers from appearing. Plant stress can cause a predominance of female flowers in cucumber. Conversely, high temperatures, long days, high light levels, and high nitrogen content in the nutrient solution can cause a predominance of male flowers. A middle ground is best for equal production. It's possible to stimu-late the development of male flowers by spraying them with gibberellic acid—used by plant breeders—at the proper concentration.

While your bloom nutrient is good for the fruiting plants, it isn't ideal for lettuce and other greens. But greens will still grow well in this nutrient if you compromise the electrical conductivity (EC) level. In general, fruiting plants require a higher EC (2.5–3.5) for good yields and quality while the lettuce and other greens prefer an EC below 1.5. You can compromise by running the EC around 2.0 and still get reasonable lettuce and tomatoes. You can help reduce the incidence of bolting in your lettuce by keeping temperatures down (avoid heat buildup under the lights) and the EC down. —L.M.

Q: With regard to the discussion I read on cucumbers, you mention artificial pollination. Can you advise how this is done?

I am growing cucumbers hydroponically in my basement and I have beautifully formed cucumbers, but they all remain about 1 inch long and don't seem to be growing any further. I am suspecting pollination (or lack thereof) is the culprit.

A: I assume you are growing an standard, short, American cucumber that has both male and female flowers and produces fruit that contains seeds. The other type is seedless (European or 'Telegraph' cucumber) and has only female flowers on the plant. Therefore, it sets seedless fruit without any pollination.

To pollinate American cucumbers, find a fully open male flower. These are the ones with a tall, yellow stamen covered in yellow, dusty-looking pollen. Pull the petals of the male flower back and wipe the pollen into the middle of the inside of a female flower. The pollen grains, once they have been applied, will rapidly germinate. The other method is to use a paintbrush and pick up some of the pollen grains from the male flower and dust them into the middle section of the female flower. You need to do this pretty much every day as the flowers open.

There are a few other reasons why the fruit may fail to form past the 1-inch-long stage, most of which are covered in an article I wrote on growing hydroponic cucumbers (see www.growingedge.com/magazine/back_issues/view_artic le.php3?AID=130332). However, I would suggest that you try some artificial pollination techniques first and see if that solves the problem. —L.M.

Q: I have a spaghetti squash plant growing but it only has male flowers on it. Is the spaghetti squash plant one that is only male for one plant and female for another? Should I have grown two?

A: Members of Cucurbita (spaghetti squash is Cucurbita pepo) sometimes have a tendency to produce many male flowers and only a few females, but they do produce both male and female flowers on the same plant. I would recommend that you be patient and wait for female flowers to appear. They look very much like male flowers but are a little smaller and are always solitary (whereas the males sometimes appear in clusters). It is true that when a few plants are grown, you can cross pollinate them when flowers appear. However, these trailing vines can take up a lot of space.

Be patient and I would imagine that some female flowers will appear soon. —D.J.P.

Q: We have been growing peppers indoors and the plants do wonderful. However, the flowers bloom and then drop off and we haven't had any luck with fruit. Is this a pollination problem or the environment indoors?

A: There are a couple of potential causes of pepper flower drop indoors. If the plants are under lights, you need to check that you have the right combination of lights for flowering and fruiting plants. Different artificial light sources give off light in different parts of the illumination spectrum. Some provide mostly light in the "blue" spectrum, which is great for photosynthesis and vegetative growth in plants. Other lights have more radiation in the "red" spectrum, which plants need when flowering for strong flower development. A combination of metal halide and high pressure sodium lamps will give both light spectrums for general purpose cropping of flowering plants.

Another likely cause is low light levels overall. Peppers are prone to flower drop under low light levels, such as might be found in a greenhouse in winter or with large plants under lights indoors. However, with indoor pepper plants, this is usually a combination of high heat caused by the lighting system and insufficient light (peppers require fairly high light levels). Flower and fruitlet drop becomes very common when the plant leaves experience air temperatures in the range of 97–100°F, so it might be a good idea to check the temperature at plant level and reassess how much light the plants actually receive. High night temperatures (above 90°F) also induces flower abscission in pepper plants.

If the plants are trying to either carry a heavy crop load of preexisting fruit on the plants or trying to produce more vegetative growth at the same time as flowering, then the plant may sacrifice the flowers in favor of more leaf development. In this case, pruning of the plant may help this process swing back in favor of flowering and fruit set.

Finally, a lack of pollination of the pepper flowers will also cause flower drop, but more commonly causes drop of the very small fruitlets. You will need to pollinate the flowers yourself in an indoor situation. —L.M.

Q: My yellow bell pepper had flowers and then baby peppers rather quickly after planting. But the peppers have been about 1 inch around for several weeks now . . . not growing at all . . . and I'm not seeing any new growth.

A: Pepper plants have a tendency to set fruit very early and low down on the plant before it has had a chance to develop a good leaf growth to support the development of fruit. Pepper growers always remove these early fruit since the plant is not able to support these and they either sit there and don't get very much larger or sometimes the fruit grows very slowly—but at the same time, this is at the expense of the rest of the plant. The best thing to do is to remove any fruit that set on the plant in the first 30 cm of stem and remove any that are obviously not getting any larger. Let the plant develop a good canopy of leaves and side branches, then start to let some flowers remain when the plant has the foliage to support the growth of fruit. The pepper fruit will then grow to a good size and the plant will be able to support a much greater number of fruit. Also, make sure the plants at this stage have a good general purpose liquid fertilizer at least twice a week (one that has nitrogen for foliage growth and potassium for fruit growth) when growing in soil. —L.M.

Q: I have just planted some pepper seedlings and would like to know if they are vines, like tomatoes. I have never grown them before.

A: Most varieties of bell pepper are tall vining plants, like tomatoes. Some bell pepper varieties develop more of a shrubby habit of growth. However, a compact, shrubby habit of growth is more common for the hotter pepper varieties and not sweet bell peppers. Young growth is herbaceous but the plants eventually become woody. Peppers are actually in the same family of plants as tomatoes, which is called Solanaceae. This family also includes potatoes, eggplant, and tobacco. However, unlike tomatoes, some bell pepper plants will develop a few main growth stems that will each produce fruit.

In order to determine exactly how your plants will grow and what their characteristics are, I would recommend that you search around for information on the specific cultivar of capsicum spp. you are growing. That way, you will know what to expect and how to train and treat your plants as they grow. —D.J.P.

Q: I have a homemade garden cart. It has three shelves and a canopy top that supports my 400-watt metal halide light. I also have a seedling shelf, the middle shelf, which has six fluorescent lights attached to the bottom of the top shelf. Hopefully you follow me. The top shelf gets warm during the course of the day, heating up the reservoirs. I currently have three DWC reservoirs. The first one has Tabasco peppers that are almost 4 feet tall and 2.5 months of age (they look great). The second has two 'Brandy' tomato plants, which look to have developed a fungus. The leaves were turning brown and drying up one side at a time, moving up the plant. The tomato plants are 1.5 months old and both are growing well and about 3 feet tall. The third has some herbs that aren't showing any problems at all.

My question is: Why aren't I showing any peppers? I've read that I may have "blossom drop" due to the fluctuation of temperature in the tubs. I believe the temperature changes 15 degrees in a day. Also, what do you think caused my tomatoes to get a fungus? The peppers get 5 teaspoons of

Dyna-Bloom and CALMAG Plus in 5 gallons water; pH is 6. Tomatoes get 4 teaspoons of Dyna-Grow and 4 teaspoons of CALMAG Plus in 4 gallons of water; pH 6. Is the temperature my problem? Should I be using a fungus control now?

A: Lack of pepper fruit is not that uncommon under certain conditions. It could be that the plants are overly vegetative and are producing masses of foliage at the expense of flowers and fruit. However, if the metal halide (MH) fixture is the only real source of good direct light, that's probably causing the lack of fruit. MH lights produce light mostly in the blue spectrum, which plants can use for vegetative growth. However, for strong flowering, plants require higher levels of red to far red light which is usually provided by high pressure sodium (HPS) and other similar bulbs. Flowering is influenced by this red to far red light. If your particular lamp does not include bulbs that combine both red and blue light spectrums than flowering will be weak and floral abortion may occur. Bulbs such as MH, that produce light in the blue spectrum, are excellent for vegetative crops such as herb and lettuce. Mixing artificial with natural sunlight would also solve this problem as sunlight has the correct light spectrums for all stages of growth.

Peppers are also prone to flower and fruitlet drop when under excessive temperatures, which might be occurring with your system. Other factors that can prevent flowering in peppers are low light levels, high EC levels, salinity, and certain pests and diseases. If the plants are under any stress, young flower buds, open flowers, and even fruit can all be aborted. This is often termed as "going vegetative." The most common cause of flower loss in peppers is high tempera-

tures. Once temperatures reach levels of 82°F during the day and 70°F during the night, flowering can be reduced. Flowers won't set at all at temperatures of 95°F during the day and 90°F during the night.

The problem with the tomato foliage drying up does sound like a disease but it could also be caused by high EC levels, salinity, or burning from high light and/or heat levels. However, the symptoms you describe sounds like it might be Verticillium or possibly Phytophthora. Verticillium is a fungal disease that's common in tomatoes. Leaf symptoms appear first on oldest leaves, moving up the plant. Leaves turn yellow, dry up (often without evidence of wilting), and drop prematurely. This fungal disease is difficult to control. The best idea would be to remove the plants from the system to prevent any spread of the diseases. —L.M.

Q: I am growing tomatoes and peppers. What other vegetables or herbs are suited to be grown with these?

A: There are actually quite a few different plants that could be grown alongside tomatoes and peppers in a hydroponic system. But generally it is the fruiting types of vegetables and the woody herbs. These would include cucumbers, eggplant, chiles (hot types), beans, artichokes, melons, marrows, pumpkins, and squash. The herbs that prefer the richer hydroponic solution needed by fruiting vegetables would include rosemary, horseradish, thyme, garlic, bay, and

A: Small fruitlet drop in capsicum is not uncommon and there can be a number of reasons why this is happening. The factors which have been known to cause this problem include high temperature, low light levels, plant stress, the presence and quantity of rapidly growing fruit on the plant, and certain pests and diseases. If the plants come under stress of any type, flower and fruitlets can all be aborted. This is often referred to as "going vegetative." Considering your climate, the most likely causal factor for the loss of the fruitlets is high temperatures. Once temperatures reach above 80°F during the day and 70°F at night, fruitlet abscission can start to occur and fruit set is also reduced. Nighttime temperatures play more of a role in fruit set and retention than day temperatures so if extremes of temperature occur at night, fruit loss can be severe. Another major causal factor with fruitlet abscission is a high crop load and low light levels—but this probably isn't the case in your situation at the moment. The main method of preventing fruitlet abscission is by selecting less susceptible cultivars that are more tolerant of warm conditions. Also, try shading the crop over summer to reduce air temperatures around the fruit and flowers. Applications of synthetic auxin (a plant growth regulator) have been found to prevent fruitlet abscission under stress conditions as they do in tomato crops, so this may also be an option. However, by keeping the EC down (below 2.3) and temperatures below 82°F, fruitlet abscission should not be such as problem. —L.M.

The main method of preventing fruitlet abscission is by selecting less susceptible cultivars that are more tolerant of warm conditions. Also, try shading the crop over summer to reduce air temperatures around the fruit and flowers.

sage. This is not to say that many other vegetables and herbs would not grow well in the same nutrient as tomatoes and peppers. But since these two plants like to have a nutrient with a reasonably high EC (electrical conductivity) with plenty of potassium for fruit quality, fruiting plants and "harder," less succulent, herbs make better companions in a mixed system. —L.M.

Q: I am growing capsicums in a 70/30 perlite/vermiculite mix outdoors and while the plants are healthy with prolific flowers, the small fruit are falling off within days of the flower petals dropping. This, as you can imagine, is very frustrating. I am using a two-part bloom/fruiting nutrient mix.

Q: I grow a variety of capsicum spp. in a flood drain bucket system. Problem is that recently flowers on all spp. aren't setting fruit. They've been flushing nicely and producing many flowers that develop and bloom but they fall when they would normally start to develop fruit. The nutrient, Pureblend Pro Bloom by Botanicare, is fresh and I keep EC the same. The plants are all mature and have fruited before. Nutrient temperature ranges from 64–72°F daily. Air temps inside their plastic "greenhouse" range from 55–85°F, sometimes getting very humid and stuffy.

A: The fruitlet abscission you are experiencing is not uncommon in capsicum plants and is due to some form of plant stress. The factors which can cause this problem include high temperature, low light levels, root zone flooding, oxygen starvation of the root zone, the presence and quantity of rapidly growing fruit on the plant and certain pests and diseases. If the plant comes under considerable stress of any type than young flower buds, open flowers as well as the young fruitlets can all be aborted and this is often referred to as going vegetative. One of the most common causes of fruitlet loss is high temperatures—conditions where the temperature reaches above 80°F by day and 70°F by night can cause a loss of fruit. Another major cause of fruitlet abscission is low light levels which are frequently found in greenhouses in winter and in indoor grow rooms. Salt injury or EC levels which are too high can also cause sufficient plant stress and initiate fruit abscission—salt levels (sodium chloride) and rapidly build up in flood and drain systems which are not regularly flushed to prevent this.

The maximum temperatures your crop is reaching, along with the high humidity stuffiness is most likely the problem since all the pepper varieties are having the same problem. This temperature stresses the plants and they will abort fruitlets as a result. Also keep an eye on the root system—with flood and drain systems it is very easy to provide to much flood and not enough drain—you only want a few minutes at each flood cycle, so that the plants are not sitting in the nutrient for any length of time. It is better to have many short flood cycles (two to four minutes) per day, rather an one or two longer (20 minutes) cycles per day. Lack of oxygen in the root zone can be a common problem in flood and drain systems which are not run correctly and this would certainly cause fruit abscission. —*L.M.*

Q: I am working to become a new hydroponic grower in the United States and I'm especially interested in growing hydroponic eggplants (aubergines). I just read the article entitled "Hydroponic Sweet Peppers and Aubergines" in the September/October 1999 issue of The Growing Edge magazine. It was very informative—especially since there is not much in print about hydroponic aubergines. But there are a few questions that I still have.

First, you mention that The Netherlands have developed a large aubergine production area under glass. Do you know of any farms or companies over there that may consider hiring a student (I'm attending the University of New Hampshire part-time) for several months? Anyone you think I should contact? I do hold an EU citizenship that might make the temporary move easier.

The other question relates to the different varieties. I've been able to find many black, purple, green, white, and pink varieties. But, I have not seen any striped, red, or yellow ones. Do you know what seed companies would be selling these seeds?

A: I'm glad to hear you enjoyed the pepper and aubergines article! Unfortunately, I can't help you with any contacts in the Dutch industry as I don't personally know any of the growers. However, you may be able to track some down via the Internet. As far as the different aubergine varieties go, I can give you the contact details of a couple of seed companies who sell the varieties you are after:

The green and white stripy aubergines are called 'Kermit,' a small variety. The orange variety is called 'Comprido Verde Claro,' a green, ribbed variety that later turns to orange. These two varieties are available from Johnny's Selected Seeds; their e-mail address is commercial@johnnyseeds.com and their Website is at www.johnnyseeds.com.

A good yellow variety is called 'Golden Egg,' which produces large, golden, egg-shaped fruit that have a rich color on a strong and sturdy plant. The other red and stripy ones are actually Solonum silo and Solonum integrifolium (other normal eggplant varieties are Solanum melongena). One of the best is the Turkish orange eggplant (Solonum integrifolium). The small fruits are actually a deep-red color, not orange as the name suggests. These are best harvested when they are turning from green to red-striped stage for best flavor—once the skin is fully red it starts to develop a bitter flavor. Another good one is the Brazilian mini eggplant (Solonum silo). These fruit start off green, ripen into orange, and then into a full red color at maturity. In New Zealand they can be brought from:

Kings Seeds NZ, Ltd.
P.O. Box 283
Katikati 3063
New Zealand

King Seeds will ship seeds overseas but you can probably find a seed dealer in your area that carries (or can order) these varieties. —*L.M.*

Q: We grew tomatillos from seed this year. While they are producing many, many flowers, the flowers are dropping off before fruit sets. I have been sensitive to watering in a consistent pattern and also fertilizing when necessary. All of our other tomatoes (romas, heirloom) are setting nicely with an abundance of fruit. We live in Salt Lake City and it is extremely hot this time of year. Temperatures are consistently in the upper 90s and low 100s with nights hovering around 70. As a final note, we gave tomatillo plants to friends, as well, and while we do not know their watering and fertilizing patterns, theirs are not producing fruit, either.

A: Tomatillos usually set fruit very easily despite warm conditions and they may well do so as the plants develop further. With tomatillos, very hot conditions (i.e., full sun) can induce flower drop. However, the cause is more likely to be a lack of pollination. Tomatillos are not like tomatoes, which self-pollinate quite easily outdoors, and only require the pollen inside one flower to be gently released to pollinate that same flower. With tomatoes, this often occurs naturally as the plants move in the breeze, when the plants are moved when you tend to them, or when bees or other insects visit the flower.

However, tomatillos need some cross pollination and this is usually carried out by insects (which perhaps are not common in your garden in the current heat). Without cross pollination, not many fruit will set and the flower will drop without any fruitlet forming. You might like to try another type or cultivar of tomatillo. Often, a different plant variety will fruit better if one does not appear to be setting fruit in your particular situation. Other factors that might also cause flower drop include soil moisture level fluctuations, lack of nutrients, and low light conditions combined with warm temperatures. —L.M.

Q: We are planning on doing hydroponic strawberries at the beginning of the school year. What advice do you have in preparation for this adventure?

A: Firstly, if you are planning on planting in August, I would suggest you obtain some day neutral cultivar plants now, trim and clean them, wrap them in plastic, and put them into refrigeration at 35°F for six weeks. This will induce the plants to flower and fruit very rapidly when planted out into warm conditions in August.

Below is a extract on hydroponic strawberry production that was presented at a hydroponic conference in 2002. It contains much detailed information on the cultivation of strawberries in hydroponic systems.

Presentation prepared for 3rd International Hydroponic Conference in Toluca, Mexico, April 18, 19, and 20, 2002.

Commercial, Hydroponic Strawberry Production

Strawberries are a popular hydroponic crop and using hydroponic methods can greatly increase yields and quality over soil based production systems. Hydroponics has a major advantage for strawberry production in that the system can be cleaned and sterilized between crops. Soil based strawberry crops rely heavily on the use of soil sterilization with chemicals to prevent plant losses from certain root rot pathogens. Strawberries are also small plants suited to a number of different hydroponic systems. They can be produced in nutrient film technique (NFT), bag, or bed systems and even in tiered or vertical systems.

There are a few essential requirements for growing strawberries. These include selection of the right cultivar, pretreatment of the runners before planting, and maintaining the right temperature levels for good fruit production. After harvest, the berries must also be handled and stored correctly to prevent many of the postharvest bruising and rot problems that downgrade the quality of the fruit.

Types and Cultivars of Strawberries Best Suited to Hydroponics and How These Are Propagated

The most widely grown type of strawberry are those called day-neutral cultivars. These will be induced to flower and fruit after a period of chilling or cool temperatures at 35–41°F. Other cultivars used for soil cropping are either "short day" or "long day" cultivars that are induced to fruit only after they have experienced short days (less than 12 hours of daylight) or long days (14 or more hours of daylight). In regions where the day length is fairly constant, day-neutral cultivars should be used.

Day-neutral types include many of the most commonly grown cultivars. These develop and initiate flowers irrespective of the day length, provided they have received a period of cold temperatures. This cold temperature is usually given to the plants or freshly dug runners for a period of around 6-12 weeks.

Plants or runners are cleaned, trimmed, and wrapped in plastic before storing under refrigeration for the 6-12 week period. After this time, they are taken out of cold storage and planted out into a hydroponic system under warm conditions. Leaves will grow and develop and then flowering will occur within a few weeks, provided the plants had a long enough time in cold storage.

Some of the most popular strawberry cultivars used in commercial production are:

• 'Camarosa,' the most widely grown cultivar in the world; it is important in climates that have mild winters
• 'Seascape'
• 'Sweet Charlie'
• 'Earliglow'
• 'Atlas'
• 'Apollo'

However, each country and growing region often has its own locally developed cultivars.

Systems for Hydroponic Strawberry Production

NFT and media based systems are most commonly used for hydroponic strawberry production. NFT, where the nutrient is recirculated through small pipes, tubes, or gullies, is popular in countries such as New Zealand and Australia. In these types of systems the plants are usually supported in small pots or cups so that the crown of the plant doesn't slip down into the nutrient causing it to rot. Some growers also use small rockwool cubes to support the young plants in NFT systems.

The ideal size for NFT channels are 6-inch-diameter rectangular gullies, although many successful crops are grown in smaller, round channels. Where smaller channels are used, a greater slope is required to prevent any ponding of the nutrient as the root systems grows and fills the channel. Adjustable slopes on NFT gullies are also a good idea for strawberry crops. NFT channels can also be arranged into tiers to make the most use of growing space.

One system in Australia used the inclined vertical pipe system. This has a continuous flow of recirculated nutrient and largely avoids any problems with nutrient ponding in the gullies. Plants in this system are supported by rockwool cubes. It also allows more plants to be grown in the same area, although its not well suited to growing conditions that have lower light levels as there can be some shading on the lower layers.

Flood and drain systems can also be used for strawberry production. Many of these systems use channels similar to those used for NFT. However, each plant is planted into a substrate or media in the base of the channels. Rockwool cubes are commonly used—as is gravel or coarse sand—to hold the plant in place when the nutrient is flooded into the channel and to retain moisture during the drain cycle. These types of systems are harder to manage once the root system has grown and filled the media in the channel. Facilitating good drainage in the system was difficult and root rot often occurred.

Small channels of media also heat up in the sun, causing a number of problems with growth and diseases. Where flood and drain systems are to be used for strawberries, a good depth of free draining media must be used and the flood cycles carefully managed.

Media Beds/Bags

Most hydroponic strawberries are actually grown in media based systems and these seem to be easier to manage than NFT for less experienced growers. There is a wide range of substrates that can be used to grow strawberries, including rockwool, expanded clay, perlite, vermiculite, gravel, coconut fiber, pumice, and untreated sawdust, to name a few. Any substrate for strawberry production needs to be sterile and reasonably free draining. Common media systems for strawberries include bag or bed systems. These contain the media and plants and nutrient applied may be recollected or is often used drained to waste.

Rockwool slab systems are common in some areas of the world for greenhouse strawberry production. Coconut fiber slabs can be used in much the same way. Usually, the nutrient is applied to a 10 percent runoff, which is drained to waste, although many growers are attempting to collect the waste nutrient and reuse it. Where rockwool or coconut fiber is used, the nutrient application has to be well managed and monitored since these media can become overly wet resulting in plant losses from crown rot.

With any media based system, planting depth is essential. The crown of the plant, which is where all the leaves and flower stems originate, must not become too damp. Only the base of the crown should be in contact with the media, with most of the plant sitting well up above the media surface. Plants that are planted too deep tend to rot very quickly. Airflow around the base of the plant and under the leaves is also important in preventing many fungal diseases, so having an elevated system up on a bench or support structure helps with air moment around the plants.

Vertical or Hanging Systems

Vertical systems are commonly used for strawberry production in some countries. Vertical systems can consist of stacked pots or buckets, such as in the Verti-Gro system, or as hanging bags of media. Vertical or hanging systems work best where there are good light levels year round, as the plants on the lower layers of these systems may not receive enough light for good production where light is low.

Hanging bag systems can be difficult to manage as the media contained within the bag can become overly wet at the lower layers causing plant losses. The greenhouse structure must also be able to support the weight of many bags of damp media. Salt buildup in the lower layers of the bag has also been found to be a problem in many commercial operations.

Aeroponics

Aeroponics is being successfully used to grow strawberries in trails in New Zealand. This system uses a continual fine misting of nutrient onto the root system and avoids many of the root rot problems associated with plant losses. The capital investment and maintenance required in aeroponics, however, means it may not be a good commercial option for most growers.

Propagation

Strawberries can be propagated by runners, which are small plantlets formed at the end of a long thin stem or stolon produced by the mother plant. They can also be produced by division of larger crowns in mature plants, by tissue culture, and from seed. However, for commercial production, strawberry plants are produced from runners. Runner production means the new plant will be the same as the parent plant so that good yields and fruit quality can be continually obtained from the cultivar chosen.

Hydroponic strawberry growers can propagate their own runners. This is usually a good idea since most prechilled runners that can be purchased are from soil raised plants and need to be washed to remove this soil before planting into a hydroponic system. Having soil grown runners or plants also increases the risk of introducing pests and root diseases into the hydroponic system, so such runners should be treated with a fungicide dip before planting out.

Obtaining new plants from runners is relatively simple. After the parent plant flowers and fruits, runners will begin to be produced. Look for a long stem or stolon where a new plantlet will form at the tip. Each stolon will produce a number of plantlets that can then be pinned down into pots of media. Roots will form on the underside of the young plant. Once the roots are well established, the new plant can be cut from the parent plant. Each parent plant can usually produce at least 15–20 new plantlets over a three-month period, although this depends on the cultivar being grown. Some cultivars produce more runners and plantlets than others. The rooted runner can now be prechilled under refrigeration for a number of weeks and then planted out to produce a new crop of strawberry fruit.

Strawberry plants can be cropped for a number of seasons. However, yield is usually highest in the first and sometimes the second season so hydroponic strawberries are often grown as an annual crop only.

Temperatures and Training

Before planting out into the NFT system, the strawberry roots may need to be trimmed. Once the chilled runners or plants have been planted out into the NFT system, plant growth and establishment should be rapid. In NFT, some form of plant support, such as small pots or tubes, should be used to hold the plants upright while the develop. Plants put into media need to planted at the correct depth so the base of the crown is in contact with the media but not buried.

The nutrient can then be applied at a low EC (around 0.5) for the first few days. Misting the newly planted strawberries with water during the warmest part of the day will help prevent too much transplant stress. After a week, the EC can be gradually increased to a full strength of around 1.8–2.4. Any plants that fail to develop should be removed and disposed of so they don't introduce rot disease into the system.

Ideal temperatures for strawberry production are in the range of 61–82°F. Low temperatures will delay the development of flowers and fruit and slow plant growth. Temperatures above 82°F can stress the plants and prevent flowering and any fruit formed will be soft with poor keeping quality. Plants growing under high temperatures and radiation levels will require shading to reduce temperature levels and plant stress. Nutrient chilling can be used in tropical climates to grow strawberry crops, although this may not be economical.

Within a few weeks, the new plants will have formed a number of leaves. Any flowers that form within these first few weeks when the plants are establishing foliage should be removed. The plant is unable to support the development of good sized berries before it has developed sufficient leaf area so flowers should only be left to develop once the plant has reached a good size. Strawberries produce flowers singly and on trusses—often with a number of small and large flowers on the same stem. Smaller flowers can be removed if necessary to increase fruit size on the rest of the stem.

Strawberries benefit from some assistance with pollination. Outside, bees and other insects carry out much of the pollination. In a greenhouse, commercial strawberry growers often use large air blowers to pollinate the plants. Small handheld air blowers also work. These release the pollen into the flower surface and pollination will then occur. Good pollination is required for evenly shaped, large sized berries. Where pollination is inadequate, misshapen or undersized berries often occur. These should be removed from the plant as soon as they are seen.

Each of the small seedlike structures on the outer surface of a strawberry produce growth hormones that act to pull in sugars and assimilates from the leaves for berry growth. Where pollination has not been successful, some of these seeds on the outer surface don't develop and, as a result, uneven berry development shape occurs.

Once the fruit have set, they grow rapidly under good growing conditions. Strawberry plants produce a high fruit yield for their relatively small size and will often crop in flushes, producing many large fruit and then resting for a few weeks before flowering and fruiting again. Yields from day-neutral strawberry plants vary considerably between growers. Anywhere from 300 grams to 1.5 kilograms per plant per season has been found, with planting densities of 10–16 plants per square meter being maintained.

Nutrition and Water Quality

Water supplies for hydroponic strawberries needs to be of good quality. Strawberries are intolerant of high levels of sodium in the water. Levels above 50 ppm sodium will reduce yields and plant health. Where sodium is present in the water supply, nonrecirculating systems should be used. Adding soluble silica to the nutrient solution will also assist the plants to grow and thrive in water that contains some sodium.

Nutrient solutions for strawberries should have good levels of potassium to support fruit growth and quality. Potassium is important for developing good flavor, firmness, and a long shelf life in the berries. Nitrogen levels also need to be maintained for continuing leaf growth and the development of runners and new plants. Strawberries can be prone to iron deficiency symptoms under conditions of low temperature or where the root system has been damaged

by transplanting or root rot diseases. A pH in the range of 5.5–5.8 is ideal for strawberries in hydroponics.

Crop Maintenance

Any older, browned, or discolored leaves should be removed. Regular crop maintenance is important as any old berries or foliage can host fungal and bacterial disease and reduce airflow around and under the plant. Deleafing old leaves should be carried out every week when the plants are actively growing, especially where conditions are warm, humid, and wet. This will reduce the occurrence of diseases.

Pests

Hydroponic strawberries can be affected by a number of pests, including mites, whitefly, thrips, aphids, caterpillars, and slugs—but the major pest of outdoor strawberry crops is birds. Birds will completely destroy crops of ripe berries and bird netting needs to be used to prevent this from occurring. Birds will also come into greenhouses where ripe berries are visible, so screens over vents become important to prevent this.

Diseases

Strawberries are very prone to a number of root rot disease and these are often the factor that results in many plant losses. Red stele or red core root rot caused by Phytophthora is a worldwide problem with strawberries and can cause significant losses. Infected plants become stunted, the leaves become a dull green color, and older leaves turn yellow or red. The plants can also rapidly wilt and die. Plants infected with red stele don't produce many roots and the stele or inside of the root turns a pink or red color. This disease comes from infected plants or soil contamination. Another root rot

Q: Is it possible to grow strawberries using exclusively artificial light? My city's latitude is 55° south and we have mountains casting shadows on it during winter. Summer is OK, but I would like to sell fruit all year. In case the answer to my question is "yes," what kind of light? What variety of strawberry will be suitable?

A: Strawberries are routinely grown entirely in artificial light. However, from a commercial perspective, it's usually better to make use of any existing sunlight and then supplement with artificial lights when necessary. The best way to accomplish this would be to grow in a controlled-environment greenhouse that is insulated for year-round use.

During the early vegetative stages of growing out strawberry runners, you can use metal halide lights, which provide more blue light for vegetative growth, to supplement sunlight. Or, if sunlight is completely absent, metal halide lights will work just fine by themselves. Then, when the straw-

berries begin to flower and fruit, you will need to supplement with high-pressure sodium lamps, which provide more red and far-red light. Again, high-pressure sodium lamps will work just fine by themselves but it is usually more economically feasible to use artificial lights to supplement natural sunlight.

It's usually advised that growers use day neutral strawberry cultivars when preparing to grow year-round. Runners for planting out should be purchased from reliable, disease-free stock that has been proven to grow well in your area. —D.J.P.

Q: I'd like to grow some day-neutral strawberries outside in hydroponic vertical towers with drip irrigation. I was told by the nursery where I buy my plants that late April is the best time to set them out. However, I can get frost up to the end of May. How do I keep the nutrient solution from freezing in the drip lines and in the towers? Do I need to irrigate the plants from overhead?

A: I would suggest that when you get your plants from the nursery in late April, hold them in cool storage (35°F) until you consider the danger of frost has passed. While it's OK to plant them in late April, they won't start to regrow until temperatures warm up anyway and you don't want the hassle of frozen drip lines. The other option would be to put an immersion heater in your nutrient and warm it to prevent frozen blockages. With the vertical towers, depending on how long they are, the drip irrigation would have one outlet in top (be careful not to let it wet the plant crowns or foliage) and one or even two placed in a planting hole about one third to half way down each vertical tower. This just gives better nutrient distribution to all the plants and safeguards against blockages in the dripper system. —L.M.

disease is black root rot caused by Pythium and Rhizoctonia species. Affected roots become black with much smaller roots than is normal. Infected plants become weak and fail to produce fruit and runners. There are a few other root rot fungi. Verticillium wilt and Fusarium can also occur. However, like most of the fungal diseases, these tend to attack weakened plants or plants that are waterlogged.

Healthy plants can usually resist attack. Addition of microbes, such as Trichoderma species and products containing other beneficial microbes, to the growing media or nutrient solution can help suppress any fungal pathogens that might be present.

Leaf or foliage diseases that can affect strawberries include leaf spot, Botrytis (or gray mold) of the leaves and fruit, leaf scorch, leaf blight, and powdery mildew. Leaf spots and other bacterial diseases can be largely prevented be not allowing the foliage and fruit to become wet. Some form of overhead crop shelter is vital where this can occur. Botrytis or gray mold is a very damaging problem where

humidity is high as it can infect the leaves and fruit. Botrytis can be controlled with fungicide applications and with use of products contenting Thrichodera spores. Powdery mildew can be prevented with applications of sodium bicarbonate sprays or silica based sprays. Adding silica into the nutrition solution may also help with disease prevention.

There are also a number of fruit rot diseases. Generally, these occur where conditions are warm and humid and there is moisture on the fruit surface. Keeping the environment dry and the berries up out of any moisture will prevent many of these. Having good air movement around the base of the plants also assists with prevention of many of the fruit rot diseases.

Harvesting

Hydroponic strawberries should be harvested when they are light-red to orange-red. Fruit must be picked when they are at least 75 percent ripe or pink for good color and flavor development after harvest. If overripe fruit are picked, these will darken and soften in storage and will not be of acceptable eating quality. If picked too green, color, flavor, and aroma will not fully develop and the fruit will be tasteless. Any fruit that are uneven in shape, undersized, or have defects or disease damage should be graded out as soon as possible after harvest. Harvesting should be carried out during the early morning before temperatures warm up too much. Warm fruit do not store as well as those picked under cooler temperature conditions.

Once picked, the berries need to be cooled as soon as possible to retain quality. This is called removing the "field heat." Berries need to be cooled down to 41°F at a high humidity (greater than 90 percent) to prevent too much moisture loss. This is usually carried out by refrigeration or with forced air cooling. High quality strawberries should store for at least 5–10 days under refrigeration.

Postharvest Handling

Strawberry fruit bruise easily and the stalks and calyxes can puncture the fruit flesh when berries are being harvested and packed. All fruit need to be handled carefully to prevent this type of damage. Any physical damage will increase the chances of postharvest rots and will result in poor keeping quality.

Growing High Flavor Berries

Many hydroponic strawberry growers aim to produce not only higher berry yields from hydroponics but also better tasting fruit. The taste or flavor of strawberries is a combination of sugars, acids, and volatile compounds. Sugars can be increased by ensuring each plant has sufficient foliage to produce assimilate and that light levels are not limiting production.

Maintaining a nutrient solution at a slightly higher EC (around 2.5) with good levels of potassium will help with sugar accumulation in the fruit. Cultivar selection is important where the flavor of the fruit is concerned. Many cultivars have fruit with naturally higher sugar levels and flavor than others, so trailing and testing different cultivars is always recommended.

Conclusion

In conclusion, hydroponic strawberries can be a challenging but profitable crop. Careful attention to propagation, chilling requirements, and planting are vital to ensure that the crop establishes well and does not develop root rots in overly damp conditions.

However, strawberries are a rewarding crop when grown well and will begin to produce fruit within a few months after planting out. Probably the greatest potential for hydroponics strawberry production is in supplying the off season market when outdoor soil grown berries are not available. Use of hydroponic technology allows this to be carried out in a cost effective way and produces high yields of good quality fruit. —L.M.

Q: I'd like to know if strawberries can be grown in a hot and humid climate like we have here in central and eastern Thailand.

A: Hydroponic strawberries, in a controlled environment, could be grown in a hot and humid climate, but this would require careful attention to details like the chilling requirement of the plants and the potential for disease problems that strawberries are prone to under these types of conditions. Probably the only way to grow high quality, high yielding crops of strawberries under the temperature conditions you have is to use hydroponics and chill the nutrient solution, thermal screens to cut light levels, and evaporative cooling, if possible, to drop temperature levels to reduce plant stress. Strawberries generally prefer temperatures of 68–82°F by day, with cooler night temperatures to maintain good fruit quality. Under warm conditions, fruit quality is reduced—the flesh becomes soft, watery, and tasteless and shelf life is reduced. There are also several potentially damaging diseases that can destroy a strawberry crop under conditions that are too warm. Preventative measures would have to be taken.

You would need to select a strawberry cultivar that has some heat tolerance and would therefore perform better in your climate. A day neutral cultivar would also be advised since short or long day cultivars would not be induced to fruit in a region where the day length is similar year round. A day neutral cultivar requires about six weeks of chilling (at 32–35°F in a refrigerator) to break dormancy and induce

the plant to flower and fruit. You can do this by wrapping the runners or young plants in plastic and putting them in a refrigerator for 6 weeks. When removed and placed in warm growing conditions, the plants will rapidly flower and fruit. You can then carry out this cycle year round to have continuous strawberry production. —L.M.

Q: I am interested in trying to grow strawberries hydroponically. I live in Taiwan and I don't know if it's possible with the heat and humidity here. The space that I would use to grow would be a rooftop. Would greenhouse shading make it possible and would the nutrients need to be cooled?

A: Yes, it would be possible to grow strawberry plants hydroponically in Taiwan in a rooftop system—provided a few simple steps are taken to ensure the plants grow well. Firstly, you will need to select a day-neutral strawberry cultivar (one that can be forced to flower and fruit irrespective of the day length). Also, if you can select a cultivar that has been bred for heat tolerance or summer conditions in areas such as California, this will help in your situation. These plants need to be chilled under refrigeration for six to eight weeks at 35–36°F. This will then induce the plants to flower and fruit when you plant them outside in warm growing conditions.

When planted out, the plants should have some shading overhead (40 percent shade cloth cover) with a good level of gentle air movement across the top of the plants to encourage transpiration. A small fan or two in the cropping area may be required. This is very important in warm, humid climates such as yours as strawberry plants are prone to a number of crown and fruit rots caused by fungal pathogens under humid conditions.

You may also need to chill the nutrient solution to get good fruiting. This could be done with the use of a chiller unit or possibly by evaporative cooling if humidity levels are not too high. The nutrient solution temperature needs to be maintained at no higher than 78°F for strawberries, so you may have to determine if it's possible to maintain this without chilling the solution. Having a large volume nutrient tank will help prevent excessive heat buildup in the solution, but this may not be possible on a rooftop garden where the weight of the system might be an issue. Cooling of the nutrient solution will not only ensure that the roots are not stressed by warm temperatures but will also help the upper region of the plant survive conditions that are a little warmer than is optimal for strawberries. —L.M.

Q: I was wondering if I can grow strawberries in Puerto Rico. In the area were I live, the temperature is between 75–85°F. Where can I find seeds or where can I purchase runners online?

A: The temperatures you mention of 75–85°F, are not excessive for strawberry production—although some form of crop shading would be recommended to keep the crop healthy and stress-free. If your environment it also very humid you will need to have a spray program designed to prevent many of the fungal and bacterial pathogens that will affect strawberry plants and fruit under warm conditions.

Generally, large-fruited strawberries are not grown from seed as the resulting plants will be very variable in terms of yields, fruit size, and berry quality. You will need to purchase runners of a day-neutral variety strawberry that has been prechilled and will then be induced to flower and fruit when planted out into warm conditions.

I am not aware of any strawberry propagators in your country (you might have to try doing a Web search in Spanish to see if there are any). Probably the best way to get some plants is to contact some strawberry growers in your country and see if you can get a list of licensed strawberry propagators in your area or nearby. —*L.M.*

Q: I am in the planning stages in regard to raising strawberries. I will be using the NFT system with channels. In researching your article in The Growing Edge, Volume 9, Number 1 (September/October 1997), I have become aware of excessive nutrient feeding. My original plan is to use 4-inch channels, five channels, side by side. What are your recommendations regarding spacing of the plants and warnings in regard to excessive or overfeeding of the nutrient? You mention the use of hanging media-filled tubes or bags. Where can I obtain information on use of these hanging tubes/bags?

A: I would suggest that you space the channels a little distance apart rather than side by side. This will allow greater airflow between and under the plants' foliage, which greatly aids disease control and plant growth. A suggested plant spacing would be 6 inches between plants in the channel and 4 inches from plant crown to plant crown in separate channels. Although your plants may appear small when you put them in, a fully mature, fruiting strawberry needs a good-sized space to grow into.

When I caution growers to not "excessively feed" the plants, I am advising them to prevent waterlogging or stagnation resulting from the stream of nutrient becoming too deep causing the roots to die. Strawberries are very prone to waterlogging and you should be aiming for a good flow rate with a thin (1–3 mm) stream of nutrient along the base of the channel—the roots should never be submerged.

To achieve this you may need to increase the slope of the growing channels as the plants grow and the root system develops so that the nutrient isn't ponding anywhere and

causing root death. Also, make sure the crowns of the plants are suspended up and out of the growing channel so they don't get wet—that could cause crown rot and plant losses.

Many growers make their own hanging bags using thick black polyethylene taped at the seam. You can also hang up large-diameter rigid PVC pipe with planting holes drilled in the side to create a more permanent system. For a custom-made growing bag, see the Mr. Tomato Website. However, these might not be in the dimensions you want for your greenhouse. Remember that whatever media you put into these bags needs to be free-draining and lightweight.

Many commercial growers have tried this system with great success and others have found it difficult to manage. The problem is that when the bags are fairly long and light levels are low, the plants in the lower layers of the bags don't receive enough light and tend to get more waterlogged than those in the higher layers, causing plant losses. So you may need to experiment with just how many plants you can grow per bag and how many bags per square meter you can have before the lower plants start to suffer.

There isn't really much published information on this type of growing system but here are a couple of scientific sources:

Linardakis, D. K.; Manios, V. I., "Hydroponic Culture of Strawberries in Plastic Greenhouses in a Vertical System," Acta Horticulturae, Vol. 287 (1991), page 317.

Mattas, K.; Bentes, M.; Paroussi, G.; Tzouramani, I., "Assessing the Economic Efficiency of a Soilless Culture System for Off Season Strawberry Production," HortScience, Vol. 32, No. 6 (1997), page 1120.

In summary, these research papers state that the media used tends to be either perlite or a mixture of perlite and peat and the bags are about 1.6–2 meters high, 16 centimeters in diameter, and are usually constructed on site of thick polyethylene. These bags are then spaced at about 0.80x1.0 meter with 1,000 bags per 0.1 hectare. Metal beams are usually used to support the bags. The recommendation is 24 plants per bag, which results in a planting density of 24,000 plants per 0.1 ha.

The nutrient solution is released with two drippers that each have the capacity of 4 liters per hour through feeding pipes into the upper and middle parts of the bags. Holes in the bottom of the bag allow the solution to be drained away into a tank. This runoff nutrient solution can then be adjusted and reused. It appears that supplying a good nutrient solution is vital for maintaining yields and quality, so I'd suggest that you have a water analysis performed and then have a good strawberry nutrient mix custom formulated.

Remember that it's important to keep a close check on potassium levels with strawberries (and other fruiting crops).

Mr. Tomato: www.mrtomato.com/

—L.M.

Q: I just picked off the first red strawberry from the plants we just recently purchased. My kids were excited to eat it, but when we tasted it, it was bitter. What could be causing this? Is there anything I can do to help the plant produce a sweeter crop this summer as it continues to grow?

A: Bitter-tasting strawberry fruit are very disappointing. However, the bitterness is more likely to be a temporary affect rather than a long term one. There are a couple of potential causes of bitterness in strawberry fruit. The most common one is a disease called Phytophthora cactorum, which is a soil-borne fungus that infects the fruit when they are close to ripening. This disease causes the fruit to develop a reddish or brownish coloration and slight softening, so you may not even notice that there is a problem. However, it also causes the fruit to taste rather bitter and unpleasant and many gardeners often wonder what is happening to their berries when this occurs. Strawberries are not overly prone to developing bitter flavors, but sometimes when the plant has been stressed with poor nutrition or a lack of water (or overwatering), the fruit may become tasteless, woody, and just not taste right.

You can assist strawberry plants to produce large, sweet berries by insuring that the plants are not prone to pathogen infection. Keep the plants dry (under a cover) and mulching around the plant so the berries can sit on a dry surface will prevent any further problems with Phythophtora diseases. Also, make sure the plant develops plenty of leaves before it is allowed to flower and set fruit. You may have to remove some of the first flowers that form so that more leaves can develop first. The plant needs good light levels, warm conditions (68–79°F), moderate amounts of water (don't overwater or saturate the soil as this will cause the plant to rot), and some fertilizer that is high in potassium once fruit are starting to grow. Apart from that, the fruit need to be picked when they are just ripe. Overly ripe fruit can develop off flavors while fruit that still have some green coloration will not have developed sufficient sugars for the best flavor. You might also need some protection from birds, which tend to come and remove strawberry fruit just as they ripen. Good luck with your strawberries. —L.M.

Q: Which is the adapted inclination of the channels for NFT strawberry cultivation? Is the 3-inch round pipe recommended to strawberries? Do differences exist in the nutrition of the June-bearing, everbearing, and day-neutral cultivars?

A: The generally recommended slope for strawberry NFT gullies as with most NFT crops is 1:40. Strawberry plants can be grown in round pipe, provided the nutrient solution flow is maintained and the root systems do not impede the flow of nutrient causing ponding and stagnation. It is particularly important with strawberries to make sure the crown of the plant is well clear of the nutrient solution and has good air circulation to prevent crown rot.

Once planted in the system there should be very little difference between the nutrient requirements of different cultivars or types of strawberries under the same environmental conditions. —L.M.

Q: I am interested in the growth of grapes for wine production with hydroponic methods. Where can I find any information, research, or documentation of any kind on this subject?

A: Grapes can certainly be grown hydroponically. Top quality table grapes are produced commercially in greenhouse hydroponic systems, so there isn't any reason why the same type of system could not be used for wine grapes (although the economics of this on a large scale would be questionable). In a hydroponic system, you could have a greater degree of control over berry quality and other factors, such as sugar levels and moisture content, than you could in a soil grown crop by manipulating the nutrient solution. Unfortunately, I have never come across any research or information on growing wine grapes hydroponically, apart from a brief mention in the book Advanced Guide to Hydroponics, by James Sholto Douglas, which I have quoted below (from page 333):

"A rather simple unit has been utilized for grape growing in Kenya. J. M. Barrow established a small vineyard south of Mombassa employing lengths of PVC piping, painted white, with openings or slots cut along the top. The trough or channel so formed was filled with aggregate and a small gully was made under the substrate to facilitate drainage. The nutrient solution was pumped from a tank, through a main leading to the channels, allowed to fill the voids in the aggregate and then returned by a discharge outlet to the reservoir. Eventually, it was intended to automate the system by using a time clock and solenoid values."

Probably the only way to find out how well this system would work is to grow a few vines and see how they produce. —L.M.

Q: I'm building a hydroponic system to produce strawberries and have some doubts. My reservoir contains cement in its structure. What are the consequences of the contact of the nutritious solution with the cement? Latex ink might be an option to prevent problems or do specific inks exists to that purpose? Another doubt that I have is the spacing of the plants. What is the minimum space among the plants that I can use? What are the ideal dimensions of the NFT channel for strawberry cultivation (height and width)?

A: If your nutrient reservoir has been in use for longer than 12 months or has been used to store water then it will be all right to use since any problem minerals will have leached out from the cement. However, if this is a new cement tank, then it will need to be either lined or coated with a non-toxic paint or resin to prevent minerals leaching from the cement into the nutrient solution. Cement tanks can be effectively sealed with use of epoxy paint (non phytotoxic).

Strawberry plants can be grown at a density of between 12–24 plants per square meter of growing space (this is dependent on factors such as age of the plants, cultivar or variety, amount of light available, ventilation around the plants etc). There really is no data on the ideal dimensions for a strawberry NFT channel. Some commercial growers use fairly small round pipe (100 millimeters in diameter) and manage to grow good crops. However, I would recommend you use a larger, flat bottomed gully in the range 100 millimeters wide by 50 millimeters deep, or even 150 millimeters wide by 100 millimeters deep. The larger channel is a better option

in warmer climates where you need to try and prevent heat build up in the channel, nutrient solution and root zone so the plants don't become temperature stressed. —*L.M.*

Q: I read in a book that is possible to maintain a strawberry plant for three years in hydroponics and that the best crops are in the second and in the third year. Is that true? How long does a strawberry plant usually produce in hydroponics? What are the necessary preventive measures that I need to take to prevent diseases? Can I use the same plants used in soil?

A: Yes, you can certainly grow the same strawberry plants for three years in the hydroponic system, but they may need some trimming or cutting back of the older foliage as it ages and to help with air flow around the base of the plant (to help prevent crown rot diseases and high humidity levels). In general, hydroponically strawberry plants grown from healthy, pre-rooted runners will produce the highest yields and best quality fruit in the first and second season, with a drop off after this time. Some growers will only crop the plants for one season, then replant with fresh, prechilled runners to get a second crop within the same year (in a greenhouse situation), other growers prefer to leave the plants in for longer—especially if they collect their own runners for new plant production.

In order to grow a long-term strawberry crop, the most important thing to remember is that the plants are very prone to crown or root rots. Maintaining airflow around the crown of the plant and keeping the crown well above the media or nutrient solution is very important. You may also want to consider some preventative fungicides if the humidity levels are high or if fungal disease are a problem. These are exactly the same problems that soil-grown strawberries also have, with the incidence of crown and root rots being more prevalent in the soil where it is more difficult to control the moisture levels and aeration around the root zone. Also, in soil grown crops, some protection from birds and other predators is usually required as they will rapidly either eat all the fruit or severely reduce the quality of the crop. —*L.M.*

Q: I was thinking of building a greenhouse. My system probably will be tired for strawberries with two levels or a system with just one level. My city is around 90 kilometers from Capricorn Tropic, near Sao Paulo city. What is best direction to construct it? North/south or east/west?

I'm using an NFT system to grow strawberries without any type of pot or media. I have a small system, but I need expand it, and I was thinking of changing the growing system to an open system—small bag culture with drip irrigation. The bag would contain about 15 kilograms of perlite, vermiculite and peat.

I know how to run an NFT system, but I've never used a media-based system. What suggests and considerations can you make on this? Around how many irrigations should I made in one day? Should I use the same nutrient solution used in NFT, with the same conductivity (1.6 mS and 1.8 mS)?

A: The best orientation for your greenhouse depends on the which way the crop rows will be running. If the greenhouse is oriented north to south, then the rows of plants should be set up to run the long way in the greenhouse (from end to end). If you want to have the crop rows placed from side to side (across the greenhouse), the greenhouse can be placed east to west. However, in your area of the world it won't make that much difference.

Strawberries will grow well in media-based bag systems with drip irrigation. You will have to decide whether the nutrient is going to be recollected from the bags or left to drain to waste. I would suggest that if your NFT system works well, that there isn't a benefit to changing to a media-based system. Doing so will add extra labor in mixing the media, filling the bags, disposing of the media after the crop, etc.

Media systems can be very simple the irrigation needs to provide at least one dripper or emitter per bag to deliver the nutrient. Nutrient needs to be applied in small quantities several times per day, depending on the environment and stage of crop development. The number of irrigations required per day not only depends on the plant and the environment but also on the water and oxygen-holding capacity of your media mixture. You want the media to remain damp (but not overly damp) between irrigations. It's not possible

As the plants develop and under warmer, higher light conditions, you will need to continually adjust the timing and amount of irrigation. Plants need to be irrigated to about 10 percent runoff. This runoff should be recollected and either reused or disposed of on an outdoor crop or plants. Setting the bags of plants in rigid plastic channels makes this a fairly simple operation to recollect the nutrient leached out of the bags. Generally, the same or a fairly similar nutrient formula can be used in inert media as is used in NFT for strawberries—unless the media already has some fertilizer additives in it. For example, the peat you use may need additions of lime and this will change the nutrient formula you should apply. Conductivity in media systems should be run a little lower than NFT as the plants will remove water between irrigations from the media and the EC in the root zone can increase. Check the conductivity of the nutrient draining from the base of some of the bags against the EC you apply and try to keep it at the same level. If the EC increases when passing through the media, lower the conductivity of the solution being irrigated into the plants. A good EC level to start with would be around 1.5 mS. —L.M.

Q: I would like to know about substrates and nutrients ratios for vertical hydroponic strawberry growing. Also, would this information apply to other berries like raspberry or blackberry?

A: Most vertical systems in the United States use perlite for growing strawberries. It is important to have a media that allows the crown of the plants to remain well aerated and is

Most vertical systems in the United States use perlite for growing strawberries. It is important to have a media that allows the crown of the plants to remain well aerated and is fairly free draining.

to say exactly how many irrigations or the amount required per day. This is something growers determine on the spot when required. As a very rough guide, a good media will only need two to three irrigations per day in the early crop development stages and up to eight in warmer conditions with a mature, fruiting plant. You will need to continually monitor the moisture levels between irrigations in the crop as well as the electrical conductivity of the nutrient draining out of the bags (to prevent salt buildup). You will also need to check the pH of your media before planting, especially since you are going to have peat in the media, and make sure all your media is sterilized before planting.

fairly free draining. However, other suitable media choices include ground bark (coarse grade), perlite and vermiculite mixtures, expanded clay, fresh sawdust, LECA stone, pumice, and various combinations of these media.

The nutrient ratios would change from being high N:K to high K:N as the plant fruit load increases. The Ca:N ratio should be maintained at above 1:1 during all stages of growth. This general rule would apply to most berry fruit, although with blackberries, raspberries, etc. the change would be less extreme due to the lower fruit load per unit leaf area of these plants. —L.M.

Q: A friend of mine is starting their own hydroponic garden and is considering what type of plants to put in it. I was wondering what the best combination of vegetables to grow together would be. We wanted to grow tomatoes, strawberries, and other edible plants, but I was looking for a combination that would be good to start out with. I was also looking into possibly growing grape vines . . . Is that a good idea? What we have to work with is a hydroponic system that will fit approximately 20–30 plants. Another possibility is tropical flowers, but we want plants that will yield something while we learn how to work the hydroponic system easily. The climate we have to work with is that of the Sierra Nevadas. Please give me an idea on how to grow a good hydroponic garden for the first time, and explain just what it is we should expect.

A: While just about all plants can be grown in the same hydroponic system, I would suggest that you divide plants into the high and low nutrient demand groups (i.e., those that need a low electrical conductivity (EC) value of the nutrient and those that need a higher EC value for good production). During the cooler months of the year, grow plants in the low nutrient demand category as many of these are also tolerant of cooler temperature conditions (you may, however, need some form of crop protection for the plants when nighttime temperatures fall too low). Plants such as lettuce, Asian vegetables, salad greens, herbs, watercress, and rocket all require a lower EC value than the fruiting plants (of around 0.8–1.2). Then, in the warmer months, temperatures should be suitable for the fruiting plants, such as tomatoes, cucumbers, strawberries, peppers, melons, squash, eggplant, etc., which can all be grown in the same system, with an EC of around 2.0–2.4.

Grape vines grow extremely well in hydroponics. The best system is a large container (20 liters minimum) filled with a free-draining media onto which the nutrient is applied two or three times per day when growth is active. When the vines are dormant in winter, irrigation once every few days is sufficient.

Probably the best advice for new hydroponic gardeners is to start off with the easiest plants (lettuce, herbs, salad greens, etc.) while you learn the basics of how to operate the system and maintain the EC and pH. Then you can move up to the more challenging crops, such as the fruiting plants. Once you have the system running well, try a few of the tropical flowers (you will need to modify the environment and provide crop protection to get the best year round quality from these types of plants). Experimenting with different plants is the best way to develop growing skills when it comes to hydroponic gardening. —L.M.

Q: Thank you for the recent article on hydroponic raspberries in the May/June 2001 issue of The Growing Edge. What are your thoughts on trying to grow other cultivars similarly? Specifically, I'm interested in highbush blueberries and the development of multiple crops (two, three, or more) in a single year in my mid-Florida area. It appears that both crops have similar needs, but the blueberry propagation is slower and labor intensive in hydro. Also, can you include any ideas on required time schedules, yield, cane manipulation, inside gathering techniques, and proper return to chill & dormancy efforts to initiate a new cycle?

Finally, any thoughts on motivating the plant's "chemistry reactions of winter" through injecting, spraying, or whatever it takes to stimulate the normal winter hormone/chemistry reactions caused by the chill hours of winter? My thought is that perhaps without inducing winter through temperature, we could simulate and generate the normal chemical responses of the wintering plant this way.

A: You outlined the difficulty with blueberries: They take much longer to propagate and produce a crop than raspberries. However, we at Suntec think that multiple cropping within a year-long cycle can be achieved and at the moment we have a few blueberry cultivars we are attempting to grow out of season in a greenhouse here in New Zealand with hydroponic techniques. It appears that producing fresh blueberry fruit during winter could be very profitable given that they have a very short season of harvest in summer (much shorter than is achieved with the different types of raspberry cultivars) and the fact that frozen fruit are simply not up to the standard of freshly harvested ones.

The system we are looking at involves growing cultivars that are naturally quite small and compact and thus suited to hydroponic cropping. Given that the plants receive all their nutrients hydroponically, the pot size can be kept small without effecting the plants. The system we plan to look at is actually an "evergreen system" of production where the plants are not permitted to go through any cold season dormancy. This is a method of production they have used successfully in Australia and in other warm—even tropical—climates. In tropical climates, they can often induce fruiting within chilling by defoliating the plants after fruit harvest. The evergreen system simply relies on preventing extremes of temperature occurring in either summer or winter, which can be achieved within a greenhouse environment.

I have listed some references on this technique below. Some of this research was carried out at the University of Florida a few years ago. Since you are in that area, they may be able to assist you further.

"Feasibility of Blueberry Production in Warm Climates," R. L. Darnell and J. G. Williamson, Acta Horticulturae, Vol. 446 (1997), page 251

"Establishment of a Non-Dormant Blueberry (Vaccinium corymbosum Hybrid) Production System in a Warm Winter Climate," R. K. Reeder, T. A. Obreza, and R. L. Darnell (Horticultural Sciences Department, University of Florida, Gainesville, Florida), Journal of Horticultural Science and Biotechnology, Vol. 73, No. 5 (1998), pages 655-663

Obviously, any system that removes the requirement for chilling—particularly chilling of potted plants—has a major advantage and this evergreen system also means that the use of dormancy breaking chemicals isn't required. This non-dormant system relies on the application of nitrogen throughout the fall and winter, which enables the plants to avoid the normal dormancy cycle and the chilling requirement. This nutritional treatment is much easier to control in a hydroponic system so the technique would appear to work well in a soilless culture system as it does outdoors in soil. Outdoor growers using the non-dormancy system in Florida use this frequent nitrogen application and freeze protection to obtain blooming in November and continue until February. Ripe berries are harvested from January through April if winter temperatures are high enough.

Given this information and the controlled climate and nutrition obtained within a greenhouse cropping situation, there is no reason why you could not crop successive blocks of plants year-round (perhaps avoiding times of the year when outdoor fresh berries are plentiful).

With regard to harvesting in a greenhouse situation, probably the best method would be to go back to using handheld vibrators that shake the berries from the plants onto a net. These were used in many blueberry crops in the 1960s before the large mechanical harvest machines that are used today were developed. Harvesting by hand only will result in each picker getting about 4 kilograms per hour of fruit off the plants. Use of vibration devices can increase the harvest rate to over 12 kilograms per hour per person.

Hopefully this will help in your search for information on greenhouse blueberry production. There are a couple of other references which you might find useful:

"Blueberry Culture in Greenhouses, Tunnels and Under Rain Covers," J.J.M. Bal, Acta Horticulturae, Vol. 446 (1997), page 327

"Pruning of Highbush Blueberries," V. Jansen, Acta Horticulturae, Vol. 446 (1997), page 333

In answer to your question regarding motivating the blueberry plants "chemistry reactions of winter," it is possible to regulate the plant dormancy requirement with a chemical substance. Chemical applications of 2 percent hydrogen cyanide (HCN) increases the rate and amount of vegetative bud break in plants that have not had any winter chilling or have received insufficient winter chilling. However, this treatment consisting of either 1 or 2 percent HCN has been reported by some researchers to cause some bud and shoot injury. This is less likely to occur in outdoor-grown blueberry bushes. It appears that the HCN acts to satisfy the chilling requirement usually necessary for good bud break in spring and hence allows the production of fruit in climates that would otherwise be too warm. This information was obtained from "Feasibility of Blueberry Production in Warm Climates" (see above reference). —L.M.

Q: While browsing through the (Growing Edge) Online Hydroponic Q&A archives, I didn't find much information on highbush blueberries . . . Is this an uncommon indoor hydroponic crop? I have a few plants under a 400-watt HPS light in coir media. What do you suggest I feed them? Would a strawberry nutrient solution suffice at 4.5 pH?

A: Yes, it's fairly uncommon to grow hydroponic highbush blueberries as an indoor crop and little information exists on this subject. I do have a few scientific papers on the feasibility of nondormant blueberry cropping in greenhouses and containers—and blueberries produce well in hydroponic systems. They seem to benefit from the precise nutrition and pH control that can be achieved with hydroponics. We've had containerized hydroponic blueberries in our greenhouse here in New Zealand for the last couple of years and have only this season had the plants produce fruit (the plants were very small when first planted).

One problem that I can foresee with indoor blueberry production under lights is that the plants grow quite large (up to 6 feet for more is common) and wide (ours are about 4 feet across and getting wider). And while they produce a large number of berries, the actual yield compared to the space they require is rather low. On the other hand, blueberries under protected cultivation seem to produce larger fruit with a higher sugar level than those outdoors—and aren't bothered by birds.

The second problem with growing blueberries under protected cultivation is pollination. Blueberries need good pollination to set fruit. Bees carry out this job in outdoor crops very successfully—provided the correct pollinator varieties are present within the crop. When grown as a commercial crop in greenhouses, blueberries are usually pollinated by portable hives of bees. In theory, pollination could also be done by hand on a few plants. However, when we attempted this last year, it resulted in poor fruit set. In the absence of bee pollinators, you would probably need to pollinate by hand every day for several weeks in order to get good fruit set.

You are correct in thinking that a strawberry nutrient formula would work—a fruiting strawberry formula should be close to ideal for blueberries. You will want an EC of around 2.5, which is slightly higher than for strawberries. The optimal pH level for containerized blueberries is 4.5–5.5, so aiming for 5.0 in hydroponics would be best. Even though blueberries like an acidic soil in outdoor crops, in hydroponics it's best to run the pH slightly higher than 4.5. Coir media should be excellent. It will provide the high moisture-holding capacity blueberries need for good growth and development.

It should be possible to get your plants to produce two crops per year indoors under lights with good control over plant nutrition, temperature, and light levels. Blueberries can be prevented from going dormant in winter if the temperature is kept above 47°F. In fact, it appears that most blueberry types don't have an absolute requirement for dormancy or chilling in order to induce fruiting, as is the case with many other fruiting crops. In warm temperatures and subtropical climates, blueberries can be completely prevented from entering dormancy. This factor makes the protected cropping of out-of-season fresh blueberry fruit an exciting possibility. —L.M.

Q: I am sales manager in a Taiwan company and in my leisure time I have raised blackberry bushes in the backyard. For three to four years, it never grew the berry fruit.

Today I read the content that Dr. Morgan responded to the readers question about growing blueberries in warm climate. In Taiwan, it is not cold in the wintertime, so it's not possible for the natural dormancy process to occur. In that article, Dr. Morgan mentioned using nitrogen throughout the fall and winter for a nondormant system.

Is it possible that Dr. Morgan could advise me how to perform that nitrogen application in fall and in winter for blackberries? I do the nursery just for fun after working hours. It might be good to draw the attention of my two young children outside away from TV and computer games.

A: Blueberry plants (Vaccinium corymbosum), can be grown in a nondormant greenhouse system. However, blackberries are very similar to raspberries in that they need a period of chilling and therefore can't be grown in a nondormant system. Blackberries can, however, be grown out of season by chilling the canes artificially and there is a great deal of information on the hydroponic production of raspberries, which are very similar to blackberries, in an article I wrote called "Growing Hydroponic Raspberries" in The Growing Edge, Volume 12, Number 5 (2001), page 59.

The researchers who have been investigating the nondormant system for blueberries have published the following scientific papers:

Reeder, R. K.; Obreza, T. A.; Darnell, R. L., "Establishment of a Non-Dormant Blueberry (Vaccinium corymbosum Hybrid) Production System in a Warm Winter Climate," Journal of Horticultural Science and Biotechnology, Volume 73, Number 5 (1998), page 655.

Darnell, R. L.; Williamson, J. G., "Feasibility of Blueberry Production in Warm Climates," Acta Horticulturae, Volume 446 (1997), page 251.

The information contained in these papers states that the success of an evergreen blueberry production system depends on the ability to maintain healthy leaves and avoid low temperatures that result in defoliation. Therefore, this system is limited to tropical or subtropical areas with mild winter temperatures that do not fall below freezing.

Southern high bush blueberries were used in these experiments in Florida to test the nondormant system. These were soil grown plants, but the results should also apply to hydroponically raised blueberries where it will be easier to control the rate of nitrogen application. The nondormant production system involves the application of nitrogen throughout the fall and winter (in Florida), which enables the plants to avoid the normal dormancy cycle and concomitant chilling requirement. In general, nitrogen rates of 252 kilograms per hectare per year increases plant canopy volume, leaf retention, and rate of new vegetative bud break.

I would suggest that in a hydroponic system, once the plants have finished fruiting (or if they are still vegetative), use a high nitrogen nutrient formula that is applied continuously. This should keep the plants active and, in time, they will flower and fruit again. Once the plants have set fruit, change the nutrient formula to a bloom or fruiting formula that has a higher ratio of potassium for fruit development. Then change back to the high nitrogen formula once all the fruit has been harvested. This should promote leaf growth rather than dormancy after fruiting. Dormancy will not occur in your climate as temperatures probably never drop low enough for long enough to induce it. You may need to experiment with different blueberry types and cultivars as it is likely that some will respond to this sort of system better than others. You will also need to ensure the flowers are pollinated either by insects or by hand (if growing in a greenhouse). Otherwise, fruit set will be inadequate. —L.M.

Q: I'm growing two dwarf Musa banana plants indoors. They are at about 4 feet in height. I have several questions.

The trees are potted in a 1 foot diameter planter at 1 foot height. Is this too small? Should they be repotted? If yes, at what size?

The lower leaves are turning brown about the edges while the new leaves are sprouting vigorously (I water twice weekly with Miracle-Gro. Is this normal for the lower leaves to brown out (I then clip to remove them)? Or is it a symptom of needing to be repotted?

How do they flower? Should I aid in pollinating them?

How tall will they grow? It appears that I'll have to support them if and when they get bananas—the trunks are at about 2 inches diameter at the potting line. Any suggestions for supporting them if they get bananas?

A: Although your bananas are a dwarf type, at 4 feet tall, they will need a bigger pot. I would suggest you pot them up now before they get any larger into a pot that is approximately 1.5 feet in diameter with a greater depth of at least 2 feet. This will give the banana root system more room. As it fills up the container, it should have sufficient support to hold itself upright when fruiting without toppling over its container.

The browning at the edges of the lower leaves is common in bananas. Often, it occurs because the humidity levels are too low (bananas are tropical plants that prefer high humidity levels). If the new leaves are growing well, don't be too concerned. However, increasing the humidity around the banana plants will benefit growth. This can be done by having a shallow pan of water underneath the plants and by misting with water (not chlorinated tap water) on a regu-

lar basis. Don't remove the lower leaves until they are well browned and obviously ready to be taken off since they will still be carrying out some photosynthesis. Banana plants do tend to look rather scruffy as the older leaves age, tear, and eventually fall off.

Bananas (provided they are a fruiting type and not just an ornamental Musa spp.), will form an inflorescence 10–18 months after initial planting of the young offset under tropical conditions. This could take several years in a climate that is not tropical and sometimes never occurs in container-grown specimens. If temperature and growth conditions are not suitable, flowers will never be initiated. However, container-grown bananas have been known to flower and fruit in many indoor situations. The flowers are large and covered by purple bracts that shed as the flower grows. Bananas of this type do not need pollination as they will be seedless. You will soon see tiny banana fruitlets emerge from the center of the flowers, which will then expand and develop.

Dwarf bananas can in fact grow rather large, but this depends entirely on which variety of dwarf banana you have. Some only reach 5–6 feet and others can be larger under good growing conditions. The "trunk," which is actually just a herbaceous stem, will thicken as the plant grows to support its height—provided they have sufficient light and nutrition for a good growth habit to develop. If they appear to be tall and thin and unable to support themselves or any fruit that develop, you can stake these by tying the stem to a wooden stake pushed into the container. The plant should then be able to support its fruit without toppling over. After

Q: Do you have a list of beans that are considered "broad leaf beans"? Is it possible to grow them hydroponically?

A: Broad beans, Vicia faba, are broken up into two general cultivars: Longpods and Windsors. Longpods are more hardy, are suited to cooler climates, and have kidney-shaped beans in long, slender pods (but they're not "kidney beans"; those are in the "haricot beans" group). Windsors are less hardy and produce rounder beans in shorter, broader pods. Some traditionally popular broad bean types are 'Aquadulce Claudia'; 'Seville'; 'Ite'; 'The Sutton' and 'Benny Lad,' which are dwarf types; 'Jubilee Hysor'; 'Hylon'; and 'Green Giant.' I've heard that 'Shiny Fardenlosa' is a popular hydroponic variety in New Zealand. Look for varieties that are disease resistant (some beans are susceptible to rust).

Beans can certainly be grown in hydroponic systems, including nutrient film technique (NFT) and media-based systems. Since they dislike waterlogged conditions, make sure broad beans are grown in free-draining media (if a media-based system is used). I would imagine that broad

beans would grow well in general purpose "growth" and "bloom" nutrient solutions (with a recommended electrical conductivity of 1.8 to 2.5). And since broad beans have an erect habit, they may not need any additional support. Most broad beans are harvested in a fairly juvenile state, when they are 2–3 inches long, and can be boiled and eaten whole. Larger pods can be frozen and the beans used in soup. Optimum temperatures for growing broad beans are 65–80°F. The principle pest that afflicts broad beans is the black bean aphid. Once the plants go into flowering, young vegetative shoots and branches can be pinched back a bit to reduce the possibility of aphid infestation.

If you are looking for a good reference text, Rob Smith covers the cultivation of beans (and many other crops) in detail in his excellent book, Hydroponic Crop Production. —D.J.P.

fruiting, the plant stem is cut back to at the base and new plantlets will then form, from which new banana plants can be propagated. —L.M.

Q: Last year, I grew banana trees in soil covering an area equal to one acre. My soil is sandy loam and the climate is very arid with minimal rainfall. I have to pump water from the ground well to supply them with water (mineral content of well water 950; maximum tolerance for this particular banana species is 1,200).

Bananas require a lot of water and fertilizers. So I was wondering if I could use an outdoor hydroponic system for planting bananas. This could potentially save much on both water and fertilizer. I was wondering If anyone has any similar experience and could guide me on the type of hydroponic system and growing medium to use. And an obvious question is how would I support these rather heavy plants? I would appreciate any thoughts.

A: Yes, bananas have been grown hydroponically and they appear to do well in media-based systems (even quite shallow systems) provided moisture levels are maintained. You may have to prevent too much evaporation from occurring from the media beds in your climate. I haven't been able to find any detailed hydroponic guides on commercial banana production, but there is much information on the use of irrigation and fertilizers. It appears that a 100 percent increase in fruit yield can be obtained when plants are continually supplied with sufficient water—up to field capacity, which

often does not occur in many soil-based systems. A hydroponic system should therefore not only conserve water and nutrients, but also give much greater yields. Bananas have been grown in greenhouses, but these systems tend to use the shorter, dwarf varieties because of the problem of support. Outdoors, wind can be a major problem, so you would probably need to construct some shelter for the plants as well as supplying a media bed of sufficient depth for the root system to develop fully and assist with plant support.

The media needs to have a good degree of water-holding capacity to prevent excessive evaporation from the media bed surface but at the same time have sufficient oxygenation and not become waterlogged. A free draining base of coarse sand or gravel layered with a more water-retentive substrate would probably suit these plants. With bananas, ensuring the media does not dry out is vitally important for maximum growth and yields and a drip irrigation system might be your best bet. —L.M.

Q: I have a banana tree growing on a small back patio. How do I control the new shoots that come up almost daily? If I just trim them, they are back the next day.

A: Banana plants multiply by sending up suckers, or young plantlets, which can be used to propagate new plants. However, if you don't want the plant spreading or sending up these suckers, you will need to continually remove them. The best way to do this is to get a sharp spade or large knife and wait until the young plant is large enough to get a good grip on. Then slice down alongside the mother plant and cut into the root system of the sucker as deep as you can while pulling away at the top. This will remove all of the young plantlet with the root system. By cutting it from the mother plant, you won't need to constantly trim back the new shoots each day. You will need to do this will all the plantlets that pop up around the base of the large plant. They will continue to grow from time to time. —L.M.

Q: I am looking for information on growing passionfruit hydroponically. Specifically I am looking for information on training, plant densities, cultivar selection, and yield expectations.

A: There has been a lot of recent commercial interest in growing hydroponic passionfruit. Producing out-of-season passionfruit can be profitable, so you're considering a promising crop. We've grown out-of-season hydroponic passionfruit in a greenhouse here in temperate New Zealand.

There are a number of aspects you need to know about the physiology of the passionfruit vine, which has very specific requirements for flowering and fruiting. There is little or no detailed information on growing passionfruit hydro-

Q: Any information on growing snow peas in an NFT system, indoors and under lights, would be helpful.

A: Snow peas are a simple crop to grow. There are two types: tall climbing cultivars and short dwarf cultivars. They do not require as much heating as many other crops such as tomatoes, etc. as they do best in a cool climate (50–60°F). Nutrient strength needs to be maintained around 2.5 EC. Lighting can be used, but to make the most of this the tall varieties should be used and strung up for best production. Harvesting timing is very important with this crop—the pods must be picked before the peas inside start to form. This can mean having to harvest every day or every second day to get them at the right stage of maturity. Also since they are harvested at an immature stage, they have a shorter post harvest life and should be put into refrigeration covered in plastic wrap to prevent wilting. —L.M.

ponically, but there are several scientific references about the crop in greenhouses and its cultivation requirements. Passionfruit have different optimum temperature levels for each stage of flowering, fruit set, and fruit development. By applying the correct temperature at the correct time, high yields can be obtained from hydroponic vines grown in containers.

The most common mistake made with passionfruit in greenhouses is the assumption that when the vine is large enough, it will flower and fruit. This is not the case. If temperatures are warm enough, the vine will continue to grow vegetatively and won't switch to flowering until a specific set of environmental conditions are provided.

Passionfruit vines are best grown for 2 years and then replaced. Vine extension in most passionfruit cultivars is best at a daytime temperature of 77°F and a nighttime temperature of 68°F and best flower development will occur at 68°F during the day and 59°F at night. Lower temperatures will inhibit both flowering and vine growth and higher temperatures—86°F day and 77°F night—completely prevent flower development in most purple passionfruit cultivars. Good environmental control is required for passionfruit production. As with many other fruiting crops we grow hydroponically, passionfruit are prone to fruit drop at high temperatures so the lower end of the temperature range must be maintained through maturity and harvest. Once the fruit have been harvested, temperatures can be increased again to promote vine growth and then lowered to induce more flowers and fruit so that two harvests per vine per year can be obtained.

Passionfruit is a large vine with many stems that need to support a number of fairly large fruit. Vines are best tied up like tomato plants when small and later formed into a trellis type of system—a bit like grape vines—so that each stem is trained up and along a wire to make the best use of greenhouse space. Vines may also need to be tipped when they become too long and are carrying sufficient fruit. Excessive or weak stems should be removed to allow maximum light and air penetration through the canopy.

Plant density is one factor that's difficult to determine since it's dependent on the cultivar, growing conditions, and the hydroponic system and training structure used. As a general rule, one vine per 1.5–2 square meters should be a good spacing—provided the vine is being trained upward and is well supported. A 2-year-old passionfruit vine will become quite large and heavy.

Cultivar selection will depend on what varieties are available locally. The large purple passionfruit, Passiflora edulis, is the most popular and there are a number of good cultivars for outdoor production that should do well in hydroponics, including 'Purple Gold' and 'Lacey.' There are also golden or yellow passionfruit types.

Yield expectations are difficult to estimate. If conditions aren't carefully controlled, no yield at all is not uncommon—you could end up with just a huge amount of vegetative vine for months on end. On the other hand, good cultivars that are given the right conditions can be very heavy croppers in the first season during the first flush of fruit, with lesser fruit produced from subsequent flushes of growth. The average vine can carry over 100 fruit with two crops per year in a heated greenhouse. Obviously, the yield will depend on fruit size, weight, and number, so the best way to estimate this is to grow a few different cultivars and see what you can achieve. —L.M.

Q: I began to read The Growing Edge as a fish hobbyist and I always enjoy the information. It's interesting and giving me tons of dreams. I keep and reread all of my old issues. I particularly like the article on important edible plants from South America in Volume 10, Number 4. Is this possible to grow those crop in Quebec, Canada? Where can I find the seeds or tubers for growing in Canada? I just found one place in the states that only has one kind of oca and they can't send it to Canada. I'm also looking for Carica papaya to start in my greenhouse. Is it possible to put me in contact with author Martin Waterman?

Also, in Volume 11, Number 2, in the heirloom article, there is a picture from Kapuler of the Chinese popcorn. Can anyone tell me where I can buy seeds? I can't find them in all the catalog I have.

A: One of the primary sources of information in "Important Edible Plants From South America" was Oregon Exotics Nursery, based outside of Grants Pass, Oregon (1065 Messinger Road, Grants Pass, Oregon 97527, (541) 846-7578, www.exoticfruit.com/). They should be able to help you find crops that would be suited to your climate. We are no longer in contact with Martin Waterman. Seeds of Diversity Canada (www.seeds.ca/) also might be able to help you find some of the plants you are seeking.

Kursa Kapular, the person who photographed the "Chinese popcorn," is the daughter of Alan Kapular of Seeds for Change (see store.yahoo.com/seedsofchange/). The Chinese corn plant can be found at store.yahoo.com/seedsofchange/corcerorchir.html. —D.J.P.

Q: Can tropical trees, which are next to impossible to grow in containers because of the root systems, be grown hydroponically? I am thinking particularly of trying mangoes. Other tropical possibilities are pistachios, cashews, jackfruit, durian, and papaya.

A: The major problem with the tropical plants, which you mentioned, is their size. They are, in general, fairly large trees. Most will grow to well over 10 meters in height at maturity. Large plants such as these have a large root system with a huge root mass that would be difficult to contain in a hydroponic system.

You would be able to get fruit from a small papaya, which is a treelike herb growing to about 2–8 meters in height, in a hydroponic system, but the other plants you mention are long lived trees of a large size. These large trees could really only be produced in hydroponics long term if you could either obtain dwarf varieties or find some way of pruning to keep size of both the tops and roots down while still getting the plants to flower and fruit. This has been done with other large trees. There are dwarf and container varieties of many citrus and stone fruit trees that will fruit in a hydroponic system.

It may be possible to use a semi-hydroponic system where hydroponic nutrients are applied to these plants that are started in an outdoor media bed, but the roots can access the soil and grow down to the depth they require to support themselves at maturity (usually several meters down into the soil). —*L.M.*

Q: I love to see plants grow so I planted pits from lemon and nectarine to see if they would grow—and they do. My lemon tree is growing like crazy. I have had to cut it off many times because is up to the ceiling but I have noticed that its leaves are getting yellow at the edges and many of them are falling off. Am I doing something wrong? I keep my tree in a place where it gets plenty of sunshine and I water it once a week. I am also wondering if it will ever grow fruit.

The tree from the nectarine pit grows very slowly but as long as it doesn't die I am happy. Would you be able to tell me how to care for my fruit trees?

A: You are to be congratulated for growing these plants from seed! This takes a lot of patience and often fails. The lemon tree, grown from a seed, is not likely to have the same characteristics of the tree the fruit originally came from. Most good quality lemon trees are grafted. A bud of a good fruiting type of lemon is attached onto a strong root stock with good rooting characteristics. Together they form a strong tree with good fruit.

A seedling lemon—under the right environmental conditions—will still, mostly likely, fruit eventually. However, the plant is not likely to be a compact, dwarf, heavy fruiting quality lemon plant. A seedling lemon tree will be quite variable in its growth and fruiting habit and is likely to grow into a large tree before fruiting. The yellowing at

the leaf edges sounds like the plant is running out of nutrients—particularly it is has gotten tall, been cut back, and regrown many times. It might need repotting into a larger container and also some liquid fertilizer on a weekly basis will help (make sure there is nitrogen and magnesium in the fertilizer).

The only common cause of leaf yellowing and drop in citrus trees is mites. These are difficult to see and will look like very small red dots on the underside of the plant leaves. You may also see some fine downy webbing. These mites rapidly suck the plant dry, making the leaves go yellow and drop off. Spraying on a regular basis with a good spraying oil and insecticide mixture should help solve the problem. For a more organic approach, regular, weekly use of a neem oil spray will also help keep the insects under control. The tree should eventually fruit, but it may need more room to grow larger before it does so.

The nectarine tree may have the same problem as the lemon tree. As a seedling, it will be very unpredictable in regard to size, when it will fruit, and the quality of the fruit. The fruit will not be as good as the named, grafted varieties that are used commercially or purchased in the garden center. However, some seedling nectarines do produce tasty fruit eventually—but it will need to be planted outside at some stage. For now, the seedling will probably benefit from some liquid fertilizer and warm conditions to speed up growth. Also, keep an eye out for many pests, such as the mites, which might also affect the young tree. —*L.M.*

Q: I was thinking about growing bamboo in my hydroponic greenhouse and was wondering what fertilizer ratios I should feed and how much water I should apply during each watering and a total for the day. My main goal is to use as much water and nutrients as possible without regard to the "best production" possible. Can you give me some advice on this or point me in the right direction?

A: Bamboo is a vigorous plant and a heavy feeder under good growing conditions and it also tolerant of damp media or soil so you should be able to get good growth rates under greenhouse conditions. You will need to apply a nutrient solution that is high in nitrogen to support rapid vegetative growth and apply sufficient water and irrigations per day to keep the root zone fairly moist without draining to waste too much nutrient. This would require monitoring as the bamboo grows and would have to be gradually increased as the plants developed. Water application should also be linked to the environmental conditions so that more is applied on sunny, warm days and less on cooler or overcast days when the plants' requirement for moisture is less.

Below are some general recommendations for nutrient levels in hydroponic nutrient solutions for hydroponic bamboo. These are only approximate and you may need to get a solution analysis carried out to fine-tune the fertilizer mix that you use.

General Hydroponic Nutrient Recommendations for Bamboo

Nitrogen	270 ppm
Phosphate	75 ppm
Potassium	210 ppm
Magnesium	65 ppm
Calcium	262 ppm
Sulfur	86 ppm
Iron	6.80 ppm
Manganese	2.98 ppm
Zinc	0.25 ppm
Boron	0.70 ppm
Copper	0.07 ppm
Molybdate	0.05 ppm

—L.M.

Q: Can capers (Capparis spinosa) be grown hydroponically (see www.hort.purdue.edu/newcrop/cropfactsheets/caper.html)? What about truffles, mushrooms, asparagus, artichokes, and black pepper (Piper negrum)?

A: Yes capers could be grown hydroponically, although they probably never have been. There is some good information on general production of these plants on the Website you mention. A very light, porous, free draining media would be suitable (similar to their natural habit on coast lines, etc.), such as coarse sand or gravel with a dilute hydroponic nutrient mix.

In theory, truffles could be grown in a soilless environment. However, in practice, this is not likely to be done. Truffles are a fungi that have a special association with the roots of certain tree species. These fungi cannot make their own food, so they send out hyphae, a threadlike structure, which coats the roots of the tree host and helps the tree absorb certain minerals. In return, the tree host provides the fungus with carbohydrates and other compounds and nutrients that are a product of the tree's photosynthesis. There is probably no reason why, after some very intensive biochemical investigation, that these organic compounds could not be isolated in a lab, recreated, and the fungi grown in an inert media. However, the truffle eating public may not like this idea and the cost involved would likely be prohibitive.

The Japanese once grew mushrooms in a media source (agar) by supplying them with the organic compounds from decomposition of straw and manures that had been syn-

Q: **Would you please let us know is it possible to produce fodder from barley in a normal room not using a container?**

A: Green fodder can be produced from barley in a normal room, as long as some light (either natural or artificial) is provided. Usually, the barely would be spread into a thick layer in plastic trays lined with absorbent paper. However, you could also spread the barely onto sheets of plastic with some drainage holes punched, which are also lined with absorbent paper. Barely takes about 10 days until it has developed sufficiently for use as a stock feed. At this stage, it will be about 8 inches tall. Water is used for the first few days, then hydroponic nutrient solution is misted onto the developing seedlings for maximum growth and quality of the fodder. At harvest, the "mats" of fodder can be rolled up and taken out to the livestock. —L.M.

thesized for this purpose. But this is not done commercially due to the cost and perception of these "artificial" products. Mushrooms require organic matter and compounds to grow and cannot be grown on an inert media with just inorganic hydroponic nutrient salts.

Yes, asparagus has been successfully grown in media-based hydroponics and even in aeroponics, mainly by home hobbyists and researchers who were investigating how the root system works. This, however, would not usually be a commercially viable option since asparagus needs a large volume of media for a mature plant's root system and crown and only crops once per year.

Globe artichokes (large, thistlelike plants) perform very well in media-based hydroponic systems—although they are large plants. In hydroponics and in controlled environments (heated), they can be induced to yield many more chokes than outdoor crops and are a reasonably fast growing plant in hydroponics. Jerusalem artichokes are a very different sort of plant that produces underground tubers. These could also be grown in media-based hydroponic systems. A couple of good Websites on both types of artichokes are given below:

orst.edu/Dept/NWREC/artichgl.html (globe artichokes)
orst.edu/Dept/NWREC/artichje.html (Jerusalem artichokes)

Black pepper is a large sprawling vine that is not normally grown in hydroponics. However, provided sufficient plant support for the vine to climb on is provided and a large enough container is used for the root system, there is no reason why black pepper could not be grown hydroponically. Pepper requires a warm climate of 82–95°F and high rainfall for good production levels. —*L.M.*

Q: Can groundnuts be effectively grown in hydroponics?

A: Yes, groundnuts—otherwise known as peanuts (Arachis hypogaea)—can certainly be grown in hydroponics. We have a small but healthy crop growing in our greenhouse at the moment and they are thriving on the hydroponic nutrients. However, peanuts can be a little difficult since they're extremely prone to fungal diseases, which rapidly destroy the plants at any stage of growth. Peanut seed should be treated or dusted with a good fungicide before being planted into the production system. We've found the best type of peanuts to grow hydroponically are the large, Virginia types. These types have yielded the best so far, although the smaller Spanish peanut types have also grown well. You need to select nuts that are large, plump, and don't show any signs of physical deformity or rot for germinating.

We've been using a pumice and coconut fiber media. Media-based bed or container systems using a free-draining, light media, such as a mixture of river sand and coconut fiber, perlite, fine pumice sand, or combinations of these make a good substrate for peanuts. The media needs to be sterilized before use and occasionally applying a fungicide spray over the developing plants is a good idea—particularly when conditions are warm and humid. Peanuts have also been grown in aeroponic units, which have the advantage that the developing nuts (called "pegs") can be viewed.

The important aspect to remember with peanuts is that once they have flowered, the developing peg—a long stem that will produce the nut under the ground—will grow from the aerial portion of the plant and then burrow down under the media to develop the young fruit. The fruit will develop and mature in about 10 weeks with favorable temperatures and moisture conditions. Well grown peanut plants can have about 30–40 pods so a container that holds at least 2.6 gallons (10 l) of media is required when growing hydroponically. The media needs to be friable and light and cannot restrict this development process. Peanuts are legumes and have the ability to use nitrogen fixed from the atmosphere by bacteria that live on the root system of the plant.

Hydroponic peanuts, just like outdoor soil-based crops, need a long, warm growing season—about 140 frost-free days—for good yields. The nuts are harvested when the foliage begins to turn yellow in late summer or early fall. The peanuts then have to be hung up in a warm, dry place for about 4 weeks. They can then be stored in airtight containers or shelled and roasted. The crop is easy to grow and

seems to yield well under hydroponic production. The small plant size also makes them a good choice for container growing in greenhouses. —*L.M.*

Q: What is the average growth period for hydroponically grown peanuts and what is the yield for farm-grown peanuts in a growth period of 120 to 140 days? Also, how many peanuts does it take to produce 1 gallon of peanut oil? What types of bacteria and fungi affect peanuts grown hydroponically?

A: Hydroponically grown peanuts have an average growth period, under good growing conditions, of approximately 120 to 160 frost-free days from sowing to harvest of the nuts. The amount of time taken for the crop depends on the climate and the variety. Farm-grown peanuts yield around 2,200 to 2,600 pounds per acre (depending on the season, location, and variety grown) in the United States (this data was taken from the National Agricultural Statistics Service of the USDA). I cannot find any data on how many peanuts it takes to get an gallon of oil . . . This probably depends on the type of peanut grown, its oil percentage at harvest, and the process of oil extraction used.

The bacteria and fungi that can affect hydroponically grown peanuts include many of the same ones that can affect field-grown peanuts, including leaf spot, rust, southern blight, Sclerotinia blight, Botrytis (gray mold), Pythium and Rhizoctonia fungi, and black mold (Aspergillus niger). The most common fungal pathogens are those that infect the plants in the early stages of germination and seedling development—most notably Pythium and Rhizoctonia, which are common under damp, warm conditions. —*L.M.*

Q: How do I grow bean sprouts from mung bean seeds? Can you provide me with everything you know? Is there a Website that I can visit?

A: Sprouts are easy to grow. Line a plastic growing container, which are commonly sold in garden centers for growing sprouts (but any shallow plastic container will do), with some absorbent capillary matting. In place of true capillary matting, paper towels can be used. Some hobbyists have also reported using a thin layer of inert, sterile media, such as horticultural sand, gravel, perlite, or vermiculite. Scatter the seeds along the base of the tray and mist with plain water. Place the tray in a moderately well lit, warm spot—not too bright or hot. The seeds should germinate and grow within a few days. As soon as they begin growing well, mist with dilute vegetative nutrient solution. After a few days, the entire crop of sprouts can be cut when the plants have grown to a few inches high. —*D.J.P.*

Q: I would like some information on how to grow rice hydroponically—what method to use (NFT?), growing medium, and nutrient requirements. Also, where can a find a list of nutrient requirements for vegetables?

A: Rice is not a common hydroponic crop, although it can be grown in soilless culture. Commercially, it would not be economical. However, on a small scale, rice is best raised in media bed systems that can be flooded with dilute nutrient on a regular basis (or remain partially flooded) like the rice plants would be in a traditional outdoor crop. The best media for this type of flood-and-drain system would be a heavy substrate that does not float when submerged. Gravel or coarse sand could be used. It is also possible to grow rice in rockwool or coconut fiber slabs that can also be flooded or keep very moist to provide the ideal conditions for rice. Rice seed should be soaked in water for 24 hours before sowing into the media or seedlings can be raised in trays and later transplanted into the media. As the rice ripens, the nutrient flooding of the media needs to be gradually lessened. Rice needs high humidity levels to pollinate well, but the presence of a flooded bed or media should provide this under warm conditions. The ideal temperature is close to 86°F at high humidity for most rapid growth, although the plants will grow slower at lower temperature levels.

Rice has fairly specific nutrient requirements for maximum growth and development in hydroponics. A nutrient formulation will require the following levels of mineral elements (in parts per million, ppm):

Nitrogen	249 ppm
Phosphorus	58 ppm
Potassium	80 ppm
Magnesium	65 ppm
Calcium	317 ppm
Sulfur	87 ppm
Silica	100 ppm
Iron	5.0 ppm
Manganese	3.0 ppm
Boron	0.70 ppm
Zinc	0.40 ppm
Copper	0.07 ppm
Molybdate	0.05 ppm

Rice also has a requirement for silica as an essential mineral nutrient. Silica ends up being up to 16 percent of total dry matter in rice plants, so a nutrient solution with at least 100 ppm silica will need to be maintained throughout the life of the plants. —L.M.

Q: Are there any estimates on biomass productivity for hydroponic grains, such as rice? Is legume-rhizobium symbiosis restricted when growing hydroponic leguminous grains? Can vegetable protein sources be grown hydroponically? Do you have any productivity estimates?

A: There are many sources of biomass productivity figures for many grain and other hydroponic crops such as rice, wheat, soybeans, potatoes, and more. Many of these values have been obtained from researchers working on Controlled Ecological Life Support Systems (CELSS) for space travel where hydroponic systems are extensively used and tested for crop production. The lists below provide some approximate figures for edible biomass production in hydroponic crops.

Crop Edible Biomass	(g/m2/day)
Potatoes	16.7
Yellow corn	14
Soybeans	12
Wheat	11.3
Quinoa	8
Brown rice	6

Q: **My basil plants, which I planted in May, have developed brown, hard stems and have gone to seed already. What is the growth period for these plants in Florida? It is only the end of July.**

A: Basil is an annual plant that tends to grow rapidly and go to seed prematurely in hot weather—often after only a couple of months. Sometimes, when conditions are really warm (over 86°F), the plants can develop woody stems and flower shoots while still only quite small before you have had a chance to harvest many leaves.

In warmer conditions, it is important to choose varieties of basil that are "slow to bolt," cut the plants back hard before they have a chance to form a flower stem, make sure that the soil or media doesn't dry out, and keep the plants well fed. Also, providing some form of shade over the plants helps to lower air temperatures and can prolong the life of the crop. Flower stems can be cut back hard as soon as you see them forming and this should force the plant to send out some new vegetative shoots from buds on the stem. However, these will also tend to flower sooner or later. Some of the smaller basil varieties, such as bush basil, can withstand higher temperatures before flowering than the larger-leaved types and are worth trying. —*L.M.*

Crop	Average Protein (g)	Productivity per 100 g of Edible Portion (g/m2/day)
Soybeans	35.9	12
Chickpeas (dried)	21.3	5
Quinoa	13.1	7.5
Wild rice	14.7	2.8
Rice, white	7.3	6
Sorghum	11.3	8
Durum wheat	13.7	13
Peanuts (fresh)	25.6	4
Sunflower seeds	19.8	5
Beans, black-eyed	23.5	13
Beans, red kidney	22.1	13
Lentils, green (dried)	24.3	13
Pigeon pea (dried)	20.0	6
Spirulina	5.9	—
Maize	8.7	13.5

Source: "The New Oxford Book of Food Plants", J. G. Vaughn; C. A. Geissler, (Oxford University Press, Oxford, United Kingdom, 1998).

In comparison, the super dwarf rice used in trials with the Advanced Life Support (ALS) system at the Utah State University Crop Physiology Lab (see www.usu.edu/~cpl/celss.html) obtained a harvest index of 60 percent (harvest index is the ratio of edible to inedible biomass from the crop). Super dwarf rice is particularly high in terms of edible biomass and is well suited to hydroponic production in limited spaces.

Legume-Rhizobium symbiosis in most hydroponic leguminous crops isn't a factor since nitrogen (N) usually isn't limited in hydroponic nutrient solutions. However, in hydroponic systems were N is limited—perhaps with some organic nutrient solutions—the N-fixation ability of Rhizobium can be extremely beneficial. Rhizobium symbiosis can occur in hydroponic systems just as it does in soil—although the crop might need to be inoculated with the correct species of nitrogen-fixing bacteria if it isn't already present.

Many sources of vegetable protein can be grown hydroponically. However, some crops are more productive in terms of protein content and biomass production than others. The crops listed in the chart above can be produced hydroponically and have a relatively high protein content.

Soybeans head the list in terms of protein content and can certainly be grown hydroponically. However, apart from being grown in ALS systems, they aren't grown in soilless systems on a commercial scale due to the extensive level of field-grown soybeans and the relatively low value of the crop. —*L.M.*

Q: Can soybeans be grown (cost effectively) in a hydroponic system? If so, what would be the approximate yield per square meter?

A: Soybeans can be grown in hydroponics. However, this is usually not cost effective. Soybeans are traditionally soil grown on a large, extensive scale and sold in bulk as a commodity, making the price fairly low per kilogram of beans. The use of mechanization for all aspects of cultivation and harvesting in the field make the price of the final soybeans also contribute to low prices. The crop does not warrant manual handling, which would be required in a hydroponic system.

But while soybeans are not grown commercially as a hydroponic crop, you could probably expect to get roughly double the yields of a soil-grown soybean crop. Soybean plants appear to grow well in both nutrient film technique (NFT) and media-based hydroponic systems using a standard nutrient formula designed for green or French beans. —L.M.

Q: Have legumes with root nodules been successfully grown in hydroponics? Also, are there medicinal plants that have been grown successfully in hydroponics?

A: Yes, legumes with root nodules have been successfully grown in hydroponics. What usually occurs in a hydroponic system is that the leguminous plant is supplied with adequate nitrogen and doesn't need to rely on the bacteria in the root nodules to fix nitrogen from the atmosphere. However, root nodules often develop on hydroponic plants where the nitrogen-fixing bacteria are present in the growing media, water supply, nutrient, or any other source, such as in dust or soil contamination. Sometimes, in very clean systems, the bacteria don't naturally exist and root nodules don't form on leguminous plants. However, we have observed that most hydroponic legume crops eventually develop nodules sooner or later. You can always inoculate the hydroponic solution or media with the correct source of bacteria to help ensure that root nodules form on the plant.

There are a number of medicinal plants that have been successfully grown in hydroponics, including St. John's wort (Hypericum perforatum), kava (Piper methysticum), echinacea (Echinacea spp.), and ginseng (Panax spp. or Eleutherococcus senticosus), to name a few. Aeroponic systems work well for cultivating medicinal plants that are grown for their roots. Aeroponic systems permit the roots of the plants to be easily viewed as they form and selectively harvested without destroying the plant. Hydroponic production also yields clean root systems that are free from soil contamination and therefore hydroponics is being examined as a commercial method for the production of many of these types of plants. It also appears that it's possible to increase the concentration of certain active chemicals in these types of plants by manipulating the nutrient solution and environment. —L.M.

Q: You have mentioned that medicinal plants, such as St. John's wort, echinacea, ginseng, and kava, have been successfully grown in hydroponics. I believe these plants are herbs and I would like to know if there has been any woody medicinal plant that has been or is currently being grown in hydroponics.

A: Woody plants often grow to a fairly large size and therefore are not widely grown in hydroponics. However Salix species (willow) have certainly been grown and studied in hydroponics, as has the tea tree, manuka, and eucalyptus—not usually for their medicinal properties, but it is possible to produce these plants in soilless culture. —L.M.

Q: Where can I find some literature on how to produce hydroponic fodder for dairy cattle?

A: There certainly are some interesting Websites on the Internet on this subject. And a number of manufacturers sell hydroponic fodder growing systems. I've listed a couple of links below. Also, there are a few hydroponic books that have information on producing fodder (also listed below).

Websites:
ISAR: Initiative for Social Action and Renewal in Eurasia (www.isar.org/isar/archive/ST/hydroponics47.html); this article is entitled "Hydroponic Techniques Sprout Healthy, Inexpensive Fodder"—it's an interesting read on the topic

Foddercon (www.tradepage.co.za/foddercon/index.htm); this is a commercial seller of hydroponic fodder containers and systems

Books:
Hydroponic Food Production, Dr. Howard Resh (Woodbridge Press, California); contains information on a grass growing system

Advanced Guide to Hydroponics, James Sholoto Douglas (Pelham Books, Ltd., London); has an account and diagrams for simple fodder production systems

—L.M.

Q: On growing barley to maturity for grain production in hydroponics: What would be the best density or spacing? What is the potential yield in kilos per crop and how many crops per year? Assuming complete artificial plus day lighting, how many levels or shelves can be sowed? All other environmental conditions will be controlled. What is the best media you recommend and what size the beds? I am in Mexico near Mexico City.

A: Growing barley to maturity for grain production is not common in hydroponics. Usually, grains are grown for only about 20 days and then feed out to livestock as hydroponic fodder. However, there isn't any reason why barley can't be grown in hydroponics for grain production, although this is not likely to be an economical option. It has been estimated that growing grains such as barely in hydroponics result in the grain portion of the planting being about 15 percent of plant dry weight and that it would take about one quarter to one half of this weight equivalent in nutrient salts to produce the grain, which is a high nutrient input for a small food value output.

However, based on the figures for soil grown barley, since there appears to be no other information on hydroponic barely grain production, a density or plant spacing of 22–25 plants per square foot appears to be the optimum level so you would sow about 30–35 grains in a square foot of growing bed to obtain this level of healthy plants. Barley crops are rapid producers in warm climates such as yours and should be ready for harvest at 90–120 days from sowing, so you could expect to get three to four crops per year in year round warm conditions (barley is much more slow growing in cool winter climates). Yields are very dependent on cultivars, climate, nutrition, etc. and I couldn't even guess at what you might achieve in a well run hydroponics system.

Barley does need good light levels for high grain yields, so only one level of crop under natural light is recommended. If you are going to high intensity artificial lighting in a shelf type system, then the number of levels or shelves (each

Q: How do I grow soybeans (or alfalfa) hydroponically on a small scale? What do I need to know about using it for feed? We have two cows, a handful of sheep, some chickens, and pigs. I need to know where to find feed values, besides how to actually grow them.

A: Growing hydroponic fodder for stock feed is a relatively simple operation. The seed is thickly spread over shallow plastic trays that contain an absorbent sheet of paper and then misted with water for the first few days. After the seeds sprout, the trays a misted several times a day with a nutrient solution so that the seedlings grow at a rapid rate. These trays can be stacked on shelves inside a greenhouse or grown outside. The fodder is then feed to the stock when it is about 8 inches high and has produced a dense mat of vegetation. This takes around 8–10 days from seeding for crops such as wheat and oats. One kilogram of seed will yield around 6–10 kilograms of green fodder—depending on what you are growing.

Usually this type of fodder production system will grow barley, oats, and wheat, which all have a high nutritional value as stock feeds. Alfalfa hay can have a range of 10–25

> *Barley does need good light levels for high grain yields, so only one level of crop under natural light is recommended. If you are going to high intensity artificial lighting in a shelf type system, then the number of levels or shelves (each with its own light source) will be dependant on whether you are going to be growing tall or dwarf varieties of barley.*

with its own light source) will be dependant on whether you are going to be growing tall or dwarf varieties of barley. You can probably get two layers of shelves if using the smaller dwarf cultivars, but only one would be practical with the tall varieties.

The best media, would be a free draining mix containing coarse sand or pumice with a percentage of fibrous material to hold moisture (such as coir fiber or ground bark). Barely would probably grow in all hydroponic media, such as rockwool, vermiculite, perlite, etc., but the more expensive media may not be justified for a grain crop.

The size of the beds is difficult to determine. The larger the better as the dense planting of grasslike plants can then support each other and will be more resistant to toppling over. However, strong dwarf varieties could be grown in fairly small trays of media. There is further information on the barely plant itself on the following Website: www.gov.mb.ca/agriculture/crops/cereals/bfb01s01.html. —L.M.

percent or more protein. Grass hay will contain between 4–18 percent protein. The reason for growing the feed hydroponically as opposed to feeding straight grain is that the green feed is 95 percent digestible, unlike unsprouted grain, which is at best 30 percent digestible.

The following Websites contain some good information on hydroponic stock fodder production and feed values:

orbita.starmedia.com/~carlosarano/page4.htm
www.isar.org/isar/archive/ST/hydroponics47.html
www.ianr.unl.edu/pubs/Range/g915.htm

—L.M.

Q: I am interested in growing hydroponic melons and woody ornamentals. I need specific information on nutrients levels and suggested media for melons. For ornamentals, I am interested in propagating woody material—conifers and some deciduous stock in large plug trays. I have experience advising growers of ornamental materials—bedding plant and woody container producers—but this is a little different. I would rather not reinvent the wheel here.

A: Melons in hydroponics need a media that will retain good moisture levels and also very high levels of oxygen (air-filled porosity). Melons plants have large leaves and a high requirement for oxygenation in the root and zone and can also lose huge amounts of moisture on hot days. A mixture of perlite and vermiculite works well, as does coconut fiber with a base of gravel or expanded clay at the bottom of the growing container for additional drainage. Optimum nutrient levels for hydroponic melons are as follows (in parts per million):

Nitrogen	215 ppm
Phosphate	86 ppm
Potassium	343 ppm
Magnesium	85 ppm
Calcium	175 ppm
Sulfur	113 ppm
Iron	6.80 ppm
Manganese	1.97 ppm
Zinc	0.25 ppm
Boron	0.70 ppm
Copper	0.07 ppm
Molybdate	0.05 ppm

Electrical conductivity (EC) levels of between 1.8 (young plants) and 2.4 (older plants) is recommended in a recirculating system. The ideal pH for melons is around 5.8.

If you are not making up your own nutrient solution, a general purpose "grow" premixed nutrient can be used until the time of flowering. At that point, the nutrient should be switched to a quality "bloom" or "fruiting" formula should be used. You might need to supplement additional potassium in order to get high-quality melon fruit.

The propagation of woody ornamentals can be carried out using a number of inert, sterile hydroponic propagation media. Rockwool or oasis comes in small plugs or cubes that can be slotted into plug trays for use in propagation. Alternatively, you can use a coarse grade of sterilized sand mixed with perlite or vermiculite. Perlite and vermiculite mixtures themselves provide the correct degree of aeration and moisture required for callus formation and root outgrowth. Once the first roots have formed, a dilute hydroponic nutrient solution (general purpose mixture) can be used to provide initial nutrition until the plants are ready for growth in another media. —*L.M.*

Q: I've tried to grow many types of cantaloupe hydroponically for two years without success. The main problem is fungal and disease problems on the leaves. The plants died before the fruits were mature if I didn't use chemical pesticides. If I used chemical pesticides, the fruit looked OK but wasn't sweet at all. A gentleman from Holland who lives here in Thailand told me that it wasn't possible to grow cantaloupe in NFT because the roots get too much water and, therefore, the fruit doesn't get sweet.

Is it harmful to consume the cantaloupes that aren't mature from the dying plant grown without pesticides? Will the fungus on the leaves get into the fruit? The fruit looks OK. Is it true that it isn't possible to grow cantaloupe in NFT?

A: Cantaloupe can be prone to fungal diseases, such as powdery mildew, in warm, humid climates. This disease will rapidly colonize the plants and destroy them if not prevented or controlled. There are some varieties of cantaloupe that have some resistance to many fungal diseases and it might be a good idea to trial some of these commercial varieties and prevent the problem from reoccurring. You will also need to use fungicides to prevent these problems. Otherwise, there will be problems with the fruit quality (if the plants survive). Often, preventive sprays of silica or sodium bicarbonate will prevent some of the fungal disease pathogens from infecting the plants.

Sweetness in cantaloupe is due to combination of genetics (i.e., the variety you are growing), the nutrition of the plant (requiring high potassium levels for good fruit quality), and the amount of sugars produced by the leaves, which are then transported into the developing fruits. So, if your plants have lost leaves or the foliage is not photosynthesizing well due to the disease problem, then the plants fruit will not be of good quality or flavor. Also, if the plant is carrying a high fruit load, the quality and size of the fruit will not be as good as plants that carry a lesser fruit load. —*L.M.*

Q: I'm interested in growing hydroponic hops. Is this possible? Where can I get information on this subject?

A: While I haven't come across any information on hydroponic hop production, I don't see any reason why it wouldn't be possible. Hops (Humulus spp.) are large, herbaceous perennials that produce annual vines from overwintering rootstock. Therefore, hop plants grown hydroponically would need to have their root system overwintered in a fairly large container or bed of inert media, which would contain the root system, including rhizomes with buds and true roots.

Hops can grow to over 20 feet, so a support system is needed for the vines. Hops need specific climatic conditions, including at least 120 frost-free days, for flowers to be produced. Also, hops are dioecious, meaning there are separate male and female hop vines. Only the female vines produce the flowering hop cones that are harvested and widely used in brewing beer.

The most important requirement for hop production is long days, of 15 hours or more, to promote vine growth. This is followed by a period of shortening day length that causes the vines to stop growing vertically and produce the side shoots that will bear the flowers. These day and season length requirements mean that hop cultivation is largely limited to areas between 35 and 55 degrees latitude. Where the day length is constant throughout the year, the vines will tend to continue growing and not produce flowers and cones. However, hops can be forced to flower by providing artificially long and then short days in a controlled environment, such as a properly outfitted hydroponic greenhouse. —*L.M.*

Q: If I grow a flat of wheatgrass, cut it, and juice it, am I still able to use the soil I grew it in to grow another batch, or is that soil now depleted of nutrients?

A: It's generally not a good idea to reuse the soil to grow another batch of wheatgrass. However, this isn't because the nutrients have been depleted (these can easily be provided with a liquid feed) but because of potential disease problems

---

Q: Can mint (Mentha spicata) be grown hydroponically?

A: Yes, mint does particularly well in hydroponics and can become quite large and invasive if not regularly trimmed and contained within the system. Mint is a cool season herb but it will grow under a wide range of climatic conditions provided there is sufficient moisture and some shade provided. Commercial growers often crop hydroponic mint underneath production benches of other plants since it can tolerate partial shade and needs little attention. Mint plants can be cropped indefinitely as they will continually reproduce themselves from stolons. However, disease outbreaks are common and rust in particular tends to infect subsequent crops after the first couple of harvests. In hydroponics, EC levels for mint should be run at around 0.8–1.2 and a pH of around 5.5–5.8. Nutrient formulas similar to those used for lettuce, dill, and fennel are suitable for mint plants in hydroponics. —*L.M.*

---

that can arise from the presence of the old wheatgrass root systems present in the soil. There is the potential that the old root system and leftover grains from the old crop could produce pathogens that could not only rapidly destroy your next crop, but could also carry over into the wheatgrass, which is then juiced and consumed without cooking. Some pathogens, such as certain bacteria and fungi (and the toxins they produce), may then be present in the wheatgrass juice when you drink it (these would be destroyed if the wheatgrass juice was heated or boiled). When growing sprouts or wheat for fresh consumption. you need to be very careful with hygiene to prevent these types of problems.

The best way to produce wheatgrass for juicing is to not use any soil or media at all. The wheat is sprouted on absorbent paper in shallow (2–3 inches deep) plastic trays (no media or soil required). Once the wheatgrass has germinated, a dilute, complete hydroponic nutrient solution is misted or sprayed on the sprouts every day to support the plant growth. You can then grow the wheatgrass in this way for as long as you like at a very high density. You can then cut the grass, juice it, and then discard the root systems, which will form a mat in the tray. The plastic tray is then cleaned and sterilized with a dilute solution of bleach, rinsed, and fresh absorbent paper and more wheat grains placed in this for another crop. The advantage is that without any media, there isn't any contamination of your cut wheatgrass crop with soil and grit and the system can remain clean with less chance of pathogen contamination. In fact, this is the same system that's used to produce oats and wheat as hydroponic fodder for cattle and other livestock in areas where the soil won't sustain pasture growth. —*L.M.*

Q: I am interested in producing barley in a hydroponic system but I don't have any idea about this method of production. Can you help me?

A: I am not sure if you are referring to growing barley as a fodder crop for supplementary feeding of livestock such as cattle or to grow the plant to maturity and produce the grain . . . Hydroponics is mostly used, with barley, to sprout and grow the grain for about 10–14 days before it is fed out to livestock in areas where pasture grass growth is severely limited by drought, low fertility, or difficult climates.

For this use, the method of production is very simple. The barley seed is first soaked in water for 12 hours. Then the barley grain is spread into polystyrene or large plastic trays that have small drainage holes in the bottom. A sheet of paper is often used on the base of the tray to hold the seed and some extra moisture. The trays are then stacked into growing sheds on shelves at a high density. Temperatures are maintained at 68°F and a humidity level of 75 percent. Maximum light levels are 16 hours per day of moderate intensity. Once they have germinated, the trays of barely get watered four or five times per day with the hydroponic nutrient solution. In about eight days, the trays are full of lush barley "grass" about 25 centimeters high, ready to feed out to livestock. One kilogram of barley seed will yield about 6-10 kilograms of fresh barley fodder, which is high in protein. The trays of fodder can be simply tipped out and transported to the livestock and then immediately replanted for another crop.

It is also achievable to grow barley to maturity for grain production in hydroponics. However, this is not often done due to the relatively inexpensive cost of mass-produced soil-grown barley grain, which can be shipped long distances and stored since it is not highly perishable. Barley, like wheat and other grains, is best grown in densely sown media beds and fed a nutrient solution several times a day. Any type of food grade plastic can be used, provided you have a depth of at least 15 centimeters of media to contain the root zone and adequate holes for drainage. —L.M.

Q: We would like information for hydroponic barley grass for animal feed.

A: Growing hydroponic fodder for animal stock has become more common over the last several years. Many commercial growing systems exist for such applications. Here are a few links to systems and information on growing fodder:

www.tradepage.co.za/foddercon/
www.greenfield-hydroponics.com/fodder.html
www.isar.org/isar/archive/ST/hydroponics47.html

I'm sure that the creators of these systems would be happy to help you in your search for information on systems for hydroponic fodder. I know that many ranchers have been growing their own hydroponic fodder to make sure that their stock are eating fodder that is free from pesticides and genetically modified organisms (GMOs).

Another good source of information might be an article published by Practical Hydroponics & Greenhouses (an Australian hydroponic magazine). You can find it online at www.hydroponics.net.au/back_issues/issue03.html.

You might also check with your local agricultural research station to see if they know about any other folks producing hydroponic fodder in your area. The Canadian hydroponic greenhouse industry has been rapidly growing. —D.J.P.

Q: I need information about the hydroponic oat and barley crops. My questions are about the nutrient solution application and irrigation frequency. I am working with hydroponic crops and don't use any substrate.

A: Depending on the temperature, light levels, and stage of crop development, hydroponic oat and barley plants without any media will need misting or flooding with nutrient several times a day. Initially, the young plants may only one or two applications of nutrient per day. But, as the plants develop, nutrient application needs to be more frequent—up to six to nine times per day depending on the type of hydroponic system you are using. In nutrient film technique (NFT) systems, the flow of nutrient is continuous. You are looking to supply the plants root systems with sufficient moisture to prevent the roots from drying out between applications of nutrient solution, so checking the moisture levels in the root zone between applications will help you to determine how often the plants need nutrient applied at different stages of plant growth. —L.M.

Q: When I am growing wheatgrass, how long will it take before I can juice the grass? When I cut it, does the seed keep sprouting?

A: It should take between 10 to 14 days from sprouting until the grass has enough foliage to extract in a juicer. So long as the grass is cut above the growing point at the base of each seedling, it will resprout. For repeat sprouting, a slightly stronger nutrient solution will be required as the grass seedling will have used up its seed reserves. —L.M.

Q: I am growing basil in a top feed drip/NFT system built out of PVC gutters turned upside down on a table lined with a pond liner. The gutters are drilled on 10-inch centers with 2-inch net pots filled with a comparable sized rockwool cube. At each plant site, I have a 1/2 gallon an hour dripper. I also have good filtration.

However, my drippers are clogging. I am using General Hydroponics Maxi Grow for my nutrient. Could I install a larger flow dripper? Is my nutrient clogging my drippers? The roots are turning brown and dying. Do I need more flow? What do you think about adding a micro jet between the plants or adding an NFT emitter system at the top of each channel? Is the nutrient I am using sufficient to grow basil or should I supplement? Not being a chemist, the basil formula you have in your article in The Growing Edge is Greek to me.

A: The clogging of your drippers may be due a problem with your water supply. Your water may feature minerals, such as iron, or a pH problem, that's causing the nutrients to react and form an insoluble precipitate that is blocking the tubes. I would suggest you check that your pH is within the 5.5–5.8 range, make sure you don't add any organic additives to the nutrient, and make sure that there are good filters within your system that could catch any stray particles of media or vegetation. Rotten vegetation and pieces of roots may be causing the blockages since it seems you have a problem in the root zone if the roots are turning brown and dying. This could be a fungal pathogen, such a Pythium, or due to some other problem within the root zone.

I would suggest that you thoroughly clean all of the system, including the drippers, media, and grow pots, between crops with a 10 percent bleach solution or hydrogen peroxide. Rinse everything well and then replant with new plants and a new nutrient solution. I am not sure what the formulation of your nutrient is, so I can't comment on whether or not it is suitable for basil. However, General Hydroponics nutrients are usually suitable for most plants. You might want to switch to a "bloom" formula for basil since that crop has a fairly high requirement for potassium when growing well.

The basil formula in my article is simply a basic "recipe." It presents the amounts of certain fertilizer salts to weigh out and dissolve in a certain volume of water and then dilute to be ready for use. Hydroponic fertilizer salts are all common horticultural nutrient salts and many growers mix up their own recipes for hydroponic formulas. There isn't any secret or chemistry involved in this process. However, when mixing up small volumes of nutrient solution—as is the case with many hobbyists—it is usually easier to buy a well formulated commercial product from a good hydroponic supplier. —L.M.

Q: I am learning to grow basil. My basil is growing quite tall and the stems do not really stand up. How can I help?

A: It is a good idea to trim the tops off of your basil plants from time to time in order to make them grow more bushy as opposed to long and tall. Trim your plants down to a reasonable height where they will be able to stand on their own. Just take a few inches off at a time. Make sure you use a clean, sterile knife or pair of scissors to make the cuts (wash the implement, douse it with bleach or hydrogen peroxide, and then rinse well). Soon, the plant will begin to develop more side shoots and it will grow into more of a shrub. As these new shoots become long, trim them as well in order to promote further development. This process also allows you to enjoy some fresh basil from time to time. Also, trim any flowers that form since these will drain energy away from fresh leaf production.

There are also some types of basil that are naturally compact and form a small shrub or bush. If your basil type continues to grow too tall, you might try growing some of the more compact types. —D.J.P.

Q: For several years, I have successfully moved my outdoor containers of Italian basil indoors to the same sunny spot in the winter without problems. This year, the leaves are papery with transparent patches that have no color. In the patches, there are many tiny brown specks. Eventually, the sick leaf withers and drops off. Can you tell me what is wrong with my plants? I'm down to one.

A: It sounds like the plants experienced some cold conditions before they were brought inside. Basil is particularly cold sensitive and a night of cool temperatures can induce this papery, bleaching of the leaves, which will then drop off. If the plants were also waterlogged and/or frosted before being brought it, this will have the same effect. There are also a number of other causes to the symptoms you describe, including pest damage, diseases, and nutritional disorders. However, what you have experienced most commonly occurs in basil after cool conditions have put the plants into thermal shock. —L.M.

Q: How can I manipulate (shorten) my basil's internodal length? Will this improve yield? Light is not a problem. When it gets warm out and my reservoir temperatures rise, I have the option of adding fresh water from the well to cool it and add more nutrient or using frozen plastic containers of water until I get it down. Which do you think is the better method?

A: The best way to get plants with shorter internodes is to grow a more compact variety of basil—even some of the bush types. The environmental conditions that encourage short internodes in basil are high light, a well balanced hydroponic nutrient that has sufficient potassium levels (basil needs high levels of potassium in the nutrient for a vegetative plant), and wide plant spacing. Basil plants that are planted close together will naturally stretch up to the light and develop longer internodes, so a wider spacing helps maintain a more compact plant. There are some plant growth regulators, such as Cultar, that are used to create very short internodes and compact, bushy plants in the nursery industry, but these should not be used on food crops. Also, cutting the plants back will encourage more stems that will be thinner and shorter than the main stem.

Shorter internodes probably will not increase yields (in terms of weight). Shorter internodes also mean smaller leaf size and, hence, less weight from each plant. However, shorter plants might be easier to manage and might be less prone to falling over, etc.

As for cooling the nutrient solution, if it gets really warm, you might find you need to continually add more and more of the cool water and nutrients. Using large volumes of fresh water for cooling will end up being expensive as more nutrients will also need to be added to maintain the electrical conductivity. The ice is a more efficient idea if you have a freezer with sufficient capacity for the ice you need and the time to add this it and monitor the temperature on a continual basis. You might like to consider a small evaporative cooler unit for your nutrient. The nutrient flows over a large pad as it returns to the tank and a fan blows air through and over this evaporative pad to cool the nutrient. This works well provided your humidity levels are not too high, which would prevent evaporation and cooling of the nutrient. —L.M.

Q: What CF should I use for growing coriander in NFT? Do you have any other tips regarding coriander?

A: The approximate CF for coriander in NFT is around 12 in summer and a little higher in winter (in heated greenhouses)—about 16. Coriander will grow well outside of this range, but it can be prone to premature bolting in summer with higher CF levels and might display weak, spindly growth in winter if the CF is run too low. Higher CF levels promote more of the aromatic substances and natural oils within the plant, but with this particular crop, sometimes the effect can be too strong! Coriander is a plant that does well in both NFT and media beds, but it does not like too much root disturbance and tends to produce more of a tap root type of root system. For this reason it's best to sow the seeds direct into rockwool or oasis cubes or small pots that can then be put directly into your NFT system. Pricking out the seedlings gives them quite a check in growth and can lead to disease attack by Pythium and other problems.

The main problem with coriander—particularly in summer when conditions are starting to get fairly warm—is premature bolting. While this is fine if you are growing the herb for the seeds, it's a major problem if you are harvesting the foliage for fresh sales or home use. Removing the growing point when you see the plant "going to seed," will prolong the harvest period of the foliage, but this crop is best grown with some degree of shading in summer to help prevent too much premature bolting from occurring.

Coriander is also best grown as a short-term crop and should be harvested and replanted on a regular basis for maximum yields and foliage quality. In winter, the crop needs to be heated to a temperature of at least 64°F for good growth, although plants will "survive" a mild winter in a greenhouse situation without heating. There is very little detailed information around on many of these herbs that are now being grown hydroponically, so often the best way to really find out about them is to get some plants and have a go. —L.M.

Q: Am having great difficulty growing coriander (from seeds)—even when I ask farmer friends to do it for me. The seeds usually germinate and shoots grow to about 10 centimeters before withering rapidly. I have tried growing them in beds, in perforated plastic bags, and in large earthenware pots on a balcony, which has lots of light without direct sunshine. As coriander plants are not available here, can you advise on particular prerequisites for growing this delightful herb that's so essential in Southeast Asian cookery?

A: Coriander is indeed a wonderful herb that is rapidly growing in popularity for use as fresh cilantro all around the world. However, it can be a little difficult to grow under certain conditions. Coriander seed should be sown directly where it is to grow or into small individual cell trays, cubes, rockwool, oasis, or some other sterilized media. It is important to make sure you use a good, free-draining, high-quality seed raising mix (not soil) or sterilized media as cilantro can be prone to damping off pathogens—and it sounds like

that's the problem you're having with the seedlings.

Coriander seedlings are not suited to bare root transplanting as the tap root system is easily damaged and results in many plant deaths or stunted plants that do not yield well. The other common problem with coriander is overcrowding and sowing too many seeds in a small area. Seed should be sown two or three per cell or individually spaced at 1.5x1.5 cm into growing beds. If the resulting seedlings are sown at too high a density, airflow around the base of the seedlings is restricted and damping off pathogens will result in the young seedlings rotting and withering at the base. Making sure the germination media is free draining and kept slightly dry on the surface after germination will also assist in preventing seedling losses. By the time the seedlings are 10 centimeters tall, they should be at a spacing of one or two plants, 10-15 centimeters apart. Attempting to grow a large mass of seedlings in a clump often results in pathogen attack under warm, damp conditions.

Coriander seed will usually germinate within five to seven days at 68–79°F. If too many seedlings have germinated, thin them as soon as the seedlings can be handled. After germination, temperatures should be maintained at no less than 68°F. Conditions cooler than this will result in plants rapidly "declining." This means that growth rates will slow and the plants will gradually wither away.

Coriander has a reasonably high heat requirement for good growth rates. On the other hand, temperatures higher than 79°F, particularly when combined with high humidity levels, can also cause growth and disease problems in coriander, so the plants could need some shading under such conditions. You might also like to try a fungicide spray at about seven to ten days after germination to help control pathogens. Using a sterilized seed raising mix, keeping the media free draining and not overly damp, and thinning the seedlings out early on should give you a successful crop.

There was also an article I wrote in the November/December issue (Volume 13, Number 2) of The Growing Edge magazine on page 26 entitled "Hydroponic Coriander and Basil Production," which might also have some helpful information. —L.M.

Q: Can I grow recao (Mexican coriander) in my hydroponic system?

A: Recao (Eryngium foetidum L.), also known as culantro, is probably not commercially or widely grown in hydroponics (yet). However, there is no doubt, given the popularity of the herb in some countries, that it will eventually be grown in some areas.

Recao has different growing requirements than other herbs, such as basil and coriander (cilantro). It is a member of the Apiacea family, which includes celery, parsley, parsnips, and carrots. Recao is a biennial herb that develops a taproot structure, much like a small parsnip, and as such needs a media bed of good depth for the root system to develop. This taproot reaches 5–6 inches at maturity, so a hydroponic media bed of at least 10 inches would be required. Seeds take at least 3 weeks to germinate and require warm temperatures of around 75°F for rapid germination. The root system can withstand some handling, so seedlings can be raised in cell trays and then planted into the hydroponic media bed at around 8 weeks after germination. Recao prefers a shaded, moist environment and direct, bright light.

Hot conditions and long days will cause the plant to bolt (flower and go to seed) prematurely (much like cilantro and some other herbs).

Although the plant can be grown in full sun, it has been found that shaded crops produce plants with larger and greener leaves that are more marketable because of their better appearance the greater pungent aroma. Under 65–75 percent shade, recao plants have been found to have bolting delayed and an increased fresh weight of the leaves, so you might like to consider shading your hydroponic system after the recao has been planted. Outdoor crops of recao are often covered with a floating row cover that cuts down light and helps prevent premature flowering. The cover also keeps the leaves as succulent as possible. Leaves of recao grown under these row covers have less chlorophyll and much softer spines. It also keeps the crop cleaner.

In a hydroponic system, a nutrient formula with good nitrogen levels is required to maintain leaf growth. A general purpose "grow" or "vegetative" nutrient formula should be suitable with electrical conductivity (EC) levels similar to those used for carrots and parsnips (around 1.6–2.2 mScm-1) with a pH of 6.0–6.2. The media needs to hold reasonable levels of moisture. A coconut fiber-based substrate would be suitable and this would also allow good growth and development of the taproot system, which ensures a healthy plant and maximum leaf growth.

Pests and diseases that might affect hydroponic recao include leaf spot (Xanthomonas spp.) and aphids, whitefly, and thrips. The plants should be ready for a first harvest at around 60 days after transplanting. The plant can then be left to regrow for multiple harvests. Recao is usually sold in bunches of 6–10 leaves per bunch held together with a rubber band or twist tie. Postharvest handling is important for recao crops. Refrigeration can cause chilling injury in cut recao and the product is best stored in similar conditions as basil, at 50°F, where the it should store for up to 2 weeks. Chilling injury in recao has been noted when stored at 37°F.

Recao is relatively easy to grow and should be treated as more of a longer lived crop than most other herbs as it is slow to establish from seed. However, multiple harvests can be obtained by letting the cut plant regrow after cutting for as long as leaf quality is maintained. —L.M.

Q: I'm looking for information on growing hydroponic herbs—specifically parsley—in South Africa.

A: The following is a condensed excerpt from my book Fresh Culinary Herb Production—a Technical Guide to the Hydroponic Production of Fresh Gourmet Herb Crops.

Parsley is a fairly easy herb to grow in hydroponics that can be produced in a "continual harvest" system for many months. There are two main types of parsley that could be grown as a commercial cut crop: curly leaved parsley (Petroselinum crispum var. crispum) and plain or flat leaved parsley (P. crispum var. neapolitanum), which is also called Italian parsley. Parsley reaches heights of up to 60 centimeters and, being a biannual plant, produces leaves in the first year of growth and, in its second year, produces the flowering stems.

Recommended cultivars of parsley that should perform well in your climate for greenhouse hydroponic production are 'Deep Green,' 'Forest Green,' 'Moss Curled,' and 'Banquet.' These are curly leaved cultivars. Flat-leaved cultivars include 'Plain Italian,' 'Dark Green Italian,' 'Gigante Catalogno,' 'Sweet Italian,' and 'Giant Italian.' However, it would be a good idea to trial a number of these cultivars to see which performs best in your system and which the market prefers in terms of leaf shape and size. For commercial production, the parsley stems, when cut, must be long with a dark green color and no yellowing or leaf bleaching after harvest.

Parsley is grown as an annual plant and discarded before its second season when the flower stalks are produced. Seed grown transplants can be raised in inert media for later planting out into the hydroponic system or direct seeded into media beds. Germination of parsley seed is slow and erratic, taking 20–25 days in some cases. However, it can be purchased as osmotically primed seed, which reduces the time need for germination and can improve plant establishment. Unprimed seed can be soaked in warm water overnight before sowing to improve germination rates. Under cooler conditions, parsley is prone to pre-emergence damping off and fungicide treatment of the seed is recommended. Seed should be covered with 3 millimeters of fine substrate and a sheet of plastic to retain moisture. A: heated propagator or bottom heat to 64°F is recommended for germination. Parsley should be raised in propagation cubes or blocks or, less preferably, cell trays as the tap root system the young plants develop does not transplant well if damaged. As with other herbs, parsley seedlings that have had some degree of root damage will tend to bolt prematurely once in the main growing system.

Parsley is a cool season crop that can tolerate light shade. For this reason, it is a good plant to produce on the lower tiers of hydroponic systems where conditions are generally cooler. Warm conditions (over 71°F) lower the quality and length of parsley stems, may induce premature bolting, and tend to result in a lighter green coloration of the foliage. Media systems should incorporate a fibrous substrate, such as coconut fiber or ground bark, for water retention, although parsley plants will not tolerate cold, overly damp media. Parsley produces well in nutrient film technique (NFT) systems, provided the seedlings are raised in small pots that are directly placed into the NFT gullies since the tap root system does not bare root well into hydroponic systems.

The first harvest of parsley leaves can usually be obtained 60–70 days after planting out and every week thereafter for several months. Any flower stalks that are tough and fibrous should be removed as they form to promote the development of more foliage. Plants will eventually run out of vigor and will need to be replaced after several months of cropping. Yield of outdoor parsley have been recorded as being approximately 5–10 tons per hectare per year. Yields of flat-leafed Italian parsley are expected to be higher due to the faster growth rate and longer harvesting life of this crop.

Parsley plants are heavy feeders and will require a well balanced nutrient high in nitrogen to maintain foliage development. Levels of mineral elements recommended for greenhouse parsley crops are:

* Nitrogen   100–150 ppm
* Phosphorus 45–75 ppm
* Potassium   75–90 ppm
* Magnesium   20–30 ppm

The pH should be maintained at 5.5–6.0. Electrical conductivity (EC) values for parsley are in the 1.0–1.6 range, depending on the environment. Lower EC levels can be run under warmer conditions and high levels under cooler conditions to maintain product quality. In recirculating systems, the level of nitrogen in the solution should be monitored since rapidly growing parsley crops can drop solution nitrogen levels in a fairly short time.

Parsley should be harvested by gently pulling the outer, older leaves from the plant rather than by cutting. Italian parsley, however, can be cut where plantings are dense as this method is less time consuming. Large bunches of both types of parsley should be packaged into plastic bags with open tops or flower sleeves for larger orders. Italian parsley may be sold in bunches, bags, or clamshell packages. Fresh cut parsley should be stored at temperatures of 32–37°F and at 95 percent relative humidity. Hydrocooling or ice can be used to remove the field heat from the harvested product. Fresh cut parsley has a long postharvest storage life and can be kept in acceptable condition for up to two months at 35°F. A controlled atmosphere of 10 percent oxygen and 1 percent carbon dioxide can help maintain green coloration and quality. —L.M.

Q: I am interested in growing basil hydroponically using organic nutrients and artificial lighting. I would like to know what type of yields to expect per 1,000-watt halide and how often plants need to be regenerated.

A: The type of yields you will get are dependent on several variables, such as the type of basil grown, the environmental conditions, skill of the grower, level of nutritional balance in the nutrient solution, etc. However, since basil doesn't have a high nutritional demand compared to say, tomatoes, organic production is certainly possible. It may be more difficult to obtain yields that are similar to proven, inorganic hydroponic techniques with an organic system but, after some experimentation and research, similar yields may be possible. One of the biggest problems with organic basil production is controlling pests and diseases with exclusively organically approved methods. According to Dr. Lynette Morgan's book Fresh Culinary Herb Production (one of the best texts on hydroponic herb production and the source for much of this information), under good conditions, a yield of 1–1.5 pounds of basil per square foot of growing area is possible per month with hydroponic production. Numbers above and below this mark are common, depending on the season.

Basil can be successively harvested for a few months. However, the precise time when a plant should be discarded is up to the grower. When plants begin to produce a successive number of flower stalks, become infested with insects, or become infected with some sort of pathogen, they should be tossed and replaced with new, young plants. As basil ages, it tends to acquire a higher concentration of oil in the leaves, which makes it bitter and unmarketable. When harvesting, don't cut off too many leaves at any one time. The current recommendation for basil harvest is to cut only about one-third to one-half of the upper portion of the plant at any one time—especially under warm conditions that might induce bolting. When in doubt, taste the leaves. If they have become bitter, it's time for the plant to go. —D.J.P.

Q: I'm growing coriander in pipes and am developing brown tip on the leaves. What should I add to my mix? Since I'm mixing my own nutrient solution, could you recommend a mix for coriander and herbs in general? I live in Queensland, Australia.

A: Coriander, just like many other herbs and salad greens, is prone to developing tipburn under certain conditions. While tipburn is usually due to a lack of calcium in the tissue of the leaf tips, this tends to be more of a calcium transport problem within the plant rather than a lack of calcium in the nutrient solution. When conditions are overly warm, often accompanied by high light and humid-

ity levels—which is probably what occurs in your climate in Queensland, Australia—the plants are unable to transport calcium into the new developing tissue at the leaf margins fast enough to prevent cell breakdown. As these cells break down, the area browns and then dries up.

The first step in prevention is to ensure that you have adequate calcium in the nutrient solution (see "Coriander Nutrient Solution Formula for Warm and High Light Climates" below). The next step is to modify your environment. Use of shade cloth covers over the crop will assist in reducing temperature and light levels without slowing crop growth. If the plants are in a greenhouse, extra ventilation might help reduce humidity levels.

However, if the environment has a low relative humidity, another form of tipburn can develop in overly dry environments. The optimum relative humidity for coriander is between 75–85 percent with a temperature of 71.6–78.8°F for optimum growth and tipburn prevention.

Coriander Nutrient Solution for Warm and High Light Climates

(Grams of Nutrient Salts to Be Dissolved Into Two 5.3-gallon (20-liter) Stock Solution Tanks; Dilution of 1:100 will Give an EC of 1.4)

Part A
Calcium nitrate 1,821
Iron EDTA 100
Potassium Nitrate 304

Part B
Monopotassium phosphate 576
Magnesium sulfate 848
Manganese sulfate 17
Zinc sulfate 2.2
Boric acid 7.8
Copper sulfate 0.6
Sodium molybdate 0.204

—L.M.

Q: I have just bought a hydroponic system. The pot is approximately 12 inches across. I want to use it outdoors on my north-facing deck. I live in Zone 9. I am wondering if you could share a couple of plant names that I can have success growing. I would like to have herbs for the kitchen but I don't know how to get started.

A: Any number of plants could be grown in your new hydroponic system. One of the most popular herbs to grow for home use is basil—especially if you enjoy Italian food. Basil is also quite easy to grow. You could either start from seed or transplant a seedling into your system. You can find more in-depth information on growing specific herbs in our Online Archives (see www.growingedge.com/community/ archive/topics.html). Most herbs can be grown from one type of nutrient solution (a vegetative mix). Just make sure you research the proper electrical conductivity (EC) level for the specific herb you decide to grow (as well as any other growing specifics, such as temperature, humidity, and light levels). Another possibility would be to grow a few different herbs in the same system—as long as they have similar EC requirements. —D.J.P.

Q: I am interested in trying hydroponics with a couple of Japanese plants, green and purple perilla and wasabi. Do you know if it is possible or not?

A: Both perilla and wasabi are grown commercially using hydroponics. However, the perilla would be the easier of the two by far to produce. Wasabi has very specific requirements in terms of water temperature, quality, nutrition, type of media, and environment and has a reputation of being one of the most difficult plants to grow and keep alive in hydroponics. There is a good Website on hydroponic wasabi at www.wasabi.org/vision.htm. Also, there was also an article about a hydroponic wasabi operation in Oregon that contains a great deal of information on this subject (see "Soilless Wasabi for the Masses," by D. Peckenpaugh, The Growing Edge, Volume 13, Number 3 (Jan/Feb 2002), page 17).

On the other hand, perilla (also called shiso), is relatively straightforward and produces well in hydroponics. Perilla is an annual herb or plant that is usually raised on a commercial scale to be sold in bulk directly to the processing industry. The plant is also raised for oil production from the foliage and seed as well as in small quantities for direct sales to Japanese restaurants and consumers. Being a warmer season plant, perilla needs a climate that is free of frosts and is thus well suited to greenhouse production when heating can be used to obtain year-round production. Warm temperatures, long day length, good moisture levels, and a well balanced nutrient formula, similar to that used for general herb production, such as for basil production, are also required for high yields of perilla.

Perilla is propagated by seed. The optimum germination temperature range is 68–71°F. Seed can be directly sown into media beds or raised in small pots or cubes of rockwool or oasis for later transplanting out into the hydroponic system. The most common method of production of green leaf perilla in Japan is under cover in glass or greenhouses since the plants need a protected environment for the production of fresh leaves. Maximum foliage production will occur under long day lengths, so supplementary light might be needed. Perilla will quickly go to seed (bolt) under short days, such

as in autumn, so this needs to be prevented. The crop can then be harvested on a continual basis. The foliage is cut when the plants are about 30 centimeters tall and the leaves are 10 centimeters long. The plant will then regenerate and can be cut several more times before replacement.

The best cultivars for hydroponic perilla production are 'Ao-oba' (green large leaf), 'Ao-jiso' (green), and 'Ao-chirimen-jiso' (green), but you can collect seed from your best plants to develop your own line of high quality perilla. The main pests and diseases of hydroponic perilla would most likely be aphids, mites, whitefly, leaf-eating caterpillars, various rust fungi, damping off (Pythium in seedlings), and mildew. Most of these problems can be prevented by careful environmental control, insect screening, preventative sprays, and so on.

There is a great deal of interest in the production of herbs such as these, so experimenting with some hydroponically grown plants might be well worth the effort! —L.M.

Q: Is it possible to grow wasabi organically in a hydroponic system?

A: The short answer to your question is yes. Most crops we currently grow hydroponically can also be grown with the use of organic hydroponic nutrients—wasabi is not an exception.

Now for the long answer . . .

With wasabi, the difficulty is not so much the "organic" part of it, but the production of the crop in general. Wasabi is a tricky crop to grow. It has specific requirements for production and needs a special, modified hydroponic system. If you are already producing hydroponic wasabi, then changing from inorganic to organic nutrients shouldn't pose too many problems—provided that a few trials are initially run with a small number of plants.

Also, it's vital—like with all hydro-organic production systems—that the correct nutrient mix is used. The nutrient needs to be balanced, contain sufficient nutrients in the correct ratios, and be biologically stable—it can't turn anaerobic or "go-off" during use. There are a couple of good commercial brands of organic nutrient available. Although they aren't yet being imported into New Zealand, growers of many crops in the United States have had positive results with these nutrients. Probably the best option in New Zealand is to produce your own organic nutrient that will meet the nutritional requirements of a wasabi crop.

However, if you haven't grown wasabi before, I would recommend that you experiment with the correct system and environment for production of these plants before you venture into using an organic nutrient solution. There are a couple of good Websites that have information on wasabi.

They might help you if you are considering going into crop production.

www.freshwasabi.com/about.html
www.mangajin.com/mangajin/samplemj/Wasabi/wasabi.htm
www.wasabi.co.nz

—L.M.

Q: I'm looking for any type of hydroponic growing information on wasabi or any other "horseradish" type plant.

A: Wasabi has very specific requirements in terms of water temperature, quality, nutrition, type of media, and environment and has a reputation of being one of the most difficult plants to grow and keep alive in hydroponics. Wasabi is a very long term crop and can take up to two years from planting to harvest. There are a few good commercial grower Websites on hydroponic wasabi:

www.wasabi.org/
www.freshwasabi.com/

Also, we have one entry in The Online Hydroponic Q&A Archives on hydroponic wasabi (see www.growingedge.com/community/archive/read.php3?s=yes&q=42).

I recently visited a large hydroponic wasabi grower and wrote an article on their operation recently in The Growing Edge (see www.growingedge.com/magazine/back_issues/view_article.php3?AID=130316). The article has a lot of information on hydroponic wasabi.

Keep in mind that wasabi (Wasabia spp.) isn't horseradish (Armoracia spp.). The plants do have similarities, but they are not interchangeable. —D.J.P.

Q: I want to grow some vegetables and herbs hydroponically. Can you tell me which vegetables and herbs are compatible with each other?

A: For a small, noncommercial hydroponic setup, most green vegetables and herbs are compatible to have in the same hydroponic system. In fact, most plants can be grown together with some compromises—the electrical conductivity (EC) of the nutrient solution is the main one. If you want to produce lettuce, salad greens, and herbs in the same system, an EC of around 1.2–1.4 is a good level with a standard "grow" formula. If you are using a heated greenhouse to keep temperatures between 59–79°F then the plants that could be grouped together that prefer warmer conditions are basil, oregano, chives, most lettuce, cilantro (leaf coriander), rosemary, tarragon, etc. Cooler season crops that could be grouped together in an outdoor system that might expe-

rience cooler conditions are mint, lettuce, thyme, parsley, chervil, and many of the green vegetables such as cabbage, cauliflower, broccoli, etc. Tomatoes, peppers, cucumbers, and other fruiting vegetables need warm conditions and can be grown with herbs, lettuce, etc., but quality of the fruit will be lower since a lower EC needs to used to maintain growth in all the different plant species in the same hydroponic system. —L.M.

Q: I am growing the hydroponic "Windowsill Wonder" with basil for a science project. We are flooding it once a day with the nutrients. Are there any other tips that you have to help keep the plants growing?

A: I'm glad to hear that you have built The Windowsill Wonder! I have four such units myself that I built and use to grow a variety of plants. I've found that they work quite well.

Basil is a pretty easy crop to grow and it works well in The Windowsill Wonder. Keep an eye on the plants to see if any insects are bothering them. Usually, a good blast of water from a spray misting bottle will discourage small numbers of pests (such as whiteflies). As the plants grow, you can pinch the tops off of the main growing stems when they have grown large to make the plants develop more side shoots, creating shorter, bushier plants with more leaves. Each main side shoot can also be pinched every so often (after it has developed sufficient growth, not when it is still small) to foster more growth.

Whenever you need to add more nutrient solution, you can just pour it directly into the growing bed. Make a mark on your nutrient solution reservoir to indicate the proper level of solution and check it every week or so to see if you need to add any fresh solution.

After you have finished your science project, you can selectively harvest the basil leaves to use in the kitchen. This means that you don't have to cut all of the leaves off the plant and then toss it out. If you just cut some of the branches and leaves off, and leave the plants in the system, they will usually grow more branches and leaves. This process can be repeated a few times before the plants will be drained of their growing energy. If you let some flowers and then seeds develop on the plants, you can harvest the seeds to provide a new generation of plants. You can also make cuttings of basil branches to root and then grow into new plants. —D.J.P.

Q: I was wondering if you had a little more detailed drawings or more detailed instructions on the "Windowsill Wonder." Sorry to bother you about the easiest system, but I'm new to hydroponics and am trying start out with the basics and work my way up. So if you could help me with a design drawing or any other tip it would be greatly appreciated.

A: Here are a few tips to keep in mind when constructing the Windowsill Wonder (see www.growingedge.com/basics/easyplans/windowsill.html). This ebb-and-flow system works on positive pressure. The pump drives air into the nutrient reservoir. When the pressure builds (make sure you make a good seals on all connections) high enough, the nutrient solution will be driven into the growing bed. Then, when the pump turns off, the pressure will be released in the nutrient reservoir, allowing air to escape at a slow rate through the bleed valve, permitting the nutrient solution to drain back into the reservoir from the growing bed. Set the bleed valve open just enough so the nutrient solution can be pumped into the growing beds.

This process is best when automated by hooking the pump to a timer. Test this process to see how long it takes to fill the growing bed. My current growing beds (I have tried several sizes) are fairly large (8 inches wide by 2 feet long each—I have two hooked to one standard pump and one large, 2+ gallon reservoir) and usually take about 1/2 hour to fill. I use expanded clay in my beds and like to grow different types of hot peppers. I have found the system to work very well.

Position the nutrient reservoir at a height just below the growing bed. That way, when the pump turns off, gravity will help drain the nutrient solution back into the reservoir. And again, make sure that all of your connections have airtight seals—use plenty of waterproof silicone caulking around the connections. The ability for this system to build pressure is key to its success. —*D.J.P.*

Q: I'm working on a project to determine the optimum growing conditions for romaine lettuce in a hydroponic system. I would like to know the optimum fertilizer mix for romaine lettuce grown in a year-round hydroponic system—likely a nutrient film technique (NFT) or deep-pool, floating raft system.

Also, which romaine lettuce varieties are best suited for hydroponic production? Are there any published trials available?

A: An "optimum" nutrient solution for lettuce would regularly be adjusted depending on the environmental conditions. The formula would also need to be specifically modified for your water supply since it may contain dissolved minerals that need to be taken into consideration. However, here is a general hydroponic lettuce formula (below) that has been used to grow commercial romaine (cos) lettuce. This formula is suitable for both NFT and raft systems since it has been formulated to provide the plants with the levels of nutrients they will remove from solution in the correct ratios.

It's important to match the variety of lettuce grown with your particular environmental conditions or climate. Most cultivars that perform well in soil in your area will do well in hydroponic systems. With romaine lettuce, like with many other types, you need to consider whether your given environmental conditions will put any stress on the crop. For example, warmer temperature levels—above 79°F—put stress on lettuce crops and often lead to problems, such as premature bolting, tipburn, etc. Low temperatures and light levels can slow growth rates and lead to coloration problems. There are many good cultivars that have been bred for specific crop production conditions.

Q: How do I grow mesclun greens in a hydroponic system? Drip irrigation seems to be the most economical but still it looks impossible considering that the requirement for mesclun is only 4 inch leaf size. I was thinking about overhead gardening in inert media. What you think about this idea?

A: Mesclun mixtures or seedling mixtures are usually grown in large, shallow trays of media that is either irrigated via drip, flood and drain, or drain to waste type systems. Trays would commonly be about 2 inches deep with a free draining media (often coarse sand and vermiculture/perlite or similar). The seeds are sown thickly into this media, covered in clear plastic, and allowed to germinate at around 60–75°F. After about 3 weeks growth, the leaves are all cut and the trays of seedlings left to regrow for another cutting in about 10 days time. Some growers get a few cuts from each tray, other completely cut down to media level and then resow again. Other producers let the seedlings get quite large then remove individual leaves as they become large enough, leaving the plants to regenerate. Mechanical harvesters like small lawn mowers are used in many larger commercial operations to harvest large volumes all at once. There are a number of different mesclun seed mixtures you can buy these days—Asian, spicy, Brassica mixtures, lettuce mixtures, and many combinations. What is probably most important is that no grit or particles from the growing media end up in the harvested leaves, as it can be difficult to remove. For this reason, some growers use rockwool slabs for mesclun production and reseed into the slab many times before discarding. —*L.M.*

Running a few trials to determine which cultivars will perform the best in your system would be wise. Some of the larger commercial seed suppliers may have also carried out trials on their different cultivars in hydroponic systems under similar environmental conditions to yours so it's worth asking their advice. We have tried some cos varieties from Johnny's Selected Seeds (www.johnnyseeds.com) in an NFT system under standard greenhouse conditions. While most performed well, the cultivars that did particularly well were 'Corsair,' 'Kalura,' and 'Rosalita.' Also, new cultivars come out every year so check with your seed supplier.

Hydroponic Romaine Lettuce Nutrient Solution
(Amount of Salts to Dissolve Into Two 20-Gallon Stock Solution Tanks)

Part A
Nutrient Salt Ounces
Calcium nitrate 903.6
Potassium nitrate 105.4
Iron EDTA 60.20

Part B
Nutrient Salt Ounces
Potassium nitrate 105.4
Monopotassium phosphate 143.3
Magnesium sulfate 307.3
Manganese sulfate 9.63
Zinc sulfate 1.33
Boric acid 4.70
Copper sulfate 0.36
Ammonium molybdate 0.123

—L.M.

Q: After 8 weeks, my lettuce ('Black Seeded Simpson') turned out bitter. It was well watered, fertilized, and the soil was light. I am located in Suriname, South America. Can you tell me why it is bitter and what is going on in the plant?

A: There are two main causes of bitterness in lettuce, which should otherwise be succulent and have no real flavor. The most likely cause is that the plant was about to "bolt" or go to seed. The development of the flower stalk results in bitter compounds being produced and accumulating in the plant at this stage. Or, the plant may have been slow growing and under stress. A lack of moisture, high salinity, over fertilization, incorrect nutrition, poor environmental control (such as overly warm conditions), will all cause a buildup of bitter flavors.

However, I think after 8 weeks, if the plant was mature and large enough to eat, then the problem was aspects of the physiology of the plant that tend to cause premature bolting under warmer climatic conditions, which you probably experience in your area of the world. Even in fairly temperate climates, bolting and bitter flavors are a problem in some lettuce types. You may not have even realized that the plants had gone into a flowering phase since in the early stages, the plant doesn't show any outward symptoms. However, as the bolting continues, inside the center of the plant, the stems starts to gradually elongate and spiral upwards. Sometimes, if you pull the leaves of the mature, harvested lettuce, you can see the stem on which the leaves are attached has started to stretch upward. At this stage and for some days beforehand, the plant has started to produce quantities of latex, a sticky, white substance that is very bitter and can be seen when the stem is cut. Bitter compounds also build up and accumulate in the leaves just before the plant begins to initiate the flower stem in the center of the plant.

The best way to prevent this is to grow the plants quickly, with plenty of moisture, just enough nutrient for growth, and try to modify the environment to keep the plants cooler. Overhead shading works well on lettuce crops to drop down temperatures levels and reduce the stress on the plants. Also, you may need to harvest the plants younger at a smaller size, before the bitterness has had a chance to develop in the foliage. —L.M.

Q: I read recently about some of the factors affecting the taste of lettuce, but cannot recall where to find it. Can you briefly give me a guideline as to the prime factors that can affect the taste of lettuce?

A: Succulent leafy crops such as lettuce can be prone to bitter flavors when the crop has been slow growing under less-than-ideal conditions (such as those often experienced in winter). Also, if the nutrient solution's electrical conductivity (EC) has been too high for the environmental conditions, this can also increase the occurrence of the compounds that cause bitter flavors. Lettuce and most other salad greens prefer a low nutrient EC level since we grow these crops for succulence rather than flavor. Higher solution conductivities are used for the fruiting crops such as tomatoes, where we are trying to increase the flavor compounds in the fruit. Bitterness in lettuce has been linked to nitrate accumulation in the foliage and this can occur in winter when plants are growing slowly, although not all bitter flavors are due to nitrates.

The best solution for this problem is to grow the crop for a few days before harvest in a dilute (one-third strength) solution. For the best crisp, succulent texture, grow as quickly as possible with a hydroponic solution concentration lower than that used for flavorful crops such as tomatoes. Lettuce does best (flavor and texture wise) at a hydroponics solution EC of 0.5–1.2.

Another cause of bitter flavors in lettuce crops is when the plants starts to "bolt" (go to seed). The production of the seed head tends to cause the development of stronger flavors and this is a major problem under warmer conditions when premature bolting can occur in even young plants. The best solution to this is to grow cultivars that are slow to bolt or have a good degree of heat tolerance. Also, using shading of the crop and cooling to drop temperatures down to acceptable levels and prevent bolting will help prevent bitter flavors.

There is also a genetic factor. Some varieties of lettuce are more prone to bitter flavors under certain conditions than others, so it's well worth carrying out a few taste tests on different varieties to ensure you are using the best cultivars for your system. —L.M.

Q: I grow lettuce, green stem pak choi, kale, coysum, and water convolvulus using an NFT system with one nutrient tank. Temperatures are very hot and very humid. Outside temperatures get up to 95°F while growing room temperatures can be 122°F during the day.

I have problems with browning of the lettuce root system and leaf wilting during the day. Eventually, all of the roots became black and the crop was lost. Sometimes, I also found stubby roots on a few plants (also lettuce). I've never had this problem before. The problems just happened on the lettuce while the other crops were still OK—but the growing rate is very slow.

For fertilizer I use N=43 ppm, P=16.5, K=52.4, Ca=34, Mg=10, and S=13. Could you give me a suggestion for fertilizer for my mixed crops and suitable ppm levels. I usually use between 600–1,000 ppm.

A: Unfortunately, the temperature conditions you mention (95–122°F) make the production of healthy lettuce plants rather difficult. When the root system becomes browned and roots die off, the plant is less able to transport the necessary water and nutrients to the foliage and wilting will commonly occur—particularly during the middle of the day.

There are a number of potential causes for the dieback in the root system. It could be simply that the temperatures in the root zone are too high. Lettuce plants will develop a thin, browned root system once nutrient solution temperatures rise above 77°F. Also, in warmer conditions, a lack of dissolved oxygen in the root system can become a major problem since nutrient at 77°F or above holds much less oxygen than cooler nutrient. Also, at the temperatures you mention, certain root pathogens can infect the plants rapidly—particularly were the plants are stressed by their growing environment.

Cooling the nutrient solution, using either refrigeration or a simple evaporative cooling system, would assist lettuce growth under these conditions. It would also be a good idea to check for the presence of pathogens. There are some quick and simple pathogen test kits on the market these days, so you could do these tests yourself.

The nutrient levels you are running are very low and do not correspond to the TDS value you are getting. If you have the levels of nutrients in your solution that you reported but your meter is reading 600-1,000 TDS, you may have a serious accumulation of sodium or other unnecessary ions in your nutrient solution. Under high light intensities in tropical conditions, once the solution and air temperatures have been corrected, a higher level of nutrients is required—especially nitrogen—for the production of lettuce and pak choi.

Hydroponic researchers in Singapore have found that increasing the conductivity factor (CF) to 20 and above (which would be an EC of 2.0 and above) and providing a corresponding increase in nitrogen allows plants such as lettuce and Chinese vegetables to develop most rapidly. However, this was in aeroponic production where the temperatures were very well controlled. In NFT in the Philippines, we have shown that growing lettuce under high light intensities and temperatures using a formula high in nitrogen and a water conditioner to prevent tipburn allowed very rapid growth and high quality production. The formula used is as follows:

Tropical Lettuce Nutrient Levels (in ppm; CF=15.3)

Nitrogen	190
Phosphorus	25
Potassium	98
Magnesium	25
Calcium	216
Sulfur	33
Iron	4.90
Manganese	1.97
Boron	0.7
Zinc	0.25
Copper	0.07
Molybdenum	0.05

Tropical Lettuce Nutrient Solution
(Grams of Fertilizer to Dissolve Into Two 100-liter Stock Solutions)
Part A

Calcium nitrate	10,803.2
Potassium nitrate	875.9
Iron chelate	500

Part B

Potassium nitrate	875.9
Monopotassium phosphate	1,191.9
Magnesium sulfate	2,554
Manganese sulfate	80
Boric acid	39
Zinc sulfate	11.013
Copper sulfate	3.022
Ammonium molybdate	1.022

—L.M.

Q: I am experimenting with deep pond technology. I have a 4x4-foot tank with 7 inches of nutrient solution. There is an air stone in the bottom, which runs continuously. Styrofoam floats are on top with plants in 3-inch net pots with rockwool cubes. I have a 1,000-watt metal halide light 7 feet above the tank. I am growing only greens. The room temperature is between 65–75°F. The pH is below 5. I am using General Hydroponics Microflora and Floragro as nutrients. Lettuce and basil are growing very well.

However, I cannot seem to get collards and Swiss chard to germinate. If they do, the plants do not develop properly. What is the secret? Also, there is a green film that has started to grow on top of the rockwool cubes. Nothing is growing in the tank or on the cubes below surface level. Any ideas on what it is and how I can get rid of it? Also, are Gordon Creaser's articles on deep pond technology available online or do I have to purchase the back issues?

A: Your floating system sounds to be well constructed with a suitable depth of nutrient and oxygenation. Temperatures of 65–75°F are within a good range for the production of most lettuce, herbs, and salad greens. You might, however, need to bring the pH of the nutrient up to at least 5.8—below 5.0 is not optimal for plant growth. You can do this with a potassium hydroxide solution—and you might want to recheck the calibration of your pH meter.

The green film on the top of the rockwool cubes is algae growing. Algae will only grow where there is sufficient light. Therefore, it is on top of the cubes, which will be receiving the artificial lighting, but not in the tank or on the parts of the cubes that do not receive any light penetration (a well-run float system should not have any light falling on the nutrient in the pond). The algae is a form of plant life itself and uses tiny quantities of nutrients. However, this should not pose any major problems if it is only on the surface of the cubes and not growing inside the pond within the nutrient solution (where it could deplete oxygen and smother plant roots). Removal of algae on the surface of the cubes would be difficult and any chemical used for this purpose is likely to damage the plants and the root system, so it will be O.K. to just leave the algae where it is growing. If you are concerned about the unsightly green slime, you could easily prevent it from growing by making some simple cube covers out of thick plastic, such as Panda film. Panda film is white on one side and black on the other and prevents light from penetrating. The white side should always be up to help reflect the light back onto the plants. You need to make a slit in the square of plastic and a small hole for the plant stem. These "plant collars" work very well for hydroponic plants that are used in other systems as well.

The problem with the collards and Swiss chard that are not germinating well could be due to a couple of causes. Normally, these plants germinate rapidly with a high germination percentage. However if the media is too wet or too hot or cold—or if the seed is old and lost viability—then germination can be affected and any plants that do germinate could be stunted or deformed. Overly damp media also induces a number of pathogens, such as Pythium, which can cause the seed to rot or the seedling to decay (called "damping off"). If you are trying to raise the seedlings in the float system, it is quite possible that the rockwool is getting too wet.

I would suggest that you sow the seeds into small rockwool propagation blocks that have been pre-dampened and sitting on a tray (not in the float system), cover with a sheet of plastic, and keep at a temperature of around 60–65°F. Do not water the cubes again until the seeds have safely germinated. If the seeds are still failing to germinate, dig up the seeds and see if they have rotted in the media. This would indicate that the media was too damp and pathogens are present. If the seed is still intact but has failed to germinate after a few weeks the seed may be old and no longer viable (buy in a fresh batch and try again). Hopefully this will help with your seedling production.

Gordon Creaser's articles are periodically offered online in our Featured Articles section (see www.growingedge.com/magazine/featured_articles/show_articles.php3 for the current selection of articles). You can also search for articles by author on the Website (see www.growingedge.com/magazine/compindex.html). —L.M.

Q: I am growing lettuce in a roof gutter flood-and-drain system with some commercial white perlite and some reddish-coated beads. I have a lot of algae forming. Is this a problem or should I ignore it? If a problem, can I get rid of it easily? This is a home-gardening situation—not commercial.

A: You definitely should try to reduce the amount of algae growing in your system. Exposure to sunlight is what makes algae grow and it will compete with your plants for nutrients in your solution. Algae also has a nasty habit of clogging tubes and other fittings. Although you didn't mention it, I would bet that you don't have a cover on your rain gutter growing trough.

If that's the case, here's what I would recommend. First, if the growing media you are using has become too infested with algae, get rid of it and replace with fresh media. Some of your media might be able to be saved if it doesn't have too much algae on it. If algae is growing on the gutter itself, you should scrub it off before replacing the plants and new media. Make sure you keep the bare roots of your plants moist while cleaning your system.

Then, you will need to create a cover for your gutter. Some home improvement stores carry gutter covers that might fit over your gully. Or you could fashion one out of plant-safe white plastic sheeting. If you can't find white, paint whatever nonphytotoxic (safe for plants) plastic you can find white. Don't use clear or black plastic. Clear will let light in and won't take care of your algae problem. Black would attract too much light and heat and cook your plants roots. You could also cover your gully with plywood. However, you will find that plastic is easier to poke holes into to accommodate your plants stems. One commercial product that is frequently used for this purpose is panda film, which should be available at an area hydroponic retailer (to find a store near you, see www.hydromall.com/stores/index.html). Also, make sure you store your mixed nutrient solution out of direct sunlight.

By blocking the light from entering your rain gutter system, you should find that algae growth is drastically reduced. —D.J.P.

Q: I am going to grow hydroponic Ipomoea aquatica (water spinach). Could you please recommend some information on the nutrient formulation, growing system, environmental conditions, and seed sources for broad-leaved water spinach? I would also like some book sources.

A: Water spinach, also known as kang kong, grows very well in hydroponics but prefers a semiaquatic environment with a flooded root system for the best growth and quality—but it will grow and produce well in nutrient film technique (NFT) systems as well. I cannot find any detailed information on the hydroponic production of water spinach. However, its requirements are similar to watercress and lettuce in terms of nutrients and a standard lettuce or herb nutrient formula will work well for this plant.

The main requirement of water spinach is warm temperatures—much warmer than lettuce or watercress. The seed germinates at around 68–95°F, with germination being poor below 68°F in most cases. Seed is best sown into containers of coarse sand and covered with clear plastic and should germinate within a few days. Ideal growing temperatures are also around 77–86°F, although it will tolerate warm conditions up to 100°F.

The easiest type of system to use is a flooded gravel bed or deep flow system with some media, such as coarse sand, to support the plants. Growth is very rapid and the crop should be ready for a first cut within 4 weeks. The plants can then be left to regrow if not completely cut back at the base. The crop does not have a high nutrient demand and does very well in aquaponic systems, using only the waste from fish as nutrients. A nutrient solution at an electrical conductivity (EC) of around 0.8–1.2 is suitable. Some more detailed information is available in my article, "Hydroponic Water Chestnuts and Other Aquatic Crops," published in The Growing Edge, Volume 9, Number 6, (July/August 1998), on page 43.

Seeds for water spinach can usually be purchased from most suppliers of Asian vegetables seed such as:

• B and T World Seeds (www.b-and-t-world-seeds.com/unique.html)
• Tropical Seeds (www.tropical-seeds.com/avlvh.html)

—L.M.

Q: What guidelines can be used to determine how much shading is needed? 35 percent? 50 percent? 85 percent? San Antonio has a high annual amount of sunlight coupled with high temperatures in the summer, commencing about April through to November. We are producing lettuce and herbs. The process has just commenced and we plan on using shade paint for a once a year application.

A: The general recommendation for climates with a high radiation level is at least 50 percent shade for crops such as tomatoes, etc. and a little higher for cool-season crops such as lettuce and herbs. This shading is not only to reduce potential damage from high radiation levels, but also to help reduce temperatures to acceptable levels (it's also much more comfortable to work under). For lettuce and herbs, the recommendation would be 55–65 percent shade over summer. This shade should be removed as soon as light levels and temperatures begin to drop in the fall. Using a 55 percent shade cloth cover, for example, will reduce average greenhouse temperatures by up to 12°F during the warmest part of the day and this, combined with good airflow, will assist the growth of cool-season crops such as those you are producing.

It can be difficult to get an exact level of shading using shade paint. If you have the type of greenhouse that will support a lightweight shade cloth cover—either over the outside or on the inside—this is a better option. Shade cloth can be purchased in a range of shade levels and made into a cover to suit your greenhouse. There is also less labor involved with a shade cloth in relation to applying and removing shade paint (which also can damage plastic greenhouse cladding). Many growers use "thermal screens," which are rigid layers of shading material that are designed to slide across supports inside the greenhouse above the crop. This is another—more costly, but permanent—option to the problem of crop shading.

Shading in summer will certainly improve the growth and quality of your herbs and lettuce and is worth the expense and time required. —*L.M.*

Q: I read Volume 11, Number 5 through Volume 12, Number 1 of The Growing Edge with much interest. The articles on hydroponics in developing countries and Dr. Morgan's article on greens related exactly to a project that I am considering. As I mentioned I am working in a low income setting hoping to help increase nutrition and, possibly, income. My problem is that I do not have any experience and very little resources. I was hoping that someone there could help me in the specifics of design, starting with the construction of the beds.

I am thinking of simple wood framed beds lined in plastic. I was thinking of 2x4-feet for ease of moving and to plant individual greens separately. Is there a minimum depth they should be? What type of plastic would be best for lining? How much area do I need per pound of greens that I want to grow?

I am also thinking of a flood and drain or a trickle flow system for nutrient delivery. Would there be a benefit of one over the other? How would I determine the specifics for plumbing? How do I size the tank and pump?

I am thinking of perlite or a combination perlite and coconut fiber for the growing media. Would that be best?

I would like to grow organically if possible. How would I find a recipe for a nutrient solution that would be sufficient? What would be the basics of other nutrients if I have problems with organics.

I live in southern Florida and would like to grow all year. Of course, heat in the summer is a major problem. What are some inexpensive ways of dealing with that? Would a simple hoop frame with shade cloth over the beds, a fan to move air, and a chiller for the nutrient be sufficient?

Do you know of any other resources (books, growers, etc.) that might be helpful to get me started?

I will appreciate any help you can offer. I'm sure I will have other questions as I proceed but this will get me started. Thanks.

A: Minimum depth of the beds you are planning would be approximately 5 inches for the crops you are planning (i.e. greens) for other fruiting plants, a greater depth would be beneficial. The best type of plastic for lining these timber beds is a strong, thick black (to help keep light out) plastic sheeting of about 0.10 or 6 ply. I would also recommend you line the base of the grow beds with newspaper or cardboard to prevent any splinters etc from puncturing the plastic sheets. If you would like further details on how to construct these types of grow beds I recommend you get a copy of Peggy Bradley and Cesar Marulanda's book Home Hydroponic Gardens (from Global Hydroponic Network, P.O. Box 151, Corvallis, Oregon 97339), as it has step by step instructions on how to build these types of systems and the materials to use.

There is no accurate way to calculate how much area you need per pound of greens, it will depend entirely on your climate, the exact type of green (e.g. these vary considerably in rate of production and weight), also on the nutrients you use, and a huge number of other factors. You will only get an approximate idea of these figures when you construct you beds and have a try at a few of the different greens crops.

I would suggest that you use a trickle and collect system. That is the nutrient is trickled into the top of the media, where it flows through and around the plant roots and then drains out a collection pipe at the base of the grow bed where it can be recollected and reused. The reason I suggest this is that the flood and drain type beds need to be heavily constructed and fairly strong to support the weight of the nutrient which would fill the bed during the flood cycle. In a 4x2-foot bed this would be a large volume of liquid which would be extremely heavy and would require the beds (if they are on legs) to have a much more sturdy construction, then if you use trickle irrigation.

I would recommend that in order to work out how large you need your pump and tank to be, that you initially construct one of the grow beds, fill it with the media you have selected and then measure how much volume of water it takes to saturate the media to the point where it begins to drain out. This gives a rough idea of how much you will have to water each grow bed to saturate the media at each watering. If you multiply this by the number of beds you intend the final system to have to get the volume that will be delivered at each watering. Make sure that when you buy the tank you intend to use that you take into account that at some later stage you may want to expand your current system, and you don't want to have to replace your tank with a bigger one each time you do this. Also, apart from the amount of solution that will be delivered to the growing beds at each watering, you need to calculate how many waterings you want from each tank top up. If you only want to top up your tank once a week, it will need to be considerably larger than if you top it up and adjust the nutrient each day. Finally, once you have worked out how much nutrient is required per day to be used by the plants, you want a extra reserve in the tank of at least 50 percent (buffer capacity). Also, in a warmer climate such as yours, the larger the volume of water in the tank, the slower the heat build up in the system and the longer it takes for the plants to get heat stressed through an overly warm nutrient solution. These types of system calculations can be fairly complicated, so I would suggest you get hold of a good book which contains these types of formulas and calculations so you can accurate work out what size equipment you should buy. There is a chapter in my book Hydroponic Lettuce Production—Chapter 5 Hydroponic System Engineering—that can give you more details and formulas for these calculations.

In my opinion the best media is coconut fiber on its own—it has close to ideal air filled porosity and water holding capacity. This is provided that the source of coconut fiber you use is low in sodium levels (some are not and this would cause problems with the production of greens). If the coconut fiber you have does indeed have a sodium problem (ask your supplier what the level of sodium is in the fiber), then perlite alone would also be a good media. I assume cost will also need to be taken into account, and coconut fiber tends to be the lower cost media anyway.

Luckily, the crops you are planning to grow (greens) have a fairly low nutrient requirement compared to crops such as tomatoes which produce fruit. If you are keen on the organic production then it might be a good idea to consider using vermicast (worm castings) as your media instead of coconut fiber, or even a combination of coconut fiber mixed with vermicast. The vermicast helps provide a good source of organic nutrients, but you would also need to apply a liquid nutrient. There are several brands of commercially available organic hydroponic nutrients (such as Earth Juice, Pure Blend and the MetaNaturals range) which will give you and excellent, balanced organic nutrient for your crops. However if cost is an option, you could make your own, and again I would recommend you consult Peggy's book Home Hydroponic Gardens pages 113–121, which details how to make compost teas, and other sources of organic hydroponic nutrients. Another option would be a form of aquaponics, which is using the waste water from a small fish farming operation to feed onto you plants, This is a proven and excellent method of organic production (if you want to grow a few fish to provide your nutrients!).

If you decide to use inorganic nutrients (nutrient fertilizer salts) than the nutrient recommendations given in my article on salad greens (Volume 11, Number 5) would be suitable for your type of system. There are also many good brands of bottled pre-made nutrient mixes that would also be suitable if you don't want to mix up your own. Below is a standard lettuce nutrient formula which is used here in New Zealand for lettuce production. This is however designed for a soft water (rainwater) based nutrient. It is important that you obtain an analysis of the water you will be using, then adjust any nutrient formula you want to use for the presence of mineral elements in your water, otherwise imbalances can occur which will compromise crop yields and quality.

Hydroponic Lettuce Formula for Soft Water
(Grams of Nutrient Salts to Be Added to 100 liters of Stock Solution; Dilution of 1:100 Gives an EC of 1.2)

Part A	
Calcium nitrate	7,549
Iron EDTA	260

Part B	
Potassium nitrate	1,703
Monopotassium phosphate	1,198
Magnesium sulfate	2,571
Copper sulfate	2
Manganese sulfate	41.7
Zinc sulfate	2.6
Boric acid	25.00
Ammonium molybdate	1.02

A good shade cloth cover over your grow beds will go a long way to keeping the temperatures down to optimal levels. Air movement will also assist and if you can keep the nutrient cool either by evaporative cooling methods or by a chiller than that would be the ideal situation. Often lettuce plants which have a cool solution can withstand higher air temperatures that they would normally tolerate and this assist with the prevention of problems such as pre mature bolting and tip burn.

Finally, I would also suggest that for a commercial operation, that apart from reading a few good books, that you hire a good consultant as soon as your operation can afford to—many people have made horrible mistakes by taking advice from various sources, or misinterpreting the details given in production books. —L.M.

Q: I've recently started a home brew hydroponics system. I bleached and rinsed the entire system before starting anything in it. I am growing lettuce in a tube system with constant nutrient flow and an air pump in the solution. I'm using a 14-gallon tank, and 9 holes for growing on the top side of the tube. There is little or no light getting to the nutrient solution. The leaf lettuce plants are 4–6 inches in height and seem to be doing just fine—so far.

A possible problem I see starting is an odd odor, much like a fish tank in a pet shop that's been with out a good cleaning for a while. It's not pervasive, you have to sniff the water to notice it or sniff your hands after they've been in the water. (This was due to clean up work, and not for laxness in avoiding contamination from the hands.)

I am using a commercial bloom/flora/micro mix and do not see "dehydrated, used aquarium water" or "dead fish" as a nutrient source.

The water seems to be as clear as it normally is. I did not notice any tint to it that was not the same as a fresh batch of growing nutrient. The hose that sits in the water and the pump did feel slimy. Wiping the hose with a towel removed the feeling.

I've re-bleached the tank, hose, and pump. I can't bleach the entire system as the roots of the plants would have the contaminate.

Ignoring the problem and wishing it would go away sounds great if I could get away from it, but I've got a lot invested in making this work, mostly pride, and I am sure it's just going to get worse.

Suggestions? Algae? Bacteria? What/How do I check to decide what it is and what do I do to correct the issue?

If a UV water sanitation device was added to the system to kill critters in the water, like that in a grocery store bottled water system, what would it do to the nutrients? Thanks for your time and advice.

A: The faint odor you notice in your hydroponic system is not uncommon, and is probably due to algal growth (even through you can't see any appreciable amount of algae within the system). The fact that pump and hose felt slimy confirms that you have algae in your system. As the algae bloom and die, they decompose and produce that faint fish tank smell. Since, the problem is not severe (i.e. no long green stings of algae growth) and the smell faint, it is probably safer to do nothing, I don't expect the problem will get much worse provided you are limiting as much as possible, any light that might be falling on the exposed nutrient anywhere in the system (it only needs to be a tiny amount for algae to grow). The problem with water sanitation of the nutrient while it is in the system is that methods such as UV, ozone, chlorination etc can not only severely damage the plants root system, but UV and ozone also have negative effects on some of the nutrients in solution, making them unavailable for plant uptake. It would be a case of the treatment being worse then the problem with UV sterilization of the nutrient. On the other hand, sterilization of the water used to make up the nutrient, before it is introduced

into the system, may slow the growth of the slime, and will kill most pathogens in the water supply, but this should not be carried out on the nutrient solution. Since the nutrient solution contains a whole range of living microbes many of which are beneficial as well as other plant life such as algae, often an equilibrium will be obtained, where there is a faint smell, but no real damage is done to the plant roots. The best advice I can give is that you ensure there is maximum oxygenation within your nutrient (i.e. by letting droplets fall back into the tank), to ensure the system does not become anaerobic and damage the roots. —L.M.

Q: I am setting up two 30x120 greenhouses during the coming 60 days with the intention of producing lettuce and herbs. Our temperatures in San Antonio, with a southeast wind from the Gulf of Mexico (lots of humidity), ranges from 96°F daytime to 76°F nighttime, almost from end of May through to end of October. I was wondering if running underground both the feed lines and return lines to the holding tank could help in keeping my nutrient solution cool. I will have a concrete holding tank underground. My only experience comes from having helped in the construction of a home with 10-inch galvanized tubing snaked underground under the home, with an exterior inlet on a shady side, then fed through the walls to exit the metal roof, had the house actually too cool. The underground temp here about 30 inches below the soil level is 65°F. I was reading your response to someone else about using a chiller, and also insulating the pipes. Would there be anything detrimental about going underground outside the greenhouse, under the cover of a growing green lawn? Most of our grass here is Bermuda or San Augustine, where if grown 3 to 4 inches leaves little for the sun to reach the soil.

A: Running your nutrient pipes underground will effectively cool your nutrient and shouldn't disturb your lawn. Cooling the nutrient is a great way to keep plants happy in a warmer climate like yours. Going down as much as 30 inches might be a bit excessive (what if you need to access the pipes in the future?). I would imagine that 15-20 inches should suffice without altering the temperature too much. —D.J.P.

I would just like to add that if you have the option, try to install the largest underground holding tank possible and to use it to full capacity. It takes considerably longer for a large volume of nutrient to increase to damaging temperatures than it does with a smaller volume and many hydroponic growers in the tropics use this method to prevent heat build up. —L.M.

Q: I am growing lettuce in my greenhouse. What depth and spacing do I need to allow for the plants?

A: Different types of lettuce will have different recommended spacings. First, you need to find out how large the plants will be at maturity. For example, if they will be 6–8 inches in width at maturity, then you should space the seedlings about 8 or more inches apart. You will want to make the maximum use of space, so when the plants are mature, ideally they should be using all available space without crowding each other and competing too much for available light.

Most lettuce plants are fairly shallow-rooted since they are a short-term crop. If you provide at least 6 inches of depth for the roots system to develop, you shouldn't have any problems. —*D.J.P.*

Q: How do you care (nutrient application, germination, room temperature, amount of light) for lettuce from its germination until you transplant it to your NFT system? I'm planning to set up simple NFT hydroponic system for study purposes and perhaps expand it afterwards after gaining some skills from it.

A half strength complete hydroponic nutrient solution with an electrical conductivity (EC) of 0.6–0.8 can start to be applied once the seedlings have their first true leaves (usually within a week of the first signs of germination). In the few days prior to transplanting, two or three applications of full strength nutrient should be given to harden off the seedlings in preparation for establishment into their new hydroponic system. Temperatures at this stage should be gradually adjusted to the levels that will exist in the NFT system's environment so that transplant shock is reduced.

There is an article in Volume 13, Number 5 of The Growing Edge entitled "Hydroponic Crop Preparation Procedures" that would provide more detailed information on this topic (see www.growingedge.com/magazine/backissues.html). Also, there is a chapter in my book Hydroponic Lettuce Production on raising lettuce seedlings from seed (see www.growingedge.com/store/books_multimedia.php). —*L.M.*

Q: How long does it take for buttercrunch and green mignonette (manoa) lettuce to germinate? Also, do you know if their tastes are similar?

Different types of lettuce will have different recommended spacings. First, you need to find out how large the plants will be at maturity. For example, if they will be 6–8 inches in width at maturity, then you should space the seedlings about 8 or more inches apart.

A: Generally, lettuce plants are fairly easy to raise and care for during the germination to transplanting stage—provided you maintain the correct environment for good development. The optimal germination temperature for most lettuce varieties is in the range of 59–68°F. Germination will be slower at temperatures below 50°F and high temperatures (above 75°F) will inhibit germination of raw seed. Lettuce seed needs light to germinate and is best barely pressed into the media or lightly covered with a thin layer of media, such as perlite or vermiculite. If you are using artificial lights, you will only need a mixture of fluorescent (blue wavelength) and red lights (one or two incandescent bulbs will work) for good germination of lettuce seeds. Once the seeds have germinated (three to seven days), lighting should be gradually increased as the young plants develop up to 100 percent full natural daylight just before transplanting. Shading of the young plants should be used in environments with high natural light and temperature levels to reduce plant stress.

A: Under ideal conditions, buttercrunch and green mignonette should both take between three to six days for the first signs of germination to occur (this will take longer under cooler conditions). I personally think they taste the same. In fact, all well grown lettuce tends to taste the same (rather "tasteless"), unless it has bitter compounds that have developed in the leaves for some reason—usually due to harvesting when overly mature or stress on the plant during growth, which can be caused by high temperature, electrical conductivity, or high light conditions. —*L.M.*

Q: How long does it take to grow lettuce from germination to harvest? Also, how can I find out this information for a variety of other fruits and vegetables?

A: A lettuce plant, under optimal conditions, will take approximately 8 weeks from the first sign of germination to harvest (this is for a green butterhead type lettuce). It can take longer for the crisp head types of lettuce as they are harvested when have formed a heavier head of lettuce. However, some lettuces, particularly the fancy ones that are common in hydroponics, are harvested very young at a small size—often as young as 5 weeks from germination. Lettuce tends to grow rather slowly in the early stages. The time from germination to planting out can be more than half the life span of the crop and the rate of growth speeds up as the plants get larger, with a greater leaf area.

The information on how long a plant will take from sowing to harvest is best obtained from the seed suppliers. The seed packet should state the "days to maturity" for the particular plant and cultivar you're sowing. There are also many seed supplier Websites that have good production guides listing average times to maturity for different crops. —*L.M.*

Q: I am having some major problems understanding hydroponics. Firstly, I am doing an science assignment which is based around which is the more effective way of growing lettuce, the normal soil way or the hydroponic method way. But I don't know what method to use—there are so many ways to grow hydroponically and I'm just confusing myself. I would like some information on how to set up my own low cost hydroponic garden to hold a few lettuces. I would like a way to give these plants their nutrient without using a pump or something. Can I give it to them in a spray bottle or something? If this is possible, I would like to have it as basic as possible.

A: There are some very easy ways to grow a few hydroponic lettuce plants. One way would be to build a small water culture system out of a small Styrofoam cooler. You can find the plans on The Growing Edge Website at www.growingedge.com/basics/easyplans/ezegro.html. One way to simplify this system is to start the lettuce seeds in a small perlite-filled pot. Build the cooler grower as indicated but don't worry about the media-filled cups. Just cut a few holes in the lid of the cooler. Then, when they have grown some and have a few sets of true leaves, just transplant them into the holes cut into the cooler lid. If they need to be supported when still rather small, use bits of clean, sterile sponge in the holes to steady the stem. Make sure the roots are hanging down into the nutrient solution in the cooler. For more details on this modified "Eze Gro" system, see the June 2000 listing at www.growingedge.com/basics/easyplans/getestlab.html.

Another possibility—and this is probably the simplest of all—would be to just grow the lettuce in a perlite-filled pot. Set the pot in a large saucer and then fill the saucer with nutrient solution. The perlite will absorb the nutrient solution from below by capillary action. See www.growingedge.com/basics/easyplans/selfwater.html for more details. The ex-

ample on the Web page uses expanded clay but for lettuce I would recommend perlite.

For your experiment, make sure you provide identical environmental conditions for the different growing setups. Remember to provide the proper growing conditions for the type of lettuce you are growing. Most varieties prefer light that isn't too intense and moderately cool temperatures. —*D.J.P.*

Q: What is the ideal weight for lettuce at harvest time? How many days required for lettuce to be harvested after planting? What is the ideal space between plants for lettuce? 10 centimeters? 15 centimeters? 20 centimeters?

A: It is difficult to give accurate figures for factors such as lettuce weight at harvest, days to maturity, plant spacing and yield per square meter as these can vary widely based on many variables of plant production. For example, some lettuce plants, particularly those grown in warmer climates are harvest at a very early, immature stage before they have a chance to bolt or go to seed, hence the ideal weight at harvest can be anything from 80–400 grams. This is also dependant on cultivar, the smaller, fancy types of lettuce are much lighter than the heavier crisp head or iceberg type of heading lettuce which may be harvested at around 300–400 grams. Often the ideal weight at harvest time is also very dependant on what the market requires—some markets prefer smaller heads, others (such as restaurants, etc.) may prefer a much larger head of lettuce.

As with the ideal weight at harvest, days to maturity again varies widely, depending on cultivar, season, the environment, nutrition and at what stage the crop is harvested. In general, hydroponic lettuce can vary from 21 days upwards (sometimes up to 90 days under unfavorable conditions), but in your climate, growth should be rapid. Also seed companies should give you an indication of the days to maturity of the different lettuce cultivars you can buy, and this would be a good guide.

Again, plant spacing depends on a number of factors, with the cultivar or type of lettuce being a major one. Also the level of light—a higher planting density can be achieved where light levels are higher. For the smaller cultivars of fancy lettuce than 16–25 plants per square meter of bed would be a general guide. This is lessened to nine plants per square meter for the larger heading types of lettuce. I hope this gives some insight into lettuce production for you—no doubt you will soon get accurate figures as the crop grows and develops, yields do tend to differ between growers, so the best data will always be that obtained from you own crop. —*L.M.*

Q: Could you please advise on the sowing of watercress to be grown in greenhouse on water?

A: Watercress seeds are easily grown into cubes of moist media such as rockwool or into cells or pots of coarse river sand and vermiculite and covered with plastic. The media needs to stay fairly moist (even have the base of the pots partially flooded, if possible) since the seeds germinate most rapidly where there is plenty of moisture. The seeds are fairly small and should be scattered over the surface of the media (a salt shaker with a mixture of fine sand and seeds can help spread these). Germination will occur within a week at 60–68°F.

Most commercial growers don't raise plants from seed as the tiny seedlings can take quite a long time before they are large enough for transplanting. Watercress is usually propagated by taking a stem (15 centimeters long) and placing the end into running water or a hydroponic system—such as a float or nutrient film technique system. Rootlets will form on the nodes (if not already prevent on the cut stem) within two days and the plant will be well established within 10 days (compared with four to five weeks from a sown seed). Smaller growers can purchase a bunch of fresh watercress stems and obtain a large number of plants within a couple of weeks by planting these out into a hydroponic system. —L.M.

Q: I have some questions about watercress. What's the correct pH level of fertilizer solution? Do I need to oxygenate the water via an oxygen pump and air stone? How many hours per day? Do I need to circulate the water via a submersible water pump? How many times per day? How many minutes or hours per cycle? When circulating the water, is it done below the water level or above the water level, causing a splashing effect? What does the root system look like? How long do the roots get? Does the root system need something to cling to or can it be free-floating?

I intend to grow this in a aquarium used to raise fish (without the fish). Is there a specific size that the aquarium must be (gallons)?

A: The optimum pH is around 5.8 but the allowable range is 5.6–6.2. If you are using a float system, the nutrient needs to be aerated 24 hours a day. A long, thin air stone is the best sort to use (one that is 1 foot or so long). If you are growing in a nutrient film technique (NFT) system, the best way to aerate the solution is to have the nutrient fall from a height back into the nutrient tank. This introduces dissolved oxygen into the nutrient in the most efficient way.

Again, if you are using an NFT system or a modified NFT system (a gravel bed system as is commonly used for watercress), the flow needs to be continuous. Watercress prefers a "streamlike" environment. This also helps keep temperatures down to optimum levels as watercress is a cool-season crop. You can use a submersible pump for this but other pumps can also be used to recirculate the nutrients.

If you can circulate the water to create a splashing effect, this will introduce some oxygen into the system and keep the water mixing. However, if you have a small fish tank, you really don't need circulation, splashing, *and* an air stone—just a good air pump and long air stone alone will be enough to introduce oxygen and generally move and mix the nutrient. The roots can certainly be free floating, provided the plant itself has some form of support, such as a polystyrene float. The root system on a mature watercress plant can be up to 1 foot long and quite dense. However, it can be trimmed and the plant will continue to grow or new stems can be easily rooted when the plants get too big for the tank. The root system in watercress is well branched and quite fibrous.

The aquarium should be fine but the tank should be covered in lightproof plastic to provide darkness in the root zone. This will prevent the growth of algae, which can be very rapid in a small, enclosed container exposed to the light. The size of the aquarium depends on how many watercress plants you want to grow. One small plant could be grown in a small fish bowl of only a couple of gallons. If you want to grow a number of watercress plants to maturity, a bigger tank is better. You will need to constantly trim the plants since watercress spreads rapidly. Make sure the plants are in a position to get good light levels. —L.M.

Q: Could you tell me how I could grow watercress in my pond in the U.K. (in the midlands)?

A: The simplest method would be to obtain some watercress seed and sprinkle this around the damp edges of your pond into some fine sand during spring. The seed should germinate rapidly and colonize all the edges of your pond. However, watercress is extremely invasive and you may end up with a major weed problem that's difficult to eradicate and could choke the surface of your pond. Watercress, once established, spreads rapidly via its creeping stems that form roots at each node. It also readily self seeds.

A better solution might be to grow some seedlings in plastic pots that could be pushed into the shallows of your pond and to regularly cut these to prevent the stems from escaping into the rest of the pond. Germinate the seeds on a mixture of coarse sand, leaf litter, and/or potting mix with a small amount of soluble fertilizer to get them going. After planting in the pond they will find their own nutrients.

A more high-tech way of growing watercress is on "floats" that will float on top of your pond—wind permitting! Floats can be made of polystyrene or timber with small holes drilled through to support the watercress seedlings. The roots dangle down into the pond and will rapidly develop into a large root mass that extracts nutrients from the pond water. This is actually an ancient type of hydroponic system that works well in sheltered areas. These floating systems are used as large-scale production systems under protected cultivation for crops such as cress, lettuce, and other salad greens—but they work well outdoors as well. The watercress plants may die back in winter under freezing conditions, but will regenerate in spring from underground root systems and from seeds dropped from the previous year. Cut stems will happily grow inside on a sunny windowsill in water for a number of weeks. —L.M.

Q: I've been growing orchids for a long time now. Recently I decided to try hydroponics and changed about 60 percent of my collection to it. So far, they are very happy and seem to like it.

But the more I read, the more confused I get. Could you please recommend a book about growing hydroponic orchids? Also, could you please tell me what is the correct recommended ppm, pH, feeding schedule, fertilization for orchids? I've heard that orchids are intolerant of high conductivity.

A: Most orchids grow and produce well in hydroponic cultivation as long as some careful attention is paid to the media, watering, and nutrition. The specific recommendations for each genus depend on the requirements of each type, which is just as true for hydroponics as for any other growing system.

Orchids comprise one of the largest plant families on Earth and consist of numerous genera, each with its own preference for environmental conditions, pH, media type, and nutrition. So we can't simply lump all orchids under the same requirements. This may be where some confusion arises. Also, a lot of misinformation is disseminated that after a while, through repetition, becomes "fact."

A very general recommendation as far as media and nutrients go for orchids would be to use a well-drained media with plenty of aeration—one that can drain completely between waterings. Most orchids come from environments where rainfall is heavy for a short time. Most commercial orchid production is carried out in coarse media, such as bark or coconut fiber chips. Hydroponic producers have been known to successfully use rockwool and sphagnum moss for Cymbidium and Phalaenopsis. Some orchid types, such as Paphiopedilum, are very intolerant of wet conditions around the base of the plant, so a coarser media is preferable.

Nutrients in hydroponics can be applied to good effect by adjusting the balance of minerals between summer and winter growth and flowering phases. For example, a nutrient of 0.8–1 EC may be applied with each watering during warm, active growth periods. This formulation may consist of an N:K ratio of 1.3:1. This ratio can be reversed for flowering periods.

The reason orchids are said to have a low tolerance of nutrient solution with a high EC is because the general recommendation is that the media should be allowed to dry partially between waterings. Excessively strong nutrient would cause salt damage to the roots as the media dried. An EC of 1.2 should be the maximum. The recommended pH level will depend to a great extent on the type of orchid being grown and where it originated. This can vary from acidic (pH 5) to alkaline (pH 7.5). Again, this is an advantage of hydroponics in that the pH can easily be customized for the plant type.

Some of the best information on growing orchids comes from the orchid societies from around the world and from specialist suppliers of orchids. Also, Jack Ross recently put out a book on hydroponic orchids called The World of Orchids—A Practical Guide to Cultivating Orchids in Soilless Culture (Casper Publications, Sydney, Australia, 2001). —L.M.

Q: I would like to know if it is possible to grow vanilla bean hydroponically.

A: Vanilla is a member of the orchid family (Orchidaceae). One of the most important aspects to producing any type of orchid in hydroponics is selection of the right kind of media. You will need an inert, sterilized media which is coarse and very free draining—this might be expanded clay, pumice, scoria, river sand, coarse bark chip, charcoal or anything which might be similar. You will also need to be careful with your nutrient, in that the plant is not overfed or over watered. A standard nutrient formula can be used, but at half the normal strength to an EC level of 0.5. The vanilla orchid is a climbing plant so you will need to provide supports for the aerial roots to attach to and if you want to produce the actual vanilla pods, then you will also need to carry out hand pollination of the flowers. Many good orchid books contain cultural information on this plant, so its well worth finding out some of these details before you attempt to grow any. —L.M.

Q: I have a couple of orchids and since I am a beginner am not sure if what is happening is common. After the orchids went through their flowering process, the very base of the stem including leaves yellows and falls off but new sprouts are growing. Is this a common growth pattern for orchids?

A: No, it is not ideal for the leaves and stem of an orchid to turn yellow and fall off. This probably means that the plant was receiving too much water. If treated properly, orchid growth will last for years. In fact, a mature orchid can usually be determined by the number of leaves it has. A healthy 3- to 5-year-old orchid might have 4-6 large leaves.

But all is not lost! I'm glad to hear that you have some new growth coming up. If you treat your orchids well, the new growth should provide new leaves and shoots. Although there are *many* different types of orchids and you should find some specific documentation on how to care for the types you are growing, here are some general guidelines.

The water you use to water your plants needs to be at room temperature. Use a special watering can or jug for your plant water and keep it full. Tap water usually contains chlorine, which is bad for plants. Fill your plant water jug (no lid) and let is stand for a few days before using it. Let the substrate dry out between waterings. Most orchids like a warm, sunny, humid environment. Cooler temperatures will cause the orchid to go into dormancy. The substrate you have the orchid planted in should be light, airy, and specifically created for an orchid environment. Orchid substrates usually consist of dried fern roots, peat moss, charcoal, pumice, and shredded bark. You can buy orchid-specific substrate at most garden centers. When a flower has finished blooming, remove it about 1 inch above the next lower "eye." This next eye should produce the next bloom.

Again, I would recommend that you find some documentation on how to specifically care for the type of orchids you are growing. You might find some good information through the American Orchid Society (www.orchidweb.org/). —D.J.P.

Q: I am an orchidist who has a great deal of success using hydroponics across many genera with excellent results. However, I wish to switch over to aeroponics instead of the passive hydrocultural method I have been using.

In regards to the special needs of orchids, namely high humidity and excellent ventilation, my observations, as well as those of my other friends and acquaintances in the AOS, is that quite a few of them do not like being continuously sprayed nor wish to be subjected to traditional ebb-and-flow systems (I am aware that Phragmipediums are one of the even fewer exceptions). Unfortunately those few happen be some of the more desirable species and hybrids.

Then I think I hit upon it: Other than some very slight structural and electrical changes, what would your thoughts be on the use of an ultrasonic fogging system?

I know I could construct a sonic transducer and delivery system suitable for my needs but I am not sure if it would work quite the way I am theorizing or if the 5 to 20 micron size droplets could suitably suspend the nutrient solution within themselves.

A: Your idea is most interesting and I cannot see a reason why it wouldn't work. I would suggest you work on the principle of providing two separate environments: the root environment in a sealed aeroponic chamber with intermittent nutrient solution misting and an aerial environment above the root chamber lid that you can modify to the correct conditions for whatever orchid species you are growing.

The best nutrient solution droplet size for aeroponics is around 20–50 microns for maximum water and nutrient absorption and uptake. You could experiment with your plants to determine just what the best droplet size is for orchids. Like most other plants, orchids can benefit from the excellent aeration that can be achieved in aeroponic systems. I would hypothesize that you will achieve an increase in growth rates and plant health in your new system. —L.M.

Q: I am interested in growing vanilla in New Zealand. The climate here is not tropical. Can it be done and how would I go about doing it?

A: While there is good information on the production of Vanilla planifolia on many Websites, (see gears.tucson.ars.ag.gov/book/chap9/vanilla.html) there seems to be a lack of any details on its hydroponic nutrient requirements. Vanilla is not widely grown hydroponically since it is a large vine that prefers to climb trees for support—up to a height of 75 feet—making it difficult for protected cultivation. I assume a standard orchid nutrient formula would be suitable for hydroponic vanilla. However, it is likely that these plants would need a specifically designed formula based on their rate of growth and tissue mineral levels.

General Hydroponic Orchid Nutrient Solution (Grams of Fertilizer Salts to Dissolve Into Two 100-liter Stock Solution Tanks; 1:100 Dilution Rate Will Give an EC of 1.5 and pH of 5.9)

Part A
Calcium nitrate 9,281.3
Potassium nitrate 1,347.7
Iron chelate 500

Part B
Potassium nitrate 1,347.7
Monopotassium phosphate 1,288.9
Magnesium sulfate 2,352.8
Manganese sulfate 80

Zinc sulfate 11.01
Boric acid 39
Copper sulfate 3.02
Ammonium molybdate 1.02

(Source: Nutron 2000+ Edition 3 hydroponic nutrient formulation software; www.suntec.co.nz/nutron.htm)

—L.M.

Q: What are the needs of pH on orchids? Also, I was wondering how an orchid is propagated?

A: Most orchid species produce the best results when grown in a pH range of 5.0–6.0. But, because there are so many different types of orchids, it would be a good idea to find out what the specific requirements are for the orchids you are growing. We have some information on growing hydroponic orchids in The Online Hydroponic Q&A Archives on our Website (see www.growingedge.com/community/archive/search.php3?query=orchid&c=all).

Although many species of orchids produce a profuse amount of seed, very specific conditions must exist for them to germinate and grow into plants. Many orchid breeders germinate seedlings by using nutrient solutions in flasks that are stabilized with agar jelly. Meristem culture, where tiny pieces of orchid tissue are grown in agar jelly under sterile conditions, is also used. These processes require a fair amount of skill and knowledge. Many orchid growers simply buy flasks of seedlings from orchid breeders or buy young plants at garden centers.

There is a good book out now on the hydroponic culture of orchids called The World of Orchids—A Practical Guide to Cultivating Orchids in Soilless Culture by Jack Ross (see www.growingedge.com/store/books_multimedia/view_item.php3?PID=54). If you are considering getting into growing soilless orchids, this might be a good book to have on your shelves. —D.J.P.

Q: Has anyone had much success growing cacti hydroponically?

A: Yes, cacti can be grown hydroponically, provided a couple of simple rules are followed. Firstly, the media used must be free draining and not retain too much moisture. Substrates such as fine gravel, river sand, scoria, expanded clay, etc. provide the idea root conditions for cacti. Secondly, the nutrient solution must be fairly dilute and not applied too frequency. A standard nutrient mix, at half the normal strength (EC of about 0.5) is suitable for most cacti and succulents. This should be applied often enough to give good growth, but the media needs to dry out a little between irrigations. Despite what many people think, cacti while being

able to survive dry infertile conditions, do actually grow considerably faster when supplied with moisture and a little fertilizer. —L.M.

Q: I have an English ivy growing in a soilless mix. I am having problems with the leaves drying out, although I am watering every day. I have recently transferred the plant into a larger container, approximately six inches. I give it half a fertilizer stick once a month. It's in a very bright location on top of the fridge in the kitchen. It seems to go through periods of full green leaves to dry leaves and this time is much worse than any other occurrence. What can I do to remedy the situation?

A: If you are growing your ivy in a soilless mix, you need to be watering it with some type of hydroponic nutrient solution—not just plain water and fertilizer. The fertilizers used in traditional, soil-based gardening are designed to supplement the nutrients that occur in healthy, good soil. But if you're growing in a soilless mix, you need to provide ALL of the nutrients the plant needs through the nutrient solution. Hydroponic nutrient solutions are designed to provide all of these necessary nutrients to your plants. If you aren't using a hydroponic nutrient solution to water your plant, I would imagine that the ivy's dry leaves are a direct result from nutrient deficiencies.

Hydroponic nutrient solutions are readily available—in both organic and inorganic configurations—at hydroponic retail stores (see www.hydromall.com/stores/index.html for a store near you) and through online stores.

I have an English ivy growing in a 50:50 mix of perlite and peat moss (soilless) that I feed with inorganic hydroponic nutrient solution as well as one in soil that I water regularly and feed with soil fertilizer every other month during summer. The plant in the soilless mix grows about twice as fast as the one in soil. —D.J.P.

Q: Can one grow maidenhair fern with hydroponics? If yes, what pH and EC would be used? Finally, what formula would be recommended for the nutritional medium?

A: Yes, maidenhair ferns grow very well in hydroponics if provided with the correct environmental conditions. The pH level is best maintained at 5.8 and the electrical conductivity (EC) in a media-based system needs to be fairly low (around 0.8 mS cm-1) since the ferns are slow growers. The plants prefer a substrate that has a good quantity of fibrous material incorporated into it, such as coarse coconut fiber (low-sodium coir) or peat, which also holds moisture well. This is best used on top of a layer of gravel for drainage. A general houseplant nutrient formula will suit most ferns in hydroponics, but the important thing to consider is the environment.

Maidenhair ferns must have reasonably high humidity levels and shaded conditions to thrive. Full sun will burn the delicate foliage and cause the plant to die back, as will high temperatures. Humidity can be increased around the plants via evaporation from the media or by regular misting of the plants under a shade. If the plants begin to show any signs of leaf tipburn, scorching or burning of the foliage, or an overall dull coloration of the leaves (as opposed to a bright green), then the plant's environment needs to be changed. —L.M.

Q: I'm growing Echinodorus blheri (Alismataceae) in a hydroponic system. From October to April the plants have shown tipburn. Could you suggest how to solve this matter?

A: Echinodours blheri, or Amazon sword plant, is an aquarium plant that's generally grown in a submerged environment, which I assume your hydroponic system is providing. Given enough light, these plants grow quite quickly and require good nutrition, although deficiencies can occur—the most common being iron and calcium. Being a tropical plant, they prefer conditions around 75–82°F with a pH of 6.5–7.5.

There are a number of factors that might cause tipburn in such a plant. A deficiency of calcium in the nutrient solution could be one factor. Also, too high light, temperature, or electrical conductivity (EC) levels may be another cause, particularly if you're noticing this condition at certain times of the year—if the plants are receiving natural light. Temperatures over 82–84°F may induce some tipburn when radiation levels are high. Also, the quality of the water may also play a role in tipburn developing. High levels of certain mineral salts or chlorine from the water supply could be the cause. If any algaecide products have been added to the water, they're likely to cause tipburn or scorch of aquatic plants. This is a common problem. Products that kill algae, which is a form of plant life, can damage aquatic plants as well. Taking a close look at the plant's environment, water quality, and nutrition should provide the answer to the tipburn problem. —L.M.

Q: I am from the island of Guam and interested in growing roses using hydroponics. We have hot, tropical weather here. Do you have any information, Websites, reading material, old articles, etc. that you could direct me to regarding this topic? Since I am a beginner at this I could also use basic information on system setup (tank, pump, nutrient solution, growing medium—the works).

A: Rob Smith, coauthor of "Hydroponic Crop Production," recommends the following regarding hydroponic roses (this information was taken from pages 287–288 of "Hydroponic Crop Production"):

• All varieties are grown successfully in hydroponic systems (generally hybrid types)

• Recirculating top-irrigated or flood-and-drain media beds are common systems used; bed depth should be 200 mm (8 inches) at a minimum; top irrigation systems usually use dripper hoses or fixed-rate emitters, with one per plant

• Most growers buy their stock from rose specialist propagators

• Nutrient solution starts out weak as plants get established, usually around an electrical conductivity (EC) of 0.4–0.8; after plants are established, this level can be raised to 1.8–2.6 EC

• Quality light is essential for good performance (minimum of 6,000 mW/m2; can go as high as 14,000 mW/m2)

• Daytime temperature should be no lower than 61°F and nighttime temperature should be no lower than 54°F; ideal temperatures are 60–64°F; maximum temperature (and this should be avoided) is around 81°F

• Relative humidity (RH) should be from 68–78 percent

• Ideal nutrient solution pH is 6.3

• The addition of silica (SiO_2) at a rate of 20 percent of content to the nutrient solution will help prevent powdery mildew

This is just a sampling of the suggested cultivation recommendations for hydroponic roses but it should be enough to get you going. Rob's text has many more instructional tips regarding hydroponic cultivation and is one of the best books on the market. He is a regular columnist for The Growing Edge. We have also run several articles in the past on roses in the magazine.

In order to get a good introductory education on hydroponics, I would recommend that you read through the Introduction to Hydroponics questions and answers on The Growing Edge Website as well as the Hydroponic Basics section. Furthermore, I would recommend that you acquire a quality text on hydroponic cultivation to read and then use as a reference guide. The aforementioned book by Rob Smith and Lon Dalton is an excellent one. Here are some other suggestions:

• "Hydroponic Food Production" by Howard Resh
• "Hydroponic Gardening" by Rob Smith and Lon Dalton
• "The Best of The Growing Edge," Volumes 1 and 2

These books can be ordered off The Growing Edge website: www.growingedge.com.—D.J.P.

Q: I am growing gerbera daisies in two types of medium, rockwool and coir. The plants in the coir are doing extremely well—better then the plants in the rockwool. The nutrients as well as the climate conditions are the same. They are in two rows next to each other in a greenhouse and receive the same amount of water. Two drip lines per plant.

The rockwool cubes are 3.5x3.5x2 inches. Six plants sit on a rockwool pad that is 3 feet by 2 inches long by 3.5 inches wide and 2 inches deep. There is quit a bit of algae growing on the pads as well as the cubes.

The plants growing in the coir are in 2.5 gallon pots. They are growing quite well and have little to no algae.

I would like to leave the plants that are already in rockwool where they are. Any suggestions where I might start looking for the problems that are inhibiting their growth?

A: It sounds like the gerberas that you have growing in coir are doing fine. But the plants in the rockwool are being forced to compete with the algae for nutrients and oxygen in the root zone. Since it would be difficult to transplant your gerberas after they have been growing in the rockwool, what you need to do is control the existing algae growth and prevent any more from starting.

Algae grows whenever moisture is exposed to the light. So you need to block light from coming into contact with your rockwool cubes and pad (also called a slab). The way many growers do this is by leaving the rockwool slab in the white plastic wrapper it usually comes in and cutting slits into the top to accommodate the rockwool cubes. Then you can cut some slits into the bottom of the plastic on the slab to facilitate drainage. Many people place the slab into a plastic container that collects the runoff nutrient solution for reuse.

If you have removed the plastic that the rockwool slab came in, you will need to get some and cover your rockwool. Make sure you use white plastic. Black plastic will trap heat and cook your plants roots. Make sure you use plant-safe plastic (nonphytotoxic). If you have your slab in a plastic growing tray, another option would be to just cover the top of the tray with white plastic and cut holes to accommodate your growing plants. —D.J.P.

Q: I have a friend interested in chrysanthemums. What is the best system, nutrient solution, and conditions for this crop? Also, do you know of any published documentation on the hydroponic culture of chrysanthemums?

A: Chrysanthemums are widely produced in many different types of hydroponic systems—most of which are media-based. However, they also grow well in recirculating systems such as the nutrient film technique and flood and drain.

The media used to grow chrysanthemums must be free-draining. Often, raised beds are filled with fine gravel, washed river sand, scoria, pumice, perlite or vermiculite, expanded clay, coconut fiber, and even granulated rockwool. The plants are propagated by cuttings in sterilized sand where they readily root. These are then transplanted into the growing beds, which are usually in a greenhouse or at least under some form of crop protection. Chrysanthemums grown for cut flowers must be of high quality so some protection from wind and rain is important. Chrysanthemum crops grown as pot plants to be sold in flower can also be grown hydroponically—usually on capillary mats that assist with irrigation.

Chrysanthemums have a range of different physiological responses. Some types are induced to flower in response to warm temperatures—59°F and above—independent of the day length (photoperiod). These are early flowering types. Another type responds to the photoperiod—short days of less than 13 hours induce flowering. So growers have to "black-out" the growing environment to provide the short days required to induce flowering. Otherwise, these types will stay vegetative. Also, by providing lighting and keeping the day length longer than 14 hours, the plants can be forced to stay vegetative and prevent flowering until it is required. This technique is used by pot plant growers of chrysanthemums who are aiming to sell their plants in bud or flower on a particular date.

Research has shown that light levels over the range 125–375 J/cm2 per day produce the best growth for many chrysanthemum cultivars and that CO_2 enrichment to a level of 900 parts per million (ppm) will accelerate growth rates. Optimal temperature levels are 71.6–78.8°F day and 64.4–71.7°F once the root system has become established. Lower temperatures of 64°F during the day and 57°F night will prolong the time to flowering. High temperatures of 86°F day 78°F night significantly reduce flower quality and yields.

Chrysanthemums have a high requirement for nutrients, particularly nitrogen (N) and potassium (K). High N is required for the first couple of months of growth but should be reduced as buds are formed. At that point, the K should be increased.

Nitrogen	150–160 ppm
Phosphorus	60–72 ppm
Potassium	120–140 ppm
Magnesium	50–60 ppm
Calcium	170–180 ppm
Sulfur	70–80 ppm

Trace elements should be provided in standard ranges. The recommended EC is 16–22 in media-based systems.

I'm not aware of any books on the hydroponic production of chrysanthemums. However, there are many excellent texts on cut flower production that will provide detailed information on growing chrysanthemums. One good book is Commercial Flower Growing by John P. Salinger, (Butterworths, New Zealand, 1985). There are also a number of other books on general chrysanthemum culture. —*L.M.*

Q: I would like to know how to get started growing vegetables at home. I have a 20x20-foot room. I would like to know how many plants I can grow in this room and how much money it will cost to set up.

A: If you are new to hydroponics and indoor gardening, your best bet would be to check out the "Gardening Indoors" series of books by George Van Patten. Specifically, I would recommend starting with "Gardening Indoors". This book covers all of the basics involved in starting a grow room. Once you have the basics down, you should check out "Gardening Indoors with H.I.D. Lighting" (also by George Van Patten).

These books will cover growing aspects such as how many plants per lamp (it varies depending on the wattage and type of grow light), how to care for your plants, how much money it will probably cost you (including utility costs), how to get the most out of your investment, and many other facets that would be too lengthy to mention here.

A 20x20-foot room will provide adequate space for a lot of plants. However, there are several other aspects you need to consider first. The main issue will be startup costs. The biggest one is how many lights can you afford (to buy and to run)? Higher wattage lamps cover more area but are more expensive. I'd recommend doing some research into startup costs, both by visiting online grow light merchants and by reading some introductory books. —*D.J.P.*

Q: I am very curious if one could grow daylilies hydroponically. If so, which is the best method and type of equipment to use?

A: Daylilies (Hemerocallis spp.) can be grown hydroponically and they do particularly well in media beds—although they can also be grown in nutrient film technique (NFT) systems. They are hardy plants and therefore are good starter plants for folks who are new to hydroponics.

The most important factors with daylilies is to use free-draining media and to adjust the frequency of nutrient application to suit the season. These are easy plants to grow and they can yield an amazing number of flowers if treated well. A media bed of approximately 12–16 inches deep is usually sufficient. Suitable media choices include expanded clay, pumice, a mixture of pea gravel and vermiculite or perlite, and coconut fiber over a 1.6-inch layer of coarse gravel on the base of the bed.

Daylilies tend to from large clumps that can be broken and divided in winter to increase your stock of plants. They can also be raised from seed. Seedlings will bloom in the second year after sowing and this is a good way to raise large numbers of plants—and possibly to develop some new flower colors. Daylilies are dormant in winter, so application of water and nutrients needs to be restricted while they are going through dormancy.

The nutrient solution should have a high potassium and phosphate ratio in spring and early summer for good flower growth and quality. The nutrient solution should be changed to include a higher nitrate ratio in late summer to ensure good vegetative growth and development, which is essential for the plant to build up reserves of assimilates in the root system for the dormancy period. —*L.M.*

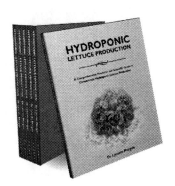

Index of questions

Hydroponic Systems

Q: p. 1
I currently use NFT as a preferred growing system. I am now going to experiment with an aeroponic system of my own making and would appreciate any comments you may have. (More)

Q: p. 1
I would like to start my own hydroponic system but I would like a possible system layout for a small-scale enterprise that will include all the necessary requirements … (More)

Q: p. 2
I am planning a new DWC hydroponic garden. I prefer to build a simple garden rather than buying a costly system. I have done extensive research and decided on this basic plan. I am looking for advice on how I can improve this DWC system. (More)

Q: p. 2
I tried using the floating system, but I have problems with less oxygen in the system. How can I avoid this problem? In other words, how can I add more oxygen to the system?

Q: p. 2
I have a question regarding the angles of decline for NFT trays—specifically an issue regarding stagnant water gathering in the trays. (More)

Q: p. 3
What is the proper slope ratio for an NFT hydroponic system with ten-foot gullies?

Q: p. 3
What are the advantages and disadvantages of modified NFT (adding inert media, such as perlite) compared to the normal NFT system?

Q: p. 3
I need to know what I need and how to construct a homemade drip system.

Q: p. 4
What ways can I power my hydroponic system without using electricity? Can I use natural gas to power it?

Q: p. 4
I'm interested in starting a small indoor hydroponic garden to experiment with growing organic produce, such as herbs, tomatoes, salad greens, and perhaps some other vegetables. (More)

Q: p. 4
What are some benefits and drawbacks of using the wick system?

Q: p. 5
What are the principles of aeroponics? What are some uses and benefits of this growing technique? And is there a simple way in which I can build a system with minimal costs?

Q: p. 5
I am new to hydroponic gardening. My intention is to set up a hobby system in a greenhouse. (More)

Q: p. 5
I live in Hawaii and would like to set up a rooftop hydroponics system. I would like to have about 50 plants growing at one time. (More)

Q: p. 6
I've been working on making my own version of an air-lift top-feeding system analogous in concept to the General Hydro Waterfarm system. However, I have run into one problem. (More)

Q: p. 6
I want to do a project on aeroponics but cannot find information about what nutrients are required for it, what the procedure is, etc. Could you kindly help me?

Q: p. 6
I am doing an experiment on hydroponics with a group of students aged 9-12 since we are on the topic at the moment. In the experiment, they are to grow seeds in hydroponic solution and in normal tap water to study and compare the growth of plants in the solutions given. (More)

Q: p. 7
My biology and chemistry class is putting together a hydroponic system. We need some basic information. (More)

Greenhouse Operations

Q: p. 8
Who builds the best greenhouse for the Pacific Northwest area? I am going to purchase a greenhouse that will also double as a pool and spa house. I will also put in a hydroponic system for personal vegetables and flowers. (More)

Q: p. 8
Where can I find information for converting my garage to a greenhouse? I have metal roof that could be replaced by translucent panels. What things do I need to think about when planning such a project?

Q: p. 8
Is it more beneficial to have a greenhouse for your hydroponic and aquaponic systems? Are there fewer or virtually no plant disease problems using these modalities?

Q: p. 8
If a greenhouse is 11 feet on the south by 16 feet on the east, how much area should be glass on the south- and east-facing sides? Is there a formula? (More)

Q: p. 9
I am planning on converting my greenhouse to hydroponic. I was wondering if I can use a combination of coconut-fiber and vermiculite as a medium for plants, using it similar to regular dirt, with a layer of rocks on the bottom, for drainage, with a layer of landscape fabric to separate the two. (More)

Q: p. 9
What would be the best greenhouse covering for a desert location? I had a very nice one that I built of dual-pane, tempered glass and redwood. (More)

Media, Materials

Q: p. 10
I am used to growing my plants in rockwool. Recently, I tried transplanting some plants into an ebb-and-flow system filled with leca. I am having problems finding a good watering schedule. (More)

Q: p. 10
I would like to know what the recommended depth or volume per plant is for hydroponic and aeroponic containers. I will most likely be using PVC piping. (More)

Q: p. 10
How long does rockwool hold its water? If it was watered well once every day, would it still have enough moisture?

Q: p. 11
My question is on the safety issues of gardening with rockwool. I am using rockwool for hobby gardening around the house and my kids are often helping. (More)

Q: p. 11
I have built a box 8 feet long, 16 inches wide, and 8 inches high out of 3/4-inch pressure-treated plywood … My problem is that I'm losing about a gallon per 1/2 hour of drip. (More)

Q: p. 12
I have been doing research and experimenting with hydroponics for a couple years now. The reason I am writing is that all the books and articles I have read so far are lacking critical information, at least for me, about methods of support for the plants in some of the different systems. (More)

Q: p. 12
How long can expanded clay and similar mediums like Gro Rocks be reused? What is the best way to clean and sterilize these types of mediums?

Q: p. 13
What is the recommended watering for plants in a Dutch garden? I am running a 404 pump with two basket emitters per Dutch pot for bush beans. (More)

Q: p. 13
I have a homemade drip system. I'm using lava rock to grow in. I have two questions. Why does my pH always bounce around? I use bottled water and BC Hydro mix. Should I keep the pump on the whole time the lights are on?

Q: p. 13
Do you know of any interesting uses for used rockwool slabs or used perlite? Can I use the used perlite with finished compost? working compost?

Q: p. 13
I am interested in finding ways of recycling used rockwool cubes. Can they be reused? If not, how does one recycle them?

Q: p. 13
I am a teacher of severely emotionally disturbed students, grades 9-12. We have a small greenhouse of about 10x16 feet and we would like to do some vegetable gardening using hydroponics. (More)

Q: p. 15
I have decided to work hydroponics into my plans. I normally have about 35 students in each class. Do you have any suggestions about starting a small greenhouse structure? (More)

Q: p. 16
What are the conditions influencing the rate of transpiration? (More)

Q: p. 16
What is the photosynthetic active radiation (PAR) needed in micromoles per meter squared for growing rice? (More)

Lighting

Q: p. 17
I know that plants require a minimum level of artificial light to grow efficiently, but is it possible to have too much light? Is there a formula for calculating the optimum light level?

Q: p. 14
I am doing an experiment on if plants need darkness to grow. (More)

Q: p. 17
In regard to specific vegetables and plants, is a vegetative light cycle a standard 18-hour on/6-hour off, and a flowering light cycle a 12/12? Or are there varying cycles to trigger the change? (More)

Q: p. 17
I have heard that you can use a six hours on six hours off cycle. Is this true & are there any benefits to using this—i.e., is it possible that the plants' metabolism is speeded up?

Q: p. 18
How close should I keep the light to the plants? The plants are two weeks old and seem to be a little leggy.

Growing Tips / Fine-Tuning for Results

Q: p. 18
In a sealed room growing environment, what would be the symptom I should look for on my plant's leaves if I had CO_2 levels set too high? Would I even see any symptoms in this situation?

Q: p. 18
I have been using three hydroponic systems in my classrooms for three years now. I get flowers but never any fruit. (More)

Q: p. 19
I have a small flood system (5-gallon reservoir). I have a problem with algae growth in the trays where the plants reside. (More)

Q: p. 19
Some of my new bean shoots are coming up with yellow leaves or yellow edges to the leaves. Can you help?

Q: p. 19
I live in the sunny South, right dab in the middle of Georgia and Alabama. I am considering a greenhouse … (More)

Q: p. 19
Our school has a DRF hydroponic system where the medium for growth is purely liquid. Recently, we have been interested in growing different kinds of flowers, such as daisies, zinnias, petunias, aster powderpuffs, carnations, and chrysanthemums. (More)

Q: p. 20

I am converting an old cow pen, about 10,000 square feet, to grow tomatoes in rockwool. (More)

Q: p. 20

In terms of plant transpiration, what is the difference between fluorescent light, home light, and sunlight?

Q: p. 20

Will ceramic tile work as thermal mass? If so, can it be ordinary ceramic tile?

Q: p. 21

I'd like to know if I can be successful in growing vegetables in my basement in South Dakota. (More)

Q: p. 22

How would you do hydroponics in an outdoor greenhouse in Kodiak, Alaska? (More)

Q: p. 22

This is my first year growing hydroponically and I've been experiencing some problems that I feel may be caused by the accumulation of salts. (More)

Q: p. 21

When growing plants with aeroponics, what are the necessary nutrients needed? (More)

Q: p. 22

I would like to know how long, in seconds, the sprayer must be on and off in an aeroponic system.

Q: p. 23

We have just started growing hydroponically. We grow all our own herbs as well as other vegetables. Currently, we grow each plant in different containers. My question is which plants use which minerals? … (More)

Q: p. 23

Is there design criteria for aerating deep pools? (More)

Q: p. 23

What is the optimal amount of time that it should take to flood a ebb-and-flow system? (More)

Q: p. 24

Other than tomatoes and bean plants, are there any other types of fruits or vegetables that are suitable for hydroponics? (More)

Q: p. 24

There is definitely a knack for being a good green thumb. I have spent a lot of money on all of the finest indoor growing supplies on the market today. I would like to know from germination to harvest the best nutrients, solutions … (More)

Q: p. 25

What is the proper method for topping plants? How much should be cut off, how often?

Q: p. 26

I have made an "aguafarm" that consists of a bucket with nutrients and another bucket with the growing media and plants and an air system … (More)

Q: p. 26

Firstly, I'll describe my setup. I have a tank of nutrient solution with an air pump into it and air stones on the end to increase the solubility of the air into the water … Now the questions: The bottom leaves are turning yellow, why? Is this too much feeding? Are there ways to improve my setup? (More)

Q: p. 25

Do you know of any wholesale or retail U.S. growers of soilless plants that can be potted in the Luwasa hydroculture pot systems?

Growing Tips / Carbon Dioxide (CO$_2$)

Q: p. 27

What type of temperature and humidity levels should I keep my grow area at for maximum carbon dioxide (CO$_2$) absorption?

Q: p. 27

Do plants use CO$_2$ during the day or during the night or both? I am wondering when I should supply extra CO$_2$.

Q: p. 27

With any successful grow room, what is the best procedure for exhaust blower operation—its duration, the best time to enrich with CO$_2$, and the best time to operate the inlet blower?

Q: p. 28

Is it safe to have a worm composter in my hydroponic grow room or would there be a risk of disease or pests transferring to my plants? I'm thinking that it might be a low-tech way to add CO$_2$.

Q: p. 28

In a tightly sealed grow room with CO$_2$ controlled at 1,500 ppm and the temperature controlled with air conditioning, is it still necessary to exhaust the room and bring in fresh air on a regular basis?

Q: p. 28

Where can I find some real data (actual data, not theory) concerning the correlation between the uptake and absorption of CO$_2$, light (lux, PAR), nutrient EC (and each element), pH, RH, and temperature?

Q: p. 29

Does CO$_2$ build up naturally from the plants in a greenhouse during no-light periods? (More)

Q: p. 29

I am a new grower in hydroponics and have just bought a ppm meter … Also, I was thinking of getting a CO$_2$ enhancer. (More)

Temperature Control / Air, Nutrient Solution

Q: p. 30

Can dry ice cool down a room that is too hot? Are there any other methods besides air conditioning that could provide cooling?

Q: p. 30

I am looking for an economical cooling solution for growing lettuce in NFT. (More)

Q: p. 30

I want to drop the temperature in a small 6x16-foot greenhouse from approximately 98°F to around 80°F. (More)

Q: p. 31

What do you think is best for room cooling? Water supply is a major problem.

Q: p. 31

Where can I find plans for an inexpensive evaporative cooling unit for cooling nutrient solution? I live in a tropical area.

Q: p. 31

I live in Phoenix, Arizona. In past years, I have shut my hydroponic garden down when solution temps reached 95°F or higher. This year, I finally set up a cooler for my solution. (More)

Q: p. 31

We have high humidity virtually all year and high temperatures after May and usually through October (75–104°F). If heating the nutrient solution helps in the colder months to warm greenhouse, can chilled solution help in the heat? (More)

Q: p. 32

My temperature in the grow room reaches 100°+ during the day. I came up with the idea of extending a duct from one of the main air conditioning ducts in the attic. Now the problem that I'm facing is that the thermostat is not in this room … (More)

Q: p. 32

I just built an aeroponic system and have an important question. How can I keep the temperature of the nutrient solution down? (More)

Q: p. 33

My nutrient solution is getting hot. (More)

Growing Tips / Tomatoes, Other Vegetables

Q: p. 33

I am just starting with hydroponics and will be growing hot peppers and tomatoes in my basement for the most part. (More)

Q: p. 34

I am building a small, 10x12-foot greenhouse. It will contain three homemade Dutch pot systems growing peppers, tomatoes, cucumbers, and cantaloupes. (More)

Q: p. 35

I would like to grow tomatoes and cucumbers in a hot country like Pakistan. (More)

Q: p. 35

I'm interested in knowing the recommended planting density for tomatoes in the tropics. (More)

Q: p. 35

I am trying to crop tomatoes in Puerto Rico. Our temperature and humidity are high so I want to know how to build a cooling system.

Q: p. 35

Can anyone help me with my tomato? The heat is terrible, low of 71°F, high of 107°F. I do not prune down the leaves anymore to provide more protection. (More)

Q: p. 36

What type of watering system would be good for tomato plants?

Q: p. 34

I want to grow tomatoes hydroponically for my 6th grade science project. I want to know where I can obtain the start up kit. (More)

Q: p. 36

What is the growth rate for tomato plants per day? For example, how many centimeters does the tomato plant grow in one day?

Q: p. 36

I am doing a science project on hydroponic tomatoes for a science fair at my school. (More)

Q: p. 38

Last year, I started a hydroponic garden in my classroom. (More)

Q: p. 39

We have just built a hobby greenhouse and are building an aeroponic system using 18-gallon containers using two spray nozzles per container and 8-inch grow pots with coco fiber and expanded clay. We plan to grow heirloom tomatoes from seed. (More)

Q: p. 40

How often do you need to increase the size of your pots before your plants become root-bound? I have six tomato plants in individual containers in a flood-and-drain system with a clay pebble and coco-fiber medium. (More)

Q: p. 40

I want to put together a drip system for hydroponic tomatoes using rockwool bags. Do I need to have drains on the bags and return the wastewater to a holding tank?

Q: p. 40

My tomatoes are in 1/2 gallon pots with holes the size of the tip of ones pinky. The pots are filled with grow rocks, and are in an ebb and flow. (More)

Q: p. 41

I have an ebb-and-flow system featuring 1/2-gallon pots. The pots are filled with grow rocks. My tomatoes are flooded for 30 minutes four times a day while in vegetative growth. (More)

Q: p. 41

I am a first-time hydroponic gardener. I have a passive system (Emily's garden) with 6 pots. How often should I be changing the nutrient solution/water mixture? (More)

Q: p. 42

What are the optimum lumens needed for 120 dwarf beefsteak tomatoes in a 32x24-ft. area with use of 1000 watt metal halide bulbs? How many bulbs?

Q: p. 42

This was my first year with trying hydroponics and I am growing outdoors. I had fair results with my tomatoes, but would like to know which varieties are best for hydroponics in Colorado.

Q: p. 42

In a drip system, is perlite OK as the sole medium or is it best mixed? (More)

Q: p. 42

I have a few questions. I originally used geolite as my medium for an ebb and flood system. Then the only change I made was switching to Hydroton, that stuff that looks like small round gum. (More)

Q: p. 43

My tomatoes keep splitting on the vine. What causes that and what can I do about it?

Q: p. 43

What would be the primary cause of small tomato size in NFT systems. The tomatoes also have streaks running down the shoulders of the fruit.

Q: p. 44

This is my first time I've tried hydroponics. I'm growing tomatoes and cucumbers in the same system in my greenhouse. Tomato vines grow very high but produce tiny tomatoes that don't seem to ripen. (More)

Q: p. 44

Our tomato plants seem to be healthy. They have many green tomatoes already. They are planted in an old bathtub filled with sandy loam and several bags of Miracle-Gro Garden Soil (about half and half). (More)

Q: p. 45

I have been growing eight tomato plants from seed over the past three months. I put the plants outside for the second time on a warm 75°F day. (More)

Q: p. 45

My 5-month-old tomato plant is 6 feet tall and has 20+ green fruit on it. The tomatoes are small for what is called a beefsteak variety, 'Trust,' and they don't show any sign of ripening. (More)

Q: p. 45

I want to grow tomatoes in my Megagarden system. It is 2x2 feet and has 15 rock baskets in it. I'm using a 400 MH. I would like to know how to keep all the plants around 1-2 feet high … (More)

Q: p. 46

I am experiencing yellowing and brittle roots in my lettuce but the arugula, basil, and tomatoes that share the same hydroponic bed and nutrient tank do not manifest such tendencies. (More)

Q: p. 46

I have tomato seedlings growing outdoors. I want to bring them inside because it does frost every now and then in San Diego in the wintertime. Would changing sunlight to indoor fluorescent light stress the plant very bad? (More)

Q: p. 47

The air coming out of my fan jet tube causes the tops of my hydroponic tomatoes to shake quite a bit. Can these windy conditions cause any physiological disorders?

Q: p. 47

I plan on growing tomatoes hydroponically in a small greenhouse (16x8). Since I live in Las Vegas where the average temperature is over 100° in the summer, I will have an evaporative cooler running to keep the temperature down. My question is, should I be concerned about the CO2 levels for proper growth?

Q: p. 48

I am trying to grow tomatoes hydroponically for the first time. The plants are outside and seem to have a very low tolerance to daytime temperatures over the mid 80s. (More)

Q: p. 48

I could really use your help regarding an improvised hydroponic system I made. (More)

Q: p. 49

I have a yellow pear tomato plant that is doing extremely well. However, the stem has developed small, white, thorny "daggers" growing on them. Do you have any idea what these daggers are?

Q: p. 49

I have several tomato plants that are just now getting tomatoes. I've noticed that some of them kind of have ridges around the sides instead of being perfectly smooth. (More)

Q: p. 49

While visiting Disney World, Epcot Center, I observed an unusual method of growing tomatoes at an attraction in The Land Pavilion. (More)

Q: p. 50

I'm growing determinate patio tomatoes under a 1,000-watt lamp indoors. How should I prune these, if at all? (More)

Q: p. 50

How do you prune roma tomatoes in a greenhouse for maximum yield?

Q: p. 47

What causes tomatoes to be floury and soft? I am growing roma tomatoes and they are disappointing. I know they should be better than they are.

Q: p. 51

How long does it usually take for a tomato bloom to become a ripe tomato? I have roma and 'Better Boy' plants.

Q: p. 51

I am growing tomato in the highlands and I have a problem regarding fruit size. (More)

Q: p. 52

I'm growing hydroponic tomatoes under eight 48-inch fluorescent tubes positioned directly above plants. The plants are doing very well. How can I support the vines? (More)

Q: p. 52

I'm in the process of preparing my tomato lineup card for my hobby hydroponic garden next spring and it would be wonderful to include some heirloom varieties … Are there any obstacles that would prevent me from growing heirloom tomatoes hydroponically? (More)

Q: p. 53

I run a nutrient film technique (NFT) system with tomatoes. I run the water every one-half hour. (More)

Q: p. 53

I installed a hydroponic system in my basement this past February. I have a tomato plant … It has blooms and is still growing at the same rate but now it has these little nodules along the base of the stem. (More)

Q: p. 53
What is the recommended growing method for hydroponic tomatoes and bell peppers? (More)

Q: p. 54
What is the best variety of tomato for hydroponics? (More)

Q: p. 55
I've been reading about hydroponics and some of the techniques used in this work. I'd like to know something about a technique called NFT (nutrient film technique). (More)

Q: p. 55
Can I remove the soil from around the tomato plants that are about 12 inches high and put them in a support media of Styrofoam cups? ... (More)

Q: p. 56
I have some interest in growing "hanging tomato plants." (More)

Q: p. 51
When growing plants in a closed greenhouse, do you need bees for pollination? If so, for which plants? tomatoes? bell peppers? cucumbers?

Q: p. 56
I grow cucumbers and many other plants from seed four to six weeks before hardening them off outside. From the first day they are outside, the cucumbers seem to have had problems. (More)

Q: p. 56
I have a cucumber plant that is blooming right now, but there aren't any male flowers, just female. I was also wondering if there was a nutrient more suited to assorted plants ... (More)

Q: p. 57
With regard to the discussion I read on cucumbers, you mention artificial pollination. Can you advise how this is done? (More)

Q: p. 58
We have been growing peppers indoors and the plants do wonderful. However, the flowers bloom and then drop off ... (More)

Q: p. 58
My yellow bell pepper had flowers and then baby peppers rather quickly after planting. (More)

Q: p. 59
I have just planted some pepper seedlings and would like to know if they are vines ... (More)

Q: p. 59
I have a homemade garden cart. It has three shelves and a canopy top that supports my 400-watt metal halide light ... My question is: Why aren't I showing any peppers? (More)

Q: p. 60
I am growing tomatoes and peppers. What other vegetables or herbs are suited to be grown with these?

Q: p. 60
I am growing capsicums in a 70/30 perlite/vermiculite mix outdoors and while the plants are healthy with prolific flowers,

the small fruit are falling off within days of the flower petals dropping. (More)

Q: p. 60
I grow a variety of Capsicum spp. in a flood drain bucket system. Problem is that recently flowers on all spp. aren't setting fruit. (More)

Q: p. 61
I am working to become a new hydroponic grower in the United States and I'm especially interested in growing hydroponic eggplants (aubergines). (More)

Q: p. 61
We grew tomatillos from seed this year. While they are producing many, many flowers, the flowers are dropping off before fruit sets. (More)

Growing Tips / Strawberries

Q: p. 62
We are planning on doing hydroponic strawberries at the beginning of the school year. What advice do you have in preparation for this adventure?

Q: p. 67
I'd like to know if strawberries can be grown in a hot and humid climate like we have here in central and eastern Thailand.

Q: p. 67
I am interested in trying to grow strawberries hydroponically. I live in Taiwan and I don't know if it's possible with the heat and humidity here. (More)

Q: p. 67
I was wondering if I can grow strawberries in Puerto Rico. (More)

Q: p. 68
I am in the planning stages in regard to raising strawberries. I will be using the NFT system with channels. (More)

Q: p. 69
I just picked off the first red strawberry from the plants we just recently purchased. My kids were excited to eat it, but when we tasted it, it was bitter. (More)

Q: p. 65
Is it possible to grow strawberries using exclusively artificial light?

Q: p. 69
Which is the adapted inclination of the channels for NFT strawberry cultivation? (More)

Q: p. 66
I'd like to grow some day-neutral strawberries outside in hydroponic vertical towers with drip irrigation. (More)

Q: p. 70
I'm building a hydroponic system to produce strawberries and have some doubts. My reservoir contains cement in its structure. What are the consequences of the contact of the nutritious solution with the cement? (More)

Q: p. 70
I read in a book that is possible to maintain a strawberry plant for three years in hydroponics and that the best crops are in the second and in the third year. Is that true? (More)

Q: p. 70

I was thinking of building a greenhouse. My system probably will be tiered for strawberries with two levels or a system with just one level. My city is around 90 kilometers from Capricorn Tropic, near Sao Paulo city. What is best direction to construct it? North/south or east/west? (More)

Q: p. 71

I would like to know about substrates and nutrients ratios for vertical hydroponic strawberry growing. Also, would this information apply to other berries like raspberry or blackberry?

Q: p. 72

A friend of mine is starting their own hydroponic garden and is considering what type of plants to put in it. I was wondering what the best combination of vegetables to grow together would be. (More)

Growing Tips / Miscellaneous Crops

Q: p. 69

I am interested in the growth of grapes for wine production with hydroponic methods. Where can I find any information, research, or documentation of any kind on this subject?

Q: p. 72

Thank you for the recent article on hydroponic raspberries in the May/June 2001 issue of The Growing Edge. What are your thoughts on trying to grow other cultivars similarly? (More)

Q: p. 73

While browsing through The Growing Edge Q&A archives, I didn't find much information on highbush blueberries … Is this an uncommon indoor hydroponic crop? (More)

Q: p. 74

I am sales manager in a Taiwan company and in my leisure time I have raised blackberry bushes in the backyard. For three to four years, it never grew the berry fruit. (More)

Q: p. 74

I'm growing two dwarf Musa banana plants indoors. They are at about 4 feet in height. I have several questions. (More)

Q: p. 76

Last year, I grew banana trees in soil covering an area equal to one acre … Bananas require a lot of water and fertilizers. So I was wondering if I could use an outdoor hydroponic system for planting bananas. (More)

Q: p. 76

I have a banana tree growing on a small back patio. How do I control the new shoots that come up almost daily? If I just trim them, they are back the next day.

Q: p. 76

I am looking for information on growing passionfruit hydroponically. (More)

Q: p. 77

I began to read The Growing Edge as a fish hobbyist and I always enjoy the information … I particularly like the article on important edible plants from South America in Volume 10, Number 4. Is this possible to grow those crops in Quebec, Canada? (More)

Q: p. 77

Can tropical trees, which are next to impossible to grow in containers because of the root systems, be grown hydroponically? (More)

Q: p. 78

I love to see plants grow so I planted pits from lemon and nectarine to see if they would grow—and they do. (More)

Q: p. 78

I was thinking about growing bamboo in my hydroponic greenhouse and was wondering what fertilizer ratios I should feed and how much water I should apply? … (More)

Q: p. 79

Can capers (Capparis spinosa) be grown hydroponically (see www.hort.purdue.edu/newcrop/cropfactsheets/caper.html)? What about truffles, mushrooms, asparagus, artichokes, and black pepper (Piper negrum)?

Q: p. 80

Can groundnuts be effectively grown in hydroponics?

Q: p. 80

What is the average growth period for hydroponically grown peanuts? … (More)

Q: p. 75

Do you have a list of beans that are considered "broad leaf beans"? Is it possible to grow them hydroponically?

Q: p. 80

How do I grow bean sprouts from mung bean seeds? (More)

Q: p. 76

Any information on growing snow peas in an NFT system, indoors and under lights, would be helpful.

Q: p. 81

I would like some information on how to grow rice hydroponically … (More)

Q: p. 81

Are there any estimates on biomass productivity for hydroponic grains, such as rice? Is legume-rhizobium symbiosis restricted when growing hydroponic leguminous grains? (More)

Q: p. 82

Can soybeans be grown (cost effectively) in a hydroponic system? If so, what would be the approximate yield per square meter?

Q: p. 83

Have legumes with root nodules been successfully grown in hydroponics? Also, are there medicinal plants that have been grown successfully in hydroponics?

Q: p. 83

You have mentioned that medicinal plants, such as St. John's wort, echinacea, ginseng, and kava, have been successfully grown in hydroponics. I believe these plants are herbs and I would like to know if there has been any woody medicinal plant that has been or is currently being grown in hydroponics.

Q: p. 83

Where can I find some literature on how to produce hydroponic fodder for dairy cattle?

Q: p. 83

On growing barley to maturity for grain production in hydroponics ... (More)

Q: p. 79

Would you please let us know is it possible to produce fodder from barley in a normal room not using a container?

Q: p. 84

How do I grow soybeans (or alfalfa) hydroponically on a small scale? (More)

Q: p. 84

I am interested in growing hydroponic melons and woody ornamentals. (More)

Q: p. 85

I've tried to grow many types of cantaloupe hydroponically for two years without success. The main problem is fungal and disease problems on the leaves. (More)

Q: p. 85

I'm interested in growing hydroponic hops. Is this possible? Where can I get information on this subject?

Q: p. 86

If I grow a flat of wheatgrass, cut it, and juice it, am I still able to use the soil I grew it in to grow another batch, or is that soil now depleted of nutrients?

Q: p. 86

I am interested in producing barley in a hydroponic system but I don't have any idea about this method. Can you help me?

Q: p. 87

We would like information for hydroponic barley grass for animal feed.

Q: p. 87

I need information about the hydroponic oat and barley crops. (More)

Q: p. 87

When I am growing wheatgrass, how long will it take before I can juice the grass? When I cut it, does the seed keep sprouting?

Growing Tips / Basil, Other Herbs

Q: p. 87

I am growing basil in a top feed drip/NFT system built out of PVC gutters turned upside down on a table lined with a pond liner. (More)

Q: p. 88

I am learning to grow basil. My basil is growing quite tall and the stems do not really stand up. How can I help?

Q: p. 88

For several years, I have successfully moved my outdoor containers of Italian basil indoors to the same sunny spot in the winter without problems. This year, the leaves are papery with transparent patches that have no color. (More)

Q: p. 88

How can I manipulate (shorten) my basil's internodal length? Will this improve yield? (More)

Q: p. 82

My basil plants, which I planted in May, have developed brown, hard stems and have gone to seed already. (More)

Q: p. 89

What CF should I use for growing coriander in NFT? Do you have any other tips regarding coriander?

Q: p. 89

Am having great difficulty growing coriander (from seeds)—even when I ask farmer friends to do it for me. The seeds usually germinate and shoots grow to about 10 centimeters before withering rapidly. (More)

Q: p. 90

Can I grow recao (Mexican coriander) in my hydroponic system?

Q: p. 90

I'm looking for information on growing hydroponic herbs—specifically parsley—in South Africa.

Q: p. 92

I am interested in growing basil hydroponically using organic nutrients and artificial lighting. I would like to know what type of yields to expect per 1,000-watt halide and how often plants need to be regenerated.

Q: p. 92

I'm growing coriander in pipes and am developing brown tip on the leaves. (More)

Q: p. 86

Can mint (Mentha spicata) be grown hydroponically?

Q: p. 92

I have just bought a hydroponic system. The pot is approximately 12 inches across. I want to use it outdoors on my north-facing deck. (More)

Q: p. 93

I am interested in trying hydroponics with a couple of Japanese plants, green and purple perilla and wasabi. Do you know if it is possible or not?

Q: p. 93

Is it possible to grow wasabi organically in a hydroponic system?

Q: p. 94

I'm looking for any type of hydroponic growing information on wasabi or any other "horseradish" type plant.

Q: p. 94

I want to grow some vegetables and herbs hydroponically. Can you tell me which vegetables and herbs are compatible with each other?

Q: p. 94

I am growing the hydroponic "Windowsill Wonder" with basil for a science project. (More)

Q: p. 94

I was wondering if you had a little more detailed drawings or more detailed instructions on the "Windowsill Wonder." (More)

Growing Tips / Lettuce, Other Greens

Q: p. 95

I'm working on a project to determine the optimum growing conditions for romaine lettuce in a hydroponic system. (More)

Q: p. 96

After 8 weeks, my lettuce ('Black Seeded Simpson') turned out bitter. (More)

Q: p. 96

I read recently about some of the factors affecting the taste of lettuce, but cannot recall where to find it. Can you briefly give me a guideline as to the prime factors that can affect the taste of lettuce?

Q: p. 97

I grow lettuce, green stem pak choi, kale, coysum, and water convolvulus using an NFT system with one nutrient tank. (More)

Q: p. 98

I am experimenting with deep pond technology. (More)

Q: p. 98

I am growing lettuce in a roof gutter flood-and-drain system with some commercial white perlite and some reddish-coated beads. I have a lot of algae forming. (More)

Q: p. 99

I am going to grow hydroponic Ipomoea aquatica (water spinach). Could you please recommend some information ... (More)

Q: p. 99

What guidelines can be used to determine how much shading is needed? 35 percent? 50 percent? 85 percent? (More)

Q: p. 100

I read Volume 11, Number 5 through Volume 12, Number 1 of The Growing Edge with much interest. The articles on hydroponics in developing countries and Dr. Morgan's article on greens related exactly to a project that I am considering. (More)

Q: p. 101

I've recently started a home brew hydroponics system. I bleached and rinsed the entire system before starting anything in it. I am growing lettuce in a tube system with constant nutrient flow and an air pump in the solution. (More)

Q: p. 102

I am setting up two 30x120 greenhouses during the coming 60 days with the intention of producing lettuce and herbs. Our temperatures in San Antonio, with a southeast wind from the Gulf of Mexico (lots of humidity), ranges from 96°F daytime to 76°F nighttime, almost from end of May through to end of October. (More)

Q: p. 95

How do I grow mesclun greens in a hydroponic system? (More)

Q: p. 103

I am growing lettuce in my greenhouse. What depth and spacing do I need to allow for the plants?

Q: p. 103

How do you care (nutrient application, germination, room temperature, amount of light) for lettuce from its germination until you transplant it to your NFT system? (More)

Q: p. 103

How long does it take for buttercrunch and green mignonette (manoa) lettuce to germinate? Also, do you know if their tastes are similar?

Q: p. 103

How long does it take to grow lettuce from germination to harvest? Also, how can I find out this information for a variety of other fruits and vegetables?

Q: p. 104

I am having some major problems understanding hydroponics. (More)

Q: p. 104

What is the ideal weight for lettuce at harvest time? How many days required for lettuce to be harvested after planting? (More)

Q: p. 105

Could you please advise on the sowing of watercress to be grown in greenhouse on water?

Q: p. 105

I have some questions about watercress. What's the correct pH level of fertilizer solution? Do I need to oxygenate the water via an oxygen pump and air stone? (More)

Q: p. 105

Could you tell me how I could grow watercress in my pond in the U.K. (in the midlands)?

Growing Tips / Orchidaceae, Other Ornamentals

Q: p. 106

I've been growing orchids for a long time now. Recently I decided to try hydroponics and changed about 60 percent of my collection to it. (More)

Q: p. 106

I would like to know if it is possible to grow vanilla bean hydroponically.

Q: p. 106

I have a couple of orchids and since I am a beginner am not sure if what is happening is common. (More)

Q: p. 107

I am an orchidist who has a great deal of success using hydroponics across many genera with excellent results. However, I wish to switch over to aeroponics instead of the passive hydrocultural method I have been using. (More)

Q: p. 107

I am interested in growing vanilla in New Zealand. The climate here is not tropical. Can it be done and how would I go about doing it?

Q: p. 108

What are the needs of pH on orchids? Also, I was wondering how an orchid is propagated?

Q: p. 108

Has anyone had much success growing cacti hydroponically?

Q: p. 108

I have an English ivy growing in a soilless mix. I am having problems with the leaves drying out, although I am watering every day. (More)

Q: p. 109

Can one grow maidenhair fern with hydroponics? If yes, what pH and EC would be used? Finally, what formula would be recommended for the nutritional medium?

Q: p. 109

I'm growing Echinodorus blheri (Alismataceae) in a hydroponic system. From October to April the plants have shown tipburn. Could you suggest how to solve this matter?

Q: p. 109

I am from the island of Guam and interested in growing roses using hydroponics. (More)

Q: p. 110

I am growing Gerbera daisies in two types of medium, rockwool and coir. The plants in the coir are doing extremely well—better then the plants in the rockwool. (More)

Q: p. 110

I have a friend interested in chrysanthemums. What is the best system, nutrient solution, and conditions for this crop? (More)

Q: p. 111

I would like to know how to get started growing vegetables at home. I have a 20x20-foot room. (More)

Q: p. 111

I am very curious if one could grow daylilies hydroponically. If so, which is the best method and type of equipment to use?

GREEN AIR PRODUCTS

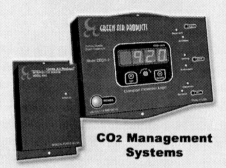

magic beans
not required.

With each issue of The Growing Edge magazine, you get the latest news and information about the growing world of hydroponics. What's more, Growing Edge experts offer in-depth how-to advice for hydroponic production of a range of familiar and exotic plants, so that you can take your hobby as far as you want to go. Order your subscription today...and get growing!

Call: (800) 888-6785
(541) 757-8477

Visit us online:
www.growingedge.com/store

THE GROWING EDGE

With this much to read,
you'll have to add on
another bathroom.